OFFENCES AGAINST WOMEN

SOCIO-LEGAL PERSPECTIVES

OFFENCES AGAINST WOMEN

SOCIO-LEGAL PERSPECTIVES

K. Kumar
Punam Rani

2024

Regency Publications

A Division of

Astral International Pvt. Ltd.

New Delhi – 110 002

social conditions and suggestive of changes needed to make law more effective. It highlights the relationship between law and social norms and the interdependence of one on the other.

The book will be of immense utility not only to lawyers and social workers but also to all men and women who like to know what is going on in the society they live in, and are interested in creating conditions in which women may get the opportunity to live with dignity and without fear.

C-9, Sector 26
Noida
24-5-1995

HARI SWARUP
(Former Judge, Allahabad High Court)

Preface

It is an irony of fate that women, who constitute nearly half of our human population and are equal partners in domestic, social and cultural activities are assigned non-descript positions and made to suffer ignoble hardships. The last two decades have seen the emergence of new forms of crimes, like infant and child-rape, dowry deaths and brutal acts by those agencies which are entrusted with the task of protecting the life and honour of the community. Time to time amendments in law and enactment of new legislations have failed to yield any fruitful results. This only reflects lack of will and initiative for strict enforcement. Majority of our people are either unaware of plights of women or are insensitive to their problems.

The present work is an effort by a father and his daughter to create an awareness among the people of the community about the plight of our women so that the community makes an endeavour to tackle the problem in right earnest.

The book is divided into 12 chapters with Prologue and Postscript as commencing and concluding Chapters. Chapter II highlights the topic of Constitutional Protection to Women. The main theme of the book has been discussed in nearly 245 pages systemized into 9 Chapters and form the core of the book. The contents are reinforced with illustrations, legal provisions and relevant case-laws.

The authors express their deep sense of gratitude to Hon'ble Justice Shri Hari Swarup for going through the manuscript, making valuable and valid suggestions and writing an inspiring foreword. Our thanks are also due to our friends and colleagues, particularly Dr. Sunil Kant Bhattacharyya, Advocate, Supreme Court of India for necessary advice and encouragement which made it possible to complete the task. The authors are thankful to Regency Publications, Delhi for bringing out this book in excellent form.

The book is dedicated to the mothers, sisters and daughters in India and abroad.

Supreme Court Bar Association
New Delhi 110 001
May 24, 1995

K. KUMAR
(*Advocate, Supreme Court of India*)

and

National Institute of Social Defence
R.K. Puram
New Delhi 110 066

PUNAM RANI

Contents

Chapter 1

Prologue

1.01 Introduction

It is said that behind every successful man there is a woman. This only shows that women are the integral part of our society and have an important role not only for rearing a child from its birth but development of man's personality, for instance; the personality of Chatrapati Shivaji was developed by his mother Jijabai. Manu, the law-giver has prescribed that a woman should not remain independent but under the control of men throughtout her life—under the dominance of her father during her childhood, husband during her youth and son in advanced age. This advice by the ancient law-giver is aimed at providing protection to a woman if so required. However, a misinterpretation of the statement has led to the forfeiture and status of rights and independence of women.

Our ancient scriptures have always worshipped woman as goddess; for instance, 'Lakshmi' the wife of Vishnu as a person controlling the wealth; 'Sarswati' the wife of Brahma, the goddess of learning and music, the finest among the fine arts. She is always projected as holding Veena, a string instrument; 'Parvati', the wife of Shiva—riding a lion; 'Kali' and 'Durga' the Goddess of power and strength, and there are many others. This country has seen many women occupying eminent positions and discharging their obligations very successfully his situation is inspite of the prevailing prejudices against them.

Table 1.02 Sex Ratio (Female Per 1000 Males) in India (States & Union Territories) (9, 10)

S. No.	States/U.T.'s	Census Year									
		1901	1911	1921	1931	1941	1951	1961	1971	1981	1991
1.	Andhra Pradesh	985	990	993	987	980	986	981	977	975	972
2.	Arunachal Pradesh	—	—	—	—	—	—	894	861	862	861
3.	Assam	918	915	908	886	886	877	876	901	810	925
4.	Bihar	1054	1044	1016	994	996	990	994	956	946	912
5.	Goa	1090	1110	1120	1090	1085	1130	1066	980	975	970
6.	Gujarat	955	945	944	945	941	952	940	936	943	936
7.	Haryana	865	835	845	844	870	871	869	867	870	875
8.	Himachal Pradesh	885	890	890	898	890	913	940	960	975	995
9.	Jammu & Kashmir	882	875	870	865	869	873	878	882	892	923
10.	Karnataka	985	960	970	965	960	970	860	957	965	900
11.	Kerala	1005	1010	1011	1022	1027	1028	1022	1019	1032	1040
12.	Madhya Pradesh	990	985	974	973	970	867	953	943	941	932
13.	Maharashtra	980	965	950	947	949	941	936	932	937	936
14.	Manipur	1035	1035	1040	1065	1055	1035	1015	980	970	960
15.	Meghalaya	1035	1015	1000	970	965	950	937	940	955	948
16.	Mizoram	1113	1120	1109	1102	1070	1040	1010	945	920	925
17.	Nagaland	975	995	990	998	1050	1000	935	870	865	890
18.	Orissa	1035	1055	1086	1017	1053	1022	1000	989	980	970
19.	Punjab	833	780	821	830	850	858	865	874	880	885
20.	Rajasthan	904	910	896	907	906	921	908	910	919	913
21.	Sikkim	915	950	970	968	920	907	905	864	835	880
22.	Tamilnadu	1045	1043	1029	1027	1012	1007	992	979	977	972
23.	Tripura	875	885	885	885	885	905	930	945	945	945
24.	Uttar Pradesh	938	915	909	904	907	910	909	883	885	881
25.	West Bengal	945	925	905	890	852	865	878	891	910	918

1. Andaman & Nicobar Islands	318	352	303	495	495	525	617	644	760	820
2. Chandigarh	770	720	743	750	765	780	850	750	770	795
3. Dadra & Nagar Haveli	960	967	940	910	925	945	965	1007	975	955
4. Daman & Diu	995	1040	1045	1090	1080	1125	1170	1100	1062	973
5. Lakshdweep	1065	985	1025	995	1020	1045	1020	980	975	945
6. Pondicherry	—	1060	1055	—	—	1030	1013	990	935	980
7. Delhi—Capital City	865	795	735	720	715	770	785	800	810	830
All India	972	964	955	950	945	945	940	930	935	929

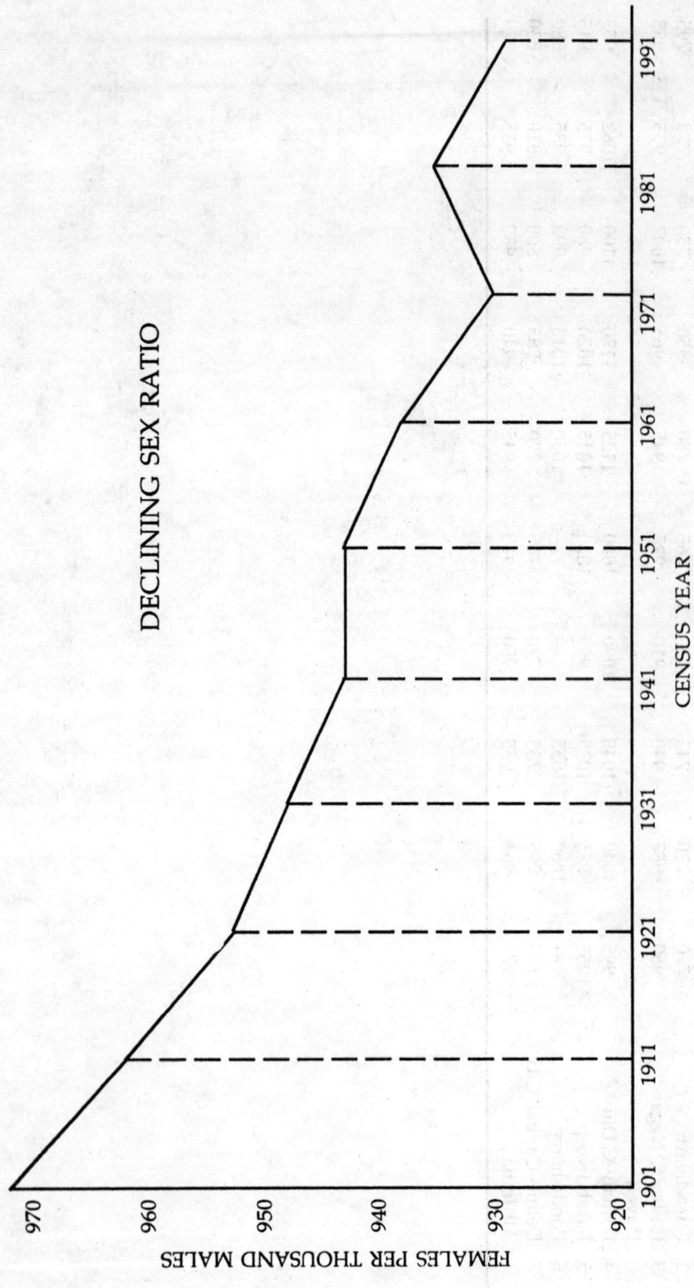
DECLINING SEX RATIO
FEMALES PER THOUSAND MALES
970
960
950
940
930
920
CENSUS YEAR
1901
1911
1921
1931
1941
1951
1961
1971
1981
1991

outnumber females. The Primary Census Abstract (PCA) released by the Deputy Chairman, Planning Commission, shows that India's population, now forms 16 per cent of the world's total population. There are over 43.92 crores males in the total population of 84,63,02,688 heads. The rest are females who account for more than 40.70 crores. It means that female population stood at 972 per one thousand males. The National Mortality Rate stood at 80. Orissa has the highest (126) and Kerala, the lowest (17).

1.04 Unaccounted Women[8]

On a global scale, 5% more boys than girls are born. Despite this, there is a preponderance of women all over the world. In U.K., France and U.S.A. man/woman ratio has been found to be represented by the following model:

Man:Woman :: 1:1.05.[10]

In the many third world countries, the male/female ratio is 1:0.90 to 1:0.95. Despite the fact that more male child is born as compared to the female child, the female outnumber male because women are hardier than their male counterpart and while living under similar conditions, the female have better survival capability. The male have comparatively poor life expectancy on account of cigarette smoking, drinking habits, deaths due to accidents and other forms of violent deaths.

In glaring contrasts to these facts, some countries have inexplicably lower females. Social factors account for the low male:female ratio in Asia and North Africa. According to an estimate millions of women are missing or are unaccounted for, in these countries. Female mortality in Europe and America is less than that in the above countries and female ratio in male-female sex ratio rises with age. The lower life expectancy and the higher fertility rates in Asia and North America would obviously lead to a lower ratio. By choosing statistics from sub-Saharan Africa where life expectancy and fertility rates are parallel, but female disadvantage does not exist, the ratio yeilded is 1 : 1.022 :: Male:Female. On this basis, 44 million of women are missing in China, 37 millions in India and more than 100 millions worldwide. Even when the Western statistices are used as a yardstick, there appears to be an overall of 60 million women remain unaccounted for.

1.05 Victims of Witch Hunting

The primitive Tribals, when faced with natural calamities like rain, drought, disease and severe domestic problems commenced worshipping natural gods and goddesses and magic grew out of them. The 'BAIGA' in the Tribals of Bastar in M.P.,[11] 'Jangurus' in Bengal[12] and 'Ojhas' in Bihar prevail upon the people in their locality as possessed of supernatural powers. Initially his magical powers were applied to the cure of diseases and ailments but in course of time, when he fails to cure a patient he would generally name a particular woman, who is either a poor person living alone or is a poor widow having no issues and in turn she is mercilessly tortured or killed. The main reasons for such killings are the following:

(1) Illiteracy and ignorance.
(2) When an unmarried sister becomes a liability to her brother or an issueless widow for the family she is managed to be killed in this way.
(3) Women are killed brandishing them as witches in order to grab their properties and also to end the liability of maintenance.
(4) Personal enmity also prompts murders after declaring the women as witches.

Records show that when the administration becomes vigilant, the miracle-man is on the run. Creating an awareness is another remedy to counteract this malady.

1.06 Unwed Motherhood

Unwed motherhood is generally thrust upon minor girls in the age group of 13–16 years who get through sentiments or are enticed by unscruplous persons of the society. The International Mission of Hope (IMH) opened two such centres, one each at Calcutta and Madras to provide shelter to unwed mothers and arrange for their children's future. The aim of such institutions, as explained by its founder Cherie Clark Prakash, is to restore the self respect of these women and make them realise that they remain human beings capable of living in the society as any other woman.[13]

Unwed motherhood is cataclysmic when the emotional bond with the unborn baby is strong and the mother has to abandon the child for social reasons.

But there should be some legislation to rope in the person who has fathered the child. With the advancement of bio-technology and genetic engineering, it can conclusively be said as to who is the biological father to the exclusion of all others. Some sort of legislation is needed to provide respectability not only to the child but to the mother as well and such persons do not slip away after having burdened the woman-girl unauthorisedly.

1.07 Female Criminality

Over the years, the females have taken to criminal activities not only as pimps or as brothel keepers or as active organisers of a Call-Girl House but such crimes as burglary, pick-pocketing, kidnapping or committing offence under the NDPS Act. There are as many as 259 women proclaimed offenders in the Capital City of Delhi alone.[14]

Every one is familiar with the bandit queen Phoolan Devi. She was a simple rustic girl on whom atrocities were perpetrated even when she had not attained teens. Circumstances forced her to take to banditry and after she allegdly took revenge she surrendered. She is rather an object of pity than anything else and the State should see that no second Phoolan Devi grows out of circumstances.

1.08 Instruments of Social Engineering

The era after Independence, witnessed the enactment of a large number of Acts sought to apply principles underlying the Constitutional guarantees. But enactments have failed to yeild the desired results partly on account of the inadequacy of the laws and partly due to lack of implementation in proper way. For instance, a number of policemen were reported to have perpetrated sexual assaults to the women inhabitants of a village in Deoghar District (Bihar) and investigation of the cases had been done by the same policemen. Some legal provision is necessary in respect of investigation in such cases, so that the prompt investigation is done in right earnest, so that the cases do not fail during trial on account of intentional poor investigation.

1.09 Conclusion

Inspite of constitutional protection provided in the Constitution of India and punishment provided under the various laws, introduction of laws to prevent immoral traffic in women and girls, commission of Sati, some amendments in the I.P.C., there is no perceptible change or decline in respect of crimes against women. It is an irony of fate that the protector of women, such as the inmates of the house including the husband, policemen, legislatures have been reported to have indulged actively in the crimes against women, detailed studies whereof shall be brought in the succeeding chapters of the book.

REFERENCES

1. "Crime Against Women", Ediotorial in *Hindustan Times* (Delhi Ed.), dated 21.7.92.
2. Delhi in Parliament—"1973 Crime Against Women", *Hindustan Times* (Delhi Ed.), dated 5.8.1993.
3. Rukmani Anandani, "Documenting Violence Against Women", *Hindustan Times* (Delhi Ed.), dated February 18, 1989.
4. Delhi in Parliament—"3186 Cases of Crime Against Women in 1991", *Hindustan Times* (Delhi Ed.), dated Dec. '17, 1991.
5. News Item from Bhubneshwar, "A Rape every 54 Minutes in India", *Hindustan Times* (Delhi Ed.), dated 29.1.1993.
6. Lok Sabha Questions—"24 P.C. Indian Women suffer from Undernourishment," Parliament News; *Hindustan Times* (Delhi Ed.), dated July 16, 1991.
7. HT Correspondent, "Women still outnumber men in Kerala," Census Report, *Hindustan Times* (Delhi Ed.), Jan. 15, 1993.
8. Bandana Malhotra (Dr.), "Where have all the Women gone?" *Hindustan Times* (Delhi Ed.), dated Feb. '14, 1993
9. "Towards Equality"—Report on the Committee on the Status of Women", Govt. of India, Min. of Education & Social Welfare, New Delhi (1974), Table 7. pp. 15.
10. Veena Mazumdar, Sex-Ratio, Female/Male, 1901–1991, *Frontline*, May 11–24, pp. 41–55.
11. K. Kumar, Gupta's Medicolegal Aspects of Sexual Offences (1990) 3rd. Edition, Published by Eastern Book Co., 34, Lalbagh, Lucknow 226001, pp. 18.
12. Sudhamoy Chatterji, "Witch Hunting—Deprivation behind Gruesome Practice", *Hindustan Times* (Delhi Ed.), dated 30.8.1993.

13. Indranil Banerji, "Unwed Mothers", *India Today*, November 15, 1986, pp. 156–165.
14. Girija Shanker Kaura, "Crime, No More a Man's World," *Hindustan Times* (Delhi Ed.), dated July 10, 1993.

Chapter 2

Constitutional Protection to Women

2.01 Introduction

Our Constitution makers were alive to the social problems associated with the emancipation of women. They had seen prevailing gender inequality during their time and had visualised that the sex-equality was crucial for the development of the country. In order to do away with the inequality and to provide reasonable opportunities and create awareness for the exercise of human rights and claim, it was necessary to promote with special care, educational and economic interests not only of men but women too and to provide necessary protection from social injustice and exploitation. The Constitution of India provides the following:

(1) Right to equality (Art. 14, 15 and 16)
(2) Right against exploitation (Art. 23)
(3) Directive Principles of State Policy (Articles 38, 39(a) & (d), 42 and 44)
(4) Fundamental Duties (Art. 51A Q (e))
(5) Elections (Art. 325)

Besides the above, the Preamble, which incorporates chief goal enshrined in the Constitution reflects the spirit of equality. A look into the Preamble will enable us to locate ideal incorporated into the Constitution.

2.02 Preamble

The Preamble of the Constitution of India, has been expressed in the following words:

> "WE THE PEOPLE OF INDIA, having solemnly resolved to constitute India into a SOVEREIGN SOCIALIST SECULAR DEMOCRATIC REPUBLIC AND to secure to all citizens:
>
> JUSTICE, social, economic and political;
> LIBERTY of thought, expression, belief, faith and worship;
> EQUALITY of status and of opportunity; and to promote among them all,
> FRATERNITY, assuring the dignity of the individual, (unity and integrity of the nation);[1]
> IN OUR CONSTITUTENT ASSEMBLY, this twenty-sixth day of November, 1949, do HEREBY ADOPT, ENACT and GIVE TO OURSELVES THIS CONSTITUTION."

The expression appearing in the Preamble were then described by Pandit Jawaharlal Nehru in the Objective Resolution which he moved in the Constituent Assembly in its First Sesssion and the Assembly adopted the same unanimously. But Nehru's Resolution itself had taken shape out of what had already been said by Mahatma Gandhi in 1931 when Mahatmaji was standing on the deck of a ship taking him to London in the capacity of the spokesman and representative of Nationalist India to the Second Round Table Conference. When asked by a correspondent at that time as to what Constitution he would bring back if he could help it, Mahatma Gandhi offered the following reply:

> "I shall strive for a Constitution which will release India from all that dom and patronage and give her, if need be, the right to sin. I shall work for an India, in which the poorest shall feel that it is their country in whose making they have an effective voice; an India where there shall not be high class and low class of people; an India in which all communities shall live in perfect harmony; there can be no room in such an India for the curse of untouchability or the curse of intoxicating drinks or drugs. Women shall enjoy the same right as men. Since we shall be at pace with all the rest of the world neither exploiting nor being exploited by

any of them. We shall have the smallest army imaginable. All interests not to be in conflict with the interests of the millions of dumb that will be respected, whether foreign or indigenous. This is the India of my dream."

The opening words of the Preamble emphasise on the ultimate authority of the people from whom the Constitution emerges. There is no sex discrimination. The words "WE THE PEOPLE OF INDIA" includes both males and females.

The Preamble outlines four objectives of the Indian Republic, viz; justice, liberty, equality and fraternity. 'Justice' implies a harmonious reconcilement of individual conduct with the general welfare of the society. The essence of justice lies in the attainment of the common good. It embraces as the preamble proclaims the entire social, economic and political spheres of human activity.

The word 'liberty' in the Preamble, signifies not only the absence of any arbitrary restraint on the freedom of individual's action but also for the creation of conditions which would provide for the necessary ingredient required for the proper development of the personality of the individual. Since society consists of individuals, social progress depends on the progress of individuals. Hence, it is in the interest of the society to ensure the maximum liberty of thought and action of the individual consistent with the circumstances and social conditions.

The two words 'liberty' and 'equality' are complimentary. Equality does not mean that all human beings are mentally and physically equal. It signifies equality of status and equal opportunity.

Emphasis has been laid on the objective of 'fraternity' in order to ensure two things, viz; the dignity of the individual and unity and integrity of the country. It is the spirit of brotherhood that is emphasised by the expression 'fraternity'. In a country like ours with diverse religion, language, culture and social system, unity can be achieved through the spirit of fraternity.

2.03 Fundamental Rights

Fundamental Rights, receives its treatment under Article 12 to 35 of the Constitution and includes such principles as right to equality, right to freedom, right against exploitation, right to religion, right to culture and education, saving of certain laws and right to constitutional remedies.

2.04 Right to Equality

"*Art 14. Equality Before Law*: The State shall not deny to any person equality before law or equal protection of laws within the territory of India."

Notes

The Constitution of India guarantees equality before law or equal protection of law to every person irrespective of the fact that he is, or he is not the citizen of India. Both the phrases aim to establish what is called the equality of status and of opportunities as envisaged in the Preamble. Article 14 of the Constitution prevents any arbitrary discrimination.

Interpreting the scope of this Article, the Supreme Court of India[2] held as under:

"(1) In considering the fundamental right of equality of opportunity, a technical pendantic or doctrinaire approach should not be made and the doctrine should not be involved even if different scales of pay, service conditions, leave etc. are introduced in different or dissimilar posts.

(2) Article 14 forbids hostile discrimination but not reasonable classification. Thus, where persons belonging to a particular class in view of their special attributes, qualities, mode of recruitment and the like are differently treated in public interest to advance and boost members belonging to backward classes, such a classification shall be outside the scope of discrimination having a close nexus with the object sought to be achieved so that in such a case, Art. 14 will be completely out of the way.

(3) Art. 14 certainly applies where equals are treated differently without any reasonable basis.

(4) Where equals and unequals are treated differently, Art. 14 would have no application.

(5) Even if there be one class of service having several categories with different attributes and incidents, such a category

becomes a separate class by itself and no difference or discrimination between such category and the general members of the other class would amount to any discrimination or to denial of equality of opportunity.

(6) In order to judge whether a separate category has been carved out of a class of service, the following circumstances have generally to be examined:
   (a) the nature, the mode and the manner of recruitment of a particular category from the very start;
   (b) the classification of the particular category;
   (c) the terms and conditions of service of the members of the category;
   (d) the nature and character of the posts and promotional avenues;
   (e) the specific attributes that the particular category possesses which are not to be found in other classes and the like."

It is difficult to lay down a rule of universal application but the circumstances mentioned above may be taken as illustrative guideline for determining the question.

In its struggle for social and political freedom, mankind has always tried to move forward to the idea of equality for all. The urge for equality and liberty has been the moving force of many resolutions. The Charter of the United Nations records the determination of the member Nations to reaffirm their faith in the equal rights of men and women.

However, fulfilment of complete equality between men and women in all spheres of life is a distant dream. The laws of a country can at best assure to its citizens only a limited measure of equality. The Constitution makers gave only political and legal equality and the status of a fundamental right. Aspects like economic and social equality were included within the scope of Directive Principles of the State Policy.

Article 15 :

Article 15 of the Constitution ensures prohibition of discrimination on grounds of religion, race, caste, sex or place of birth. Stated in words, it stands as follows:

(1) The State shall not discriminate against any citizen on grounds only of religion, race, caste, sex, place of birth or any of them.

(2) No citizen shall, on grounds only of religion, race, caste, sex, place of birth or any of them be subject to any disability, liability, restriction or conditions with regard to

(a) access to shops, public restaurants, hotels and places of public entertainment; or

(b) the use of wells, tanks, bathing ghats, roads and places of public resort maintained wholly or partly out of state funds or dedicated to the use of general public.

(3) Nothing in this Article shall prevent the State from making any provision for women.

[3][(4) Nothing in this Article or in Clause (2) of Art. 29 shall prevent the State from making any special provision for the advancement of any socially and economically backward classes of citizens or for the Scheduled Castes and Scheduled Tribes.]

Art. 15 guarantees non-discrimination on special grounds, that is religion, race, caste, sex, place of birth or any of them. But, this right is available to citizens only.

Art. 15(1) is conferred on a citizen as an individual and is a guarantee against his being subjected to discrimination in the matters of rights, privileges and immunities pertaining to him by virtue of his status as a citizen.

The significance of Art. 15 is that it is a guarantee against every form of discrimination by the state on the basis of religion, race, caste or sex. Art. 15 strikes at the root of provincialism by prohibiting discrimination based upon one's place of birth. It is also in conformity with the ideal of a single citizenship which the Constitution establishes for the whole of the country.

Art. 15, however, has provided a couple of exceptions in its application. Art. 15(3) allows the state to make any special provision for women and children. Art. 15(4) permits the state to make any special provision for the advancement of socially and educationally backward classes or for the Scheduled Caste or Scheduled Tribes. The treatment meted out to women and children is in the larger and longer range interest of the community.

Art. 15(e) was included in the Constitution as a result of the First Constitutional Amendment in 1951.

Article 16 :

This Article guarantees equality of opportunity in matters of public employment. It is stated in the following words:

(1) There shall be equality of opportunity for all citizens in matters relating to employment or appointment to any office under the state.
(2) No citizen shall, on grounds only of religion, race, caste, sex, descent, place of birth, residence or any of them be ineligible for, or discriminated against in respect of any employment or office under the state.
(3) Nothing in the Article shall prevent Parliament from making any law prescribing, in regard to a class or classes of employment to an office[4] (under the Government of, or any local or other authority within a state or Union Territory, any requirement as to residence within that State or Union Territory) prior to such employment or appointment.
(4) Nothing in this Article shall prevent the state from making provision for the reservation of posts in favour of any backward class of citizen which, in the opinion of the state is not adequately represented in the services under the state.
(5) Nothing in this Article shall affect the operation of any law which provides that the incumbent of any office in connection with the affairs of any religious or denominational institution or any member of the Governing body thereof shall be a person professing a peculiar religion or belonging to a particular denomination.

Notes

Under Article 16(1), the general rule laid down is that there shall be equal opportunity for all citizens in matters of public appointment under the State, thereby the univarsality of Indian citizenship is emphasised.

Art. 16(2) prohibits discrimination to any citizen in respect of appointment on grounds of religion, caste, race, sex, descent, place of birth or residence, should that appointment be under the State.

Art. 16(3) to 16(5) are in the nature of exceptions. According to Art. 16(3), residence, qualifications may be made necessary in case of appointments under the state for particular positions. The discretion, however, does not rest with the state but within the powers of the Parliament. Art. 16(4) empowers the state Government to make reservation of positions in public employment for any backward class. The state is empowered to declare a class of people as backward class. The exceptions embodied in Art. 16(5) seek to take out of the scope of the general principle, the management of the affairs of any religious or denominational institutions under any special law providing for the same.

What Art. 15(1) and 16(2) prohibit is that discrimination should not be made only on the ground of sex. However, these Articles do not prohibit the state from making discrimination on the ground of sex coupled with other considerations. In case titled *"Yusuf Aziz* Vs. *State of Bombay* and *Hussainbhoy Laljea ,"*[5] sex was held to be a permissible classification. While dealing with this aspect of the matter, the Supreme Court remarked as under:

> "Art. 14 is general and must be read with the other provisions which set out the ambit of fundamental rights. Sex is a sound classification and although there can be no discrimination in general on that ground, the Constitution itself makes special provisions in respect of women and children. The two Articles when read together validate the impugned chance in Sec. 497 I.P.C."

Justice Krishna Iyer in the case titled *Ms C.B. Muthamma* Vs. *Union of India*[5] expressed somewhat similar views in the following words:

> "We do not mean to universalise or dogmatise that men and women are equal in all occupations and all situations and do not exclude the need programatise where the requirement of particular employment, the sensitivities of sex or the peculiarities of social sectors or the handicaps of either sex may compel sensitivity. But save, where the differentiation is demonstrable, the rule of equality must govern."

In case *Air India* Vs. *Nargesh Mirza,*[6] the Supreme Court observed that having taken the air hostess in service and after having utilised her services for four years, to terminate her services by the management in the event of her becoming pregnant amounts to compelling the poor air hostess not to have any children and thus interfere with and divert the ordinary course of human nature. The termination of the services of an air hostess under such circumstances is not only a callous and cruel act but an open insult to Indian womanhood, the most sacrosant and cherished institution. Such a course of action is extremely detestable and abhorant to the notion of a civilised society. Apart from being grossly unethical, it smacks of a deep rooted sense of an utter selfishness at the cost of all human values. Such a provision, therefore is not only manifestly unreasonable and arbitrary but contains the quality of unfairness and is, therefore, clearly violative of Art. 14.

The Supreme Court[7] while dealing with a rule barring married women from working in a particular firm criticised the validity of the rule in the following words:

> "We are not impressed by these reasons for retaining a rule of this type... Nor do we think that because the work has to be done as a team, it cannot be done by married women. We also feel that there is nothing to show that married women would be more likely to be absent than unmarried women or widows. If it is the presence of children which would account for greater absentation of married women, that would be so with the widows having children. The fact that the work has to be carried out by the workers as a team and presence of all these workmen, is in our opinion no disqualification. So far as married women or widows are entitled to such leave as the rule of the Respondent's Firm provide and they would be availing themselves of these facilities."

2.05 Right Against Exploitation

The following expression constitute the relevant portion in Art. 23 of the Constitution:

"*Prohibition of traffic in human beings and forced labour*: (1) Traffic in human beings and 'begar' and other similar forms of forced labour are prohibited and any contravention of this provision shall be an offence punishable in accordance with law.

(2) Nothing in this Article shall prevent the State from imposing compulsory service for public purposes and in imposing such service, the State shall not make any discrimination on grounds only of religion, race, caste or class or any of them."

Art. 23 may be compared to the 13th Amendment of the Constitution of America which abolished slavery. In our country, at the time of adoption of the Constitution, there was no such practice like slavery in our country but there existed large scale exploitation of forced bonded labour practiced by upper caste people upon the unprivileged section of the society. There existed a practice under which people mortgaged their labour to the upper caste masters in lieu of the interest that would accrue on the principal amount taken as loan and this bondage could continue from generations to generations. The labour working under this situation had no right to seek employment without his master's approval and consent. His dependence on his master or landlord was so severe that it virtually amounted to slavery.

Evils like the practice of *devdasi, jogan* and other similar practices in the Southern, Western part of the country and some of the temples in Orissa particularly bordering Andhra Pradesh were rampant and are still existing. According to this practice, women or girls were either sold or dedicated to the temples in the name of gods, where they could become an object of lust and instrument of sexual exploitation so long as their youth existed.

The ideal of human dignity which though pervades the entire Constitution has been expressed in explicit terms in the form of this Article. The expression 'Traffic in Human Beings' means disposal by way of sale or hire or otherwise of human beings more or less in the same manner as man does with the disposable articles.

The trafficking in women and girls in the male dominated society has been the evil practice since old times. Medieval feudalism brought down the position of women to a very low mark. Prostitution became rampant and flesh trade established itself with agents and pimps and the dignity of women had gone down to the lowest ebb. To counter this, the Parliament enacted "The Suppression of Immoral Traffic in Women and Girls Act, 1956." This Act was renamed as "Immoral Traffic (Prevention) Act, 1956" and was substituted by Act No. 44 of 1986 with effect from Jan 26, 1987. The Act was enacted by the Parliament in persuance of the ratification by India of the International Convention of the Suppression of Traffic in persons and of the prostitution by others, signed in New York in 1950 on May 9. (Detailed study of this problem is being dealt with in the Chapter on Prostitution.)

2.06 Cultural and Educational Rights

Under Article 29 and Article 30, certain cultural and educational rights are guaranteed. The Art. 29 is stated as under:

> 29. *Protection of interests of minorities:* (1) Any section of the citizen residing in the territory of India or any part thereof having a distinct language, script or culture of its own, shall have the right to conserve the same.
>
> (2) No citizen shall be denied admission into any educational institution maintained by the State or receiving aid out of State funds on grounds only of religion, race, caste, language or any of them.

Thus sex is a prohibited ground of discrimination under Art. 15 and Art. 16, but not under Art. 29. Courts, however, have come to settle down with an interpretation which means that sex as a basis of classification may be a suspect but cannot altogether be prohibited. Special laws for women can be made in different kinds of cases notwithstanding the fact whether they are favourable or unfavourable to women. It has only to be seen in such a situation that such orders may not only be reasonable but also seem to be reasonable. The following cases are cited by way of example:

(1) In case titled *Anjali Roy* Vs. *The State,*[8] the fact involved was that after opening of a college exclusively for women, girl

students were denied admission into another college which was a co-educational institution. Accordingly one Anjali Roy was denied admission in the co-educational college under the orders of the Director of Public Instruction of the Government of West Bengal. The petitioner challenged the orders of the D.P.I. as arbitrary, malafide and unreasonable. The Hon'ble High Court of Calcutta dismissed the Writ Petition holding that the order prohibiting the admission of the girl students to the former co-educational institution was with the intention to make the girl students to take admission in women's college so that the same could be popular and well established and thus, become a self sufficient. This was thus, a special provision as contemplated by Art. 15(3) for the benefit of women and in consequence the provision of Art. 15(1) was not available for this. It was further held that Art. 15(1) was of wider implications as compared to Art. 29(2) and prohibited discrimination on the ground of sex on all matters and so it included discrimination in matters of admission into educational institutions with the result that Art. 15(1) should control Art. 29(2).

(2) In case titled "*University of Madras* Vs. *Santhabai* and another[9] The High Court of Madras took a different view to deny admission to *Santhabai* in a newly opened college. The Court held the view that the University of Madras is not a `State' as defined in Article 12 of the Constitution and thus its regulation will not be subject to prohibition of Art. 15(1) of the Constitution of India. Another point is that admissions are regulated within the ambit of Art. 29(2) and the regulation of the University required that colleges should have the necessary infra-structure to provide essential facilities for women before they could be admitted. This fact is not discriminatory on ground of sex.

So far as the scope of Art. 15(3) is concerned, the High Court expressed that notwithstanding Art. 15(1), it was lawful for the state to establish educational institutions solely for women and the exclusion of men students from such institutions does not contravene Art. 15(1). The cumulative effect of Art. 15(3) and 29(2) is that while male students have no right to get admission in women's college, the women's right to admission to other colleges is a matter within the regulation of authorities.

Art. 29(2) contains the controlling provisions where the question relating to admission to colleges involves.

The scope of Art. 29(2) came up for detailed interpretation before the Apex Court[10] in two cases, both of which were appeals against the judgement and order of Madras High Court relating to admission to Educational institutions maintained by the state. The Supreme Court, after a threadbare discussion, observed as follows:

> "It will be noticed that while Cl.(1) protects the language, script or culture of a section of the citizen, Cl.(2) guarantees the fundamental right of an individual, who is citizen. The right to get admission into any educational institution of the type appearing in Cl.(2) is a right which an individual has as a citizen and not by virture of belonging to a any community or class of citizen. The right of the citizen is not to be denied to him on grounds only of sex, religion, race, caste, or language or any of them. If a citizen, who seeks admission into any such educational institution but does not possess the requisite academic qualifications and on this account is denied admission on that ground only, certainly he cannot be held to complain of any infraction of his fundamental rights under the Constitution within the framework of this Article. In the event of his having the required academic qualifications if he is refused admission only on grounds of religion, race, caste, language or any of them, then it amounts to clear violation of his fundamental rights."

On behalf of the state, it was contended that Art. 46*, charged the state with promoting with special care, the educational and special interests of the weaker section of the people and in particular of the SC/ST and with protecting them from social justice and all forms of exploitation. But, the court rejected this argument holding that this was a Directive Principle—a non-justiciable right—and it could not over-ride a Fundamental Right which was justiciable. It was the duty of the court to enforce a

**Art. 46. Promotion of educational and economic interests of the Scheduled Castes, Scheduled Tribes and other Weaker Sections.* The State shall promote with special care the educational and economic interests of the weaker sections of the people, and in particular, of the Scheduled Castes and the Scheduled Tribes, and shall protect them from social injustice and all forms of exploitation.

Fundamental Right.

The passing of the 42nd Amendment of the Constitution of India in 1976, Sec. 3, w.e.f. January 1, 1977 ensured the Supremacy of the Parliament and gave primacy to Directive Principles over Fundamental rights. In view of the passing away of this Amendment, the aforesaid argument of the Court has little force.

2.07 The Right to Constitutional Remedy

The declaration of Fundamental Rights becomes infructuous unless there is an effective instrument for enforcement of the right. Art. 32 of the Constitution** provides a remedy for the enforcement of the fundamental rights. The remedy is in the forms of specific Writs mentioned in the Article. Hence, if there is an aggrieved person who seeks a remedy from the court through a particular Writ, the nature of the remedy itself is clear both to the aggrieved person and to the court.

The Writs mentioned in the Constitution are:

(1) *Habeas Corpus:* This is a Latin term which literally means "You May Have The Body". The Writ was regarded in English as a foundation of the human freedom and the British citizen insisted upon this privilege wherever he wanted whether for business or for colonisation. This is how it found a place in the Constitution of the United States when the British colonies in America won their independence and established a new State under the Constitution.

In India, the power to issue a Writ vests only in Supreme Court and the High Court. The Writ is a direction of the court

---

** *Art. 32. Remedies for enforcement of rights conferred by this Part.* (1) The right to move the Supreme Court by appropriate proceedings for the enforcement of the rights conferred by this Part is guaranteed.

(2) The Suspreme Court shall have power to issue directions or order of Writs, including Writs in the nature of habeas corpus, mandamus, prohibition, quo warranto and certiorari, whichever may be appropriate, for the enforcement of any of the rights conferred by this part.

(3) Without prejudice to the powers conferred on the Supreme Court by Clauses (1) and (2), Parliament may, by law empower any other court to exercise within the local limits of its jurisdiction all or any of the powers exercisable by the Supreme Court under Clause (2).

(4) The right guaranteed by this Article shall not be suspended except as otherwise provided for by this Constitution.

to a person who is detaining another, commanding him to bring the body of the person in his custody at a specified time to a specified place for a specified purpose.

The Writ has only one purpose, that is; to set at liberty a person who is confined without legal jurisdiction; to secure release from confinement of a person detained unlawfully. The Writ, in accordance with circumstances, can be issued against the state and its authorities as well as private individual or organisation.

(2) *Mandamus:* This is a Latin expression and means "WE ORDER". The Writ of Mandamus is an order of the Supreme Court or the High Court commanding a person or a body to do that which is his or its duty to do so. For instance an appointing authority is obliged to issue a letter of appointment to a candidate if all the formalities of selection is over and the candidate is declared fit for appointment to the post. But despite the fulfilment of such condition, if the officer or the authority concerned refuses or fails to issue the appointment letter, the aggrieved person has a right to seek the remedy through a Writ of Mandamus.

(3) *Prohibition:* A Writ of Prohibition is issued primarily to prevent a lower court from exceeding its jurisdiction, or acting contrary to the rules of natural justice. For instance, a judge may be restraint from adjudication upon a case wherein he is personally interested. The Writ of Prohibition is a counterpart of the Writ of Certiorari and an aggrieved person may make an application to the issue of both the Writs, that is 'Prohibition' and 'Certiorari'.

(4) *Certiorari:* It is a Writ which orders the removal of a suit from any court to another which is superior to the first. It may be used before a trial commences to prevent an excess or abuse of jurisdiction and to transfer the case for trial before a higher court. It may be invoked after trial as well in order to quash an order which has been made without jurisdiction or in defiance of the Rules of Natural Justice.

(5) *Quo Warranto:* An application for Writ of Quo Warranto seeks an order from the Supreme Court or High Court to restrain a person from acting in an office to which he is not entitled. It may also seek the office to be declared as vacant. What the court has to do is to determine where there has been

usurpation of an office of a public nature. For instance, a member of a Municipal Corporation may, through an application of Writ of Quo Warranto, challenge the authority of the Mayor, if he is of opinion that the Mayor was not properly elected.

The High Court can issue Writ under the provisions of Art. 226 and Art. 227 of the Constitution.

Art. 226. Powers of High Courts to issue Writs :

(1) Notwithstanding anything in Article 32, every High Court shall have power, throughout the territories in relation to which it exercises jurisdiction to issue to any person or authority, including in appropriate cases, any Government, within those territories, directions, orders or Writs, including Writs in the nature of habeas corpus, mandamus, prohibition, quo warranto and certiorari, or any of them, for the enforcement of any of the rights conferred in Part III and for any other purpose.

(2) The power conferred by Clause (1) to issue directions, orders or Writs to any Government authority or person may also be exercised by any High Court exercising jurisdiction in relation to the territories within which the cause of action, wholly or in part, arises for the exercise of such power, notwithstanding that the seat of such Government or authority or the residence is not within those territories.

(3) Where any party against whom an interim order, whether by way of injunction or stay or in any other manner, is made on, or in any proceeding relating to, a petition under Clause (1), without

(a) furnishing to such party copies of such petition and all documents in support of the plea for such interim order; and

(b) giving such party an opportunity of being heard, makes an application to the High Court for the vacation of such order and furnishes a copy of such application to the party in whose favour such order has been made or to the counsel of such party, the High Court shall dispose off the application within a period of four weeks from the date on which the copy of such application is so furnished, whichever is later, or where the High Court is closed, on the last day of that period, before the expiry of the next day afterwards on which the High Court is open, and if the application is not so disposed off, the interim order, shall, on the expiry of that period, or as the case may be, the expiry of the said next day, stand vacated.

(4) The power conferred on a High Court by this Article shall not be in derogation of the power conferred on the Supreme Court by Clause (2) of Article 32.

Art. 227. Power of superintendence over all courts by the High Court :

(1) Every High Court shall have superintendence over all courts and tribunals throughout the territories in relation to which it exercises jurisdiction.

(2) Without prejudice to the generality of the foregoing provisions, the High Court may:

(a) call for returns from such courts;

(b) make and issue general rules and prescribe forms for regulating the practice and proceedings of such courts; and

(c) prescribe forms in which books, entries and accounts shall be kept by the officers of any such courts.

(3) The High Court may also settle tables of fees to be allowed to the sheriff and all clerks and officers of such courts and to attorneys, advocates and pleaders practising therein.

Providing that any rules made, forms prescribed or tables settled under Clause (2) or Clause (3) shall not be inconsistent with the provision of any law for the time being in force, and shall require the previous approval of the Governor.

(4) Nothing in this Article shall be deemed to confer on a High Court powers of superintendence over any court or tribunal constituted by or under any law relating to the Armed Forces.

2.08 Directive Principles of the State Policy

The Directive Principles of State Policy constitute the 4th Part of the Constitution and are unique and novel in so far as they depict the ambitions and aspirations of the fathers of the Constitution. It was laid down that these provisions are not enforceable in any court but they are fundamental in the governess of the country and it was the duty of the State to apply these principles in making laws.[11]

Art. 39. Certain Principles of Policy to be followed by the State:

The State shall, in particular direct the policy towards securing:

(a) that the citizens, men and women, equally have the right to an adequate means of livelihood;

(b) that the ownership and control of the material resources of the community are so distributed as best to subserve the common good;

(c) that the operation of the economic system does not result in the concentration of wealth and means of production to the common detriment;

(d) that there is equal pay for equal work for both men and women;

(e) that the health and strength of workers, men and women, and the tender age of children are not abused and the citizens are not forced by economic necessity to enter a vocation unsuited to their age of strength;

(f) that the children are given opportunities and facilities to develop in a healthy manner and in conditions of freedom and dignity and that childhood and youth are protected against exploitation and against moral and material abandonment.

Notes

The picture, so far as it relates to the Constitutional Provision of equal pay for equal work for both, men and women is concerned, it is very grim. According to the "REPORT OF THE COMMITTEE ON THE STATUS OF WOMEN",[12] wage discrimination is very much practised in the form of fixing lower wage rate for women as compared to their male counterparts. The minimum wages fixed for non-skilled male workers is Rs. 7 to 9 per day for 8 hours a day whereas the wages for women for the same type of work and for the same period is Rs. 4 to 7 per day.[13]

A case came up for consideration before the Supreme Court which involved the question of equal pay for equal work for both men and women. The facts of the case was that Andrey D'Costa, a confidential lady stenographer of the company was being paid renumeration at the rate less favourable than her male colleague doing the same work. The company opposed it by saying that she was not doing the same work. The Supreme Court[14] held that the discrimination between the male and female stenographer of the company was only on the ground of sex and the Act does not permit the management to pay to a section of its employees doing the same work or a work of similar nature lesser pay contrary to the provisions of Section 4(1) of Equal Renumeration Act, 1976 (No. 25 of 1976).

Art. 42. Provision for just and humane conditions of work and maternity relief :

The State shall make a provision for securing just and humane conditions of work and for maternity relief.

Art. 44. Uniform Civil Code for the Citizen :

The State shall endeavour to secure for the citizens a uniform Civil Code throughout the territory of India.

Notes

The passing of a uniform Civil Code is not an easy proposition in a country where the population is composed of diverse religion and ethnic groups and different customs and rituals are being practised by each one of them. The passing of the Hindu Marriage Act (1955) and the Hindu Succession Act (1956) are examples of such efforts. However, on the question of giving maintenance to Shah Bano by the Supreme Court in accordance with Sec. 125 of Cr P.C. (Act 2 of 1974) generated sufficient opposition from a section of the society and the Govt. of India was pressurised to make a separate Act for Muslim women. Nevertheless, the courts in our counrty are granting maintenance applying Sec. 125 Cr P.C. to Muslim women in appropriate cases.

The absence of a uniform Civil Code in India puts Musilim women to disadvantage as according to Sariat, a Muslim male can marry and keep up to four wives as against the Hindus, Parsis, and Christian etc. Thus, converting to Islam to gain a new spouse is being practised by a few Hindus. The following cases are being cited by way of example.[15]

(1) JM, a businessman married to N are having three children out of this wedlock, over a period of fifteen years, changed his religion and embraced Islam. He took a Muslim alias and married a girl friend S @ F and when confronted by N ended the matter saying that his relationship with S @ F was perfectly justified and legitimate as both had embraced Islam. And after three months of his conversion, JM declared through an oath his decision to become a Hindu.

(2) The case of RK, whose marriage to VK dates back to the year 1978 was equally expedient. From the very beginning of the marriage VK alleged harassment by her in-laws over the question of dowry. One day RK brought home another women 'A' and legitimised their relationship through conversion to Islam and weeks later reconverted to Hinduism in a temple.

Thus, the convenience afforded by the Islamic personal law to opportunistic Hindu men with bigmay in their mind is misutilised to gain a new spouse as well as to escape payment of maintenance. The thing becomes all the more difficult for the discarded wife as the onus to prove bigmay is on the complainant and where can she get evidence to prove this.

REFERENCES

1. Subs. in the Constitution (42nd Amendment) by Act 1976, S. 2, w.e.f. 3.1.1977.
2. *AIR India* V. *Nargis Mirza and Others*, AIR 1981 SC 1829=1981 (4) SCC 335=1982 (1) SCR 882=1982 (2) SLR 117.
3. Added by Constitution (1st Constitution, Amendment Act), 1951, S. 2.
4. Subs. by Constitution (7th Amendment) Act 1956, Sec. 29 and Sch. for under any STATE specified in the 1st Sch. or any local or other authority in its territory and requirement as residence within that.
5. (1979) 4 SCC 260=AIR 1979 SC 1868.
6. AIR 1981 SC 1829=1981 (4) SCC 335=1982 (2) SCR 882=1982 (1) SLR 117.
7. *Bombay Labour Union* Vs. *International Franchises*, (1966) 2 SCR 493=AIR 1966 SC 492.
8. AIR 1952 Cal. 822.
9. AIR 1954 Madras, 67.
10. Prof. (Dir.) M.V. Pylee, "Constitution of India" Competition Success Review, May 1982, pp. 75–76.
11. Vide Art. 37 of the Constitution.

12. "Towards Equality", (Report of the Committee on the Status of women in India, Government of India, Ministry of Education and Social Welfare, Department of Social Welfare, December' 74. Table XIII, pp. 165–166—Source, Directorate of Economics & Statistics, Ministry of Agriculture, Government of India.
13. Gupta A.K., (Edited by) "Class Status and its Awareness" by R. Saran, from Women and Society, Criterion Publications, pp. 269.
14. *Mackinnon Mackenzie & Co. Ltd.* Vs. *Audreys D' Costa and Another*, AIR 1987 SC 1281=1987 Lab. IC 961=(1987) 2 SCC 469 =1987 SCC (Lab.) 100=(1987) 3 JT 34=1987 (2) SLR 690.
15. Diva Arora, "When one is not enough", *Sunday Times of India* review (Delhi Edition), dated 22.8.93, pp. 2.

Chapter 3

Female Infanticide and Female Foeticide

3.01 Infanticide

Infanticide means murder of an infant or a newly born baby. Infanticide as such has not been defined in the I.P.C. but since it amounts to the killing of a living person, the sections dealing with murder under the penal code is applicable to the offence of infanticide. Those who kill infants or newly born babies cannot claim the benefit of the right of private defence.

Infanticide is motivated by the necessity of getting rid of an illegitimate child as well as unwelcome offsprings whom the parents cannot afford.

3.02 Possible Causes of Infanticide

Infanticide of the female children in India is usually done out of the undermentioned necessity:

(1) Family vanity among the groups of warrior class.
(2) Inflated dowry demand by the parents as well as eligible bridegrooms and inability of the bride's parents to meet the same.
(3) Heavy expenses required to be incurred by the bride's party during marriages. The present day practice in a majority of societies is that, in addition to making payments of huge dowry, the bride's parents are required to meet the

expenses of both the parties and the groom's parents, at times, shamelessly demand it.

(4) At times, craze for a male child drives a family to sacrifice a daughter's life on account of superstitions under the influence of the miracleman of the community.

The killing of girl babies is frequently practiced in Thar desert area of Rajasthan, particularly among the Bhil Rajput family.[1] The infant is subjected to asphyxial deaths through mannual strangulation or through administration of opium. The male-female ratio in this area is 750 females per one thousand males, against All India figure of 929 and Rajasthan figure of 913 females per one thousand males. The figure of Jaisalmer district is 800 female per thousand males and among the Bhatti Rajput family, it is very low, that is 550 females per one thousand males.

In October 1986, the Central Government ordered an inquiry into the alleged killing of a baby girl into the family of a Legislature.[2] A C.I.D. enquiry was conducted by two officers, an Additional Superintendent of Police and an Assistant Superintendent of Police. The common thing in both the enquiries was that there is truth in the matter but since the Gujjar family in Rajasthan are well off and carry on money-lending business and, therefore, no one was coming forward to give evidence.[3] In the meantime a Public Interest Litigation (P.I.L.) case was filed before the Rajasthan High Court by Ms Summita Satyarthi, a Human Rights Activist, who prayed for a direction to be issued for holding a C.B.I. enquiry. After a great interest shown by the people a case of murder was registered against the Legislature.[4]

Among the Kellar community of landless farmers having a strength of about two lakhs, the economic condition of the people are so deplorable that it is difficult for any family to foot the bill of marriages of their daughters. However, the people somehow manage the marriage of one daughter but the marriage of two daughters is an impossibility. Therefore, a second daughter on being born, becomes an unwelcome child and is quickly done to death by administering a paste made from poisonous oleander berries. The menfolk dig a pit outside the house, watch the cries of baby and when it is stopped, the dead body is slipped into the pit and buried. Hardly there is any family where some or other child is not buried.[5]

According to a Times of India news report, from Madurai, a 26 years old woman of Chokknathpuram, who had vowed to carry "Agni Chatti" (firepot) to a nearby temple during the "Panguni Uthiram" festival could not keep up her vow as her husband declined to provide fund for that and in frustration, she doused her three daughters with kerosene oil and set them on fire. Thereafter she herself attempted to commit suicide. On hearing, the neighbours rushed and retrieved the children and hospitalised them. Cnly one could survive. It is pertinent to mention that she had a male child as well who was spared.[6]

3.03 Foeticide

Foeticide is the unlawful expulsion of foetus. It is also called "criminal abortion" or "causing miscarriage". When used in the legal sense, it includes both abortion and premature labour. As per medical sense, premature labour means expulsion of a child that has attained viability. The term "abortion" or "miscarriage" signify the expulsion of foetus or ovum at an earlier period.[7]

3.04 Classification of Abortion

Abortion may be classified into:
(a) natural and
(b) artificial

Natural Abortion: Natural abortions are common phenomena and many occur due to such reasons as mother's ill-health, local disease, or diseases of the generative organs, shocks, fear, excessive joy, accidental falls etc. Hence, appropriate care is required in respect of the health of the pregnant woman.

Artificial Abortion: Premature evacuation of foetus, whether medically, surgically or through indigenous method is known as artificial abortion. Artificial abortion is a criminal offence punishable under Sections 312–316 of the Indian Penal Code. The Sections run as under:

Sec. 312. Causing miscarriage:

Whoever voluntarily causes a woman with a child to miscarry, shall, if such miscarriage be not caused in good faith for the purpose of saving the life of the woman, be punished with imprisonment of either description for a term which may extend to three years, or with fine, or with both; and, if the woman be quick with child, shall be punished with imprisonment of either description for a term which may extend to seven years, and shall also be liable to fine.

Explanation: A woman who causes herself to miscarry, is within the meaning of this section.

Sec. 313. Causing miscarriage without woman's consent:

Whoever, commits the offence defined in the last preceeding section without the consent of the woman, whether the woman is quick with child or not, shall be punished with imprisonment for life, or with imprisonment of either description for a term which may extend to ten years, and shall be liable to fine.

Sec. 314. Death caused by act done with intent to cause miscarriage:

Whoever, with intent to cause the miscarriage of a woman with child, does any act which caused the death of such woman, shall be punished with imprisonment of either description for a term which may extend to ten years, and shall also be liable to fine.

If Act done without woman's consent—and if the act is done without the consent of the woman, shall be punished either with imprisonment for life, or with punishment above mentioned.

Explanation: It is not essential to this offence that the offender should know that the act is likely to cause death.

Sec. 315. Act done with intent to prevent child being born alive or to cause it to die after birth:

Whoever, before the birth of any child does any act with the intention of thereby preventing that child from being born alive or causing it to die after its birth, shall, if such act not caused in good faith for the purpose of saving the life of the mother be punished with imprisonment of either description for a term which may extend to ten years, or with fine, or with both.

Sec. 316. Causing death of quick unborn child by act amounting to culpable homicide:

Whoever, does any act under such circumstances, that if he

thereby causes death he would be guilty of culpable homicide, and does by such act cause the death of a quick unborn child, shall be punished with imprisonment of either description for a term which may extend to ten years, and shall also be laible to fine.

Illustration

A, knowing that he is likely to cause the death of a pregnant woman, does an act which, if it caused the death of the woman, would amount to culpable homicide. The woman is injured but does not die; but the death of an unborn quick child with which she is pregnant is thereby caused, A is guilty of the offence defined in this section.

3.05 Legalisation of Pregnancy Termination

Except for saving the life of the pregnant woman, termination of pregnancy (Bhrun Hatya) was a penal offence in accordance with the provisions of the aforesaid sections of the I.P.C.

After India achieved independence and with the passage of time, population started growing rapidly with such an alarming speed that it began to be seen that available resources would not be adequate to meet the necessities of the people in the country. Thus, several family planning programmes were evolved and propagated among the people of the country through mass media. It was further thought that a legislation to legalise termination of pregnancy was another means by which the growing population could be checked. Thus Medical Termination of Pregnancy Act (1971) was enacted as a means of population control. According to it (Sec. 3), the objective of termination of pregnancy are two fold:

(1) *Therapeutic*: When the continuance of pregnancy is likely to endanger the life of the pregnant woman and could cause grave injuries to her physical and mental health.

(2) *Eugenic*: When there is the risk of the child being born with serious physical or mental handicap. This may occur, if the pregnant woman in the first three months of her pregnancy suffers from (a) German measles; chicken pox or small pox, viral infection including viral heptitis, toxoplasmonia or any

other disease which would have affected the health of the woman. (b) The pregnant woman takes certain medicines, whether under medical advice or otherwise which affect the foetus; (c) The pregnant woman receives radio or any invisible-ray therapy and (d) Insanity of the either of the two or both spouse.

(3) *Humanitarian*: When the pregnancy is in consequence of sexual assault.

(4) *Social*: When the pregnancy has occurred on account of failure of contraceptive device.

3.06 Genetic Technology[8]

Contraceptive means to ensure sex without reprodution. Surrogate motherhood, *in-vitre* fertilisation and artificial insemination are advancements in genetic technology in which reproduction is possible without sex. New techniques have enabled the determination of the abnormalities as well as the sex of the child in advance much before the birth of the child. The pre-natal sex-determination is done through aminocentasis, wherein amnetic fluid is drawn through the uterus of a pregnant woman. It is normally possible to determine after sixteen weeks at which stage abortion is risky and can cause injury to the foetus on account of the removal of amnetic fluid. Any defect or physical deformity in the child can, therefore, be attributed on to the parents or the doctor, who drew the fluid. Since the child cannot sue either the parents or the doctor, the state is expected to institute legal proceedings against the wrong-doers.

The determination of sex is also possible through Chorionic Villi Sampling (CVS) by vaginal extraction from eight to sixteen weeks of pregnancy. This method is also dangerōus as it causes the pregnant woman to infect and in effect spontaneous abortions can take place. It may as well result in fatality of the pregnant woman.

The other method of sex determination is through ultrasound scanning which though non-invasive is unreliable, even at the advanced stage of pregnancy.

3.07 Misuse of Aminocentasis[9]

The scientists have developed the genetic technology in order to ascertain in advance if the child in the mother's womb has any deformity. However, unscrupulous people in the society are using the know-how to reduce the female population in an organised and systematic manner. The Medical Termination of Pregnancy Act, 1971 only ensures a legal sanction to a Medical Practitioner to abort a female foetus. Thus, the two together, that is MTPA and Sex-determination Technology has put India on its way to technological and legal femicide. Unregulated technology and the legal Act have created a new problem in bringing a decline in female population.

According to the Provision of Section 3 of the Act, a Registered Medical Practitioner is entitled to abort a foetus within twelve weeks of pregnancy and two of them can abort a pregnancy having a length of 12 to 20 weeks. In either case they will have to take a stand that abortion was necessary in the interest of the health of the woman.

The anguish of a pregnancy by sexual assault is presumed to constitute a grave injury to a woman's mental health. However, the failure of a contraceptive device cannot cause any such damage to the mental health. Assessment of the anticipated risk is rather vague and gives a licence to abort female child with the aid of pre-natal sex determination test.

However, business in abortion became possible and flourishing on account of provisions of Section 5 of the MTP Act, 1971 which is an enabling provision for an emergent situation and permits non-application of provisions of Section 3 and Section 4 of the Act. The Section enables a doctor without any experience in gynaecology and obstetrics to operate after having formed an opinion with due care and attention that termination of pregnancy is immediately necessary to save the life of the pregnant woman. It may be pertinent to mention that while making a provision of the Section, care to provide any safeguard has not been introduced to prevent its misuse. A doctor can now be prosecuted under the I.P.C. only. The Act suffers from the following flaws:

(i) The Act does not provide any guidelines for calculating the commencement of pregnancy and to assess the period of twelve weeks or twenty weeks. The matter has been left entirely to the wisdom the doctor.

(ii) The Act does not require that the pregnant woman countersigns or affixes her signature/thumb impression on the key column of the register containing details regarding the duration of pregnancy. Thus, any evidence, which, otherwise could have been provided, is always missing.

(iii) The evidentary value of matter is further weakened by the type of consent Form C prescribed under the Central Rules. There is no column that the doctor makes a declaration that he has explained to the pregnant woman the reasons for the termination of her pregnancy.

(iv) As usual, the Act further ensures a cover for the doctor as per Section 8 of the Act which lays down that no suit or proceedings shall lie against the doctor if he has acted in good faith. It is very difficult to prove that the doctor did not exercise reasonable care and lacked good faith.

The dangerous form of genetic engineering by selectively aborting the new born child has been flourishing in the capital city of India as well as in several big and small cities of the state on account of no value being attached to a female child in comparison to the male counterpart. According to a rough estimate around 78,000 female foeticide were aborted after prenatal sex determination test through aminocentasis. In 1983, Bombay had only three sex-clinics and over a period of next five years, it had multiplied to 258 private clinics in addition to the sixteen recognised Government clinics. No permit or licence is required to set up a clinic of this type. On account of the coming up of a large number of clinics, there is a competition in the market and the fees charged (which had become between Rs. 150 to Rs. 500) is within the reach of a common man. The popularity of the method has spread to small places in far-flung areas. The samples now can be carried to Bombay or Delhi or Calcutta or any big city of the country from the nearby places. A survey made by Women's Centre has revealed that out of 8000 abortions checked, 7999 were in respect of females.[8,10]

One clinic in Bombay is reported to have advertised that the cost of abortion is cheaper than the amount required for the marriage and payment of dowry.

The availability of medical technology which could assist pre-selection of sex has enraged some feminist groups, voluntary organisations and these organisations have demanded a total ban. The lobby of doctors who perform these tests, on the other hand, oppose the demand on the ground that if the ban is enforced, abortions would be performed by quakes, who, even now handle about 16 per cent of the cases in Bombay. There is some force in the demand of the doctors also. The whole issue is dependent upon the attitude of the people towards the female child. At the rate, the pre-natal sex determination tests are gaining popularity and being used in aborting female foetus, the day is not far when the woman may become an endangered species.[11]

Initially in seven states of the country, nearly one dozen doctors offered to perform these tests which, for the first time was introduced in All India Institute of Medical Sciences, Delhi, primarily to discover genetic disorders in foetus in those cases where the parents had the history of abnormality. Since in course of the determination of the genetic disorder, it was found that the method reveals the sex of the unborn child, it became popular as a method for determination of pre-natal sex of the child. The Medical Termination of Pregnancy Act, 1971, made it a convenient tool for selective abortion.

Consequent upon a widespread resentment against this test, the Maharashtra State has taken a lead and the Legislature of Maharashtra Assembly passed the Regulation; "Use of Pre-natal Diagnostic Techniques Act, 1988." The salient features of the Act as under:

3.08 Salient Features of the Act

(a) Section 3 of the Act prohibits carrying of the pre-natal diagnostic tests by an unregistered genetic centre laboratory or clinic.

(b) Section 4 of the Act lays down the fulfilment of five conditions for the performance of diagonistic tests. The important conditions are that woman should be near about the age of 35 years and she has a history of at least a couple of abortions, family history of mental retardation and/or physical abnormalities. These provisions, if strictly enforced, can do away with the genetic tests conducted for clandestine purposes.

(c) Sub-section (3) of Section 4 of the Act outlines the purposes which indirectly aims at preventing a child having genetic abnormalities to be born. However, some genetic characteristics are sex-linked. So if one knows such abnormalities, he comes to know of the sex of the child in that case. Section 5 of the Act, prohibits the carrying out of the tests for sex determination of the foetus as it is implied that if he knows the sex of the child, he will disclose the same to the parents.

(d) Section 2(k) defines, "Pre-Natal Diagnostic Tests" and mentions some of the tests but does not cover pre-selection techniques like Eriocsem's test (the test which separates sperms to identify these carrying the male 'Y' Chromosomes) and the Japanese Method which selectively centrifugates chromosomes in two bands.

3.09 Central Act on Foeticide (Pre-Natal Sex Determination Test)[12,13]

After having passed the Act, The Maharashtra Government forwarded a copy of the Bill to the Union Law Ministry to examine whether the States have the Constitutional Authority to undertake legislation in this regard or only parliament has the competence to pass an Act. The Government of India has constituted an eight member committee in 1987 to go into the details of the Act. The members are drawn from the legal and medical profession. The terms of reference of the committee include preamble or regulation of 'Pre-Natal Diagnostic Techniques' guidelines for regulation of Genetic Centre, Laboratory or Clinic including the place/institutions as recognised genetic centres/clinic or laboratory and steps for creating an awareness among the members of the public about the sex determination legislation.

The proposed ban on the 'Pre-Natal Sex-Determination Test' or its regulation to restrict its use would certainly cover doctors, institutions, nursing homes and couples desirous of aborting the female foetus. The Government may consider the total ban on the pre-natal sex determination test and if that be not possible may restrict its general use and confine the use to the recognised institutions. The Government of India, may, perhaps, consider the de-recognition of doctors on ethical ground by the Medical

Council by way of punishment to those who conduct such tests for the purposes of female foeticide.

3.10 Conclusion

No legislation or legal measures can succeed unless the same is enforced honestly and with stern hands. If it is not done with honesty of purpose, it provides opportunity to unscrupulous persons to earn corrupt money. Unless better living conditions in respect of females are enforced and an improvement in their status is brought out, no measures could be successful. The reservation policy of the Government in Government jobs may, perhaps, be revised to provide a substantial percentage of posts to the women eligible candidates in addition to what they acquire on merit.

REFERENCES

1. S. Dhaundhial, "Ek Kanya Pujak Desh Ke Kanya Drohi" *Saptahik Hindustan* (Hindi), Vol. VII(1), No. 39, 13 to 19 November, 1988, pp. 16–21.
2. A. Qureshy, "Killing Baby Girls a Social Practice", *Hindustan Times News Item*, New Delhi, October 30, 1988.
3. H.T. Correspondent, 'CBI Probe in Female Infanticide cases urged.' *Hindustan Times* (Delhi Ed.), dated 29.10.1988.
4. News item from Jaipur, "Case filed against Brijender Singh" *Hindustan Times* (Delhi Ed.), dated Nov. '4, 1988.
5. Venkata Raman in Uslipatti, "Born to Die", *India Today*, June 15, 1986 pp. 26–33.
6. "Mother Kills two Female Kids", *Times of India* (Delhi Ed.), dated 3.4.1993.
7. Weddel, L.A., Lyons Medical Jurisprudence for India, Vth. Edition (1914), Thacker Spink & Co., Calcutta and Shimla. pp. 288.
8. Sandhya Jain, "Central Law on Female Foeticide Likely", *Hindustan Times* (Delhi Ed.), dated June 4, 1988.
9. Krishna Mahajan, "Legal Perspective: Women Vs. Girl Child", *Hindustan Times*, dated Oct. '1987.
10. S. Tripathy, "Child Birth-Paying Heed, Ban on Sex Determination", *India Today*, Jan. '31, 1988, pp. 55.
11. H.T. Correspondent, "Woman become Endangered", *Hindustan Times* (Delhi Ed.), November 25, 1988.
12. Hindustan Times News Item, "State's Views sought on Sex Test Rule", *Hindustan Times*, dated June 2, 1988.
13. Sandhya Jain, "Central Law on Female Foeticide likely", *Hindustan Times* (Delhi Ed.), dated June 4, 1988.

MAHARASHTRA REGULATION OF USE OF PRE-NATAL DIAGNOSTIC TECHNIQUES ACT, 1988 (MAHARASHTRA ACT NO. XV OF 1988)*

An Act to provide for the regulation of the use of medical or scientific techniques of pre-natal diagnosis solely for the purpose of detecting genetic or metabolic disorders of chromosomal abnormalities or certain congenital abnormalities or sex-linked disorders and/or prevention of the misuse of these techniques for the purpose of pre-natal sex determination leading to female foeticide, and for matters connected therewith, or incidental thereto.

Whereas it is expedient to regulate the use of pre-natal diagnostic procedures like Amniocentasis or any other present or future techniques solely for the purpose of detection of genetic or metabolic disorders or chromosomal abnormalities or certain congenital anomalies or sex-linked disorders and to prevent the misuse of such techniques for pre-natal sex-determination leading to female foeticide, and to provide for matters connected therewith or incidental thereto, it is hereby enacted in the thirty-ninth year of the Republic of India as follows:

CHAPTER I

PRELIMINARY

1. *Short title, extent and commencement:*

(1) The Act may be called the Maharashtra Regulation of use of Pre-natal Diagnostic Techniques Act, 1988.

(2) It shall extend to the whole of the State of Maharashtra.

(3) It shall come into force on such date as the State Government may by notification in the Official Gazette; appoint.

2. *Definition:*

In this Act, unless the context otherwise requires:

(a) "*Advertisement*" means any notice, circular, label, wrapper, printed matter or other document on display and also includes any announcement or visible representation made with the help of light, sound, smoke, gas, cinematograph films or video tapes;

* Received the assent of the Governor in Maharashtra Government Gazette on the 28th, April 1988.

(b) *"Appropriate Authority"* means the State Appropriate Authority consitituted by the State Government under Section 6;

(c) *"Genetic Clinic"* or *"clinic"* means a place registered under this Act for the purpose of carrying out the activities of a Gazette Counselling centre as well as a Genetic Laboratory;

(d) *"Genetic Counselling Centre"* or *"centre"* means an institute, hospital, nursing home or any place by whatever name called registered under the Act for providing genetic counselling to patients and for performing obstetrical or gynaecological procedures such as foetoscopy, taking samples of amniotic fluids, chorionic villi, blood or any tissue of a pregnant female for being sent to genetic clinic or laboratory for pre-natal diagnostic test;

(e) *"Genetic Laboratory"* or *"laboratory"* means a place registered under this Act which provides facility for carrying out the analysis or tests of samples received from Genetic Counselling Centres for pre-natal diagnostic test;

(f) *"Gynaecologist"* means a person who has acquired a post-graduate qualification in Gynaecology after obtaining M.B.B.S. degree;

(g) *"Local Vigilance Committee"* means a Committee appointed under Section 16;

(h) *"Medical Geneticist"* means a person who has acquired a degree or diploma or certificate in Medical Genetics in the field of pre-natal diagnostic techniques or has experience of at least two years of work in the field after obtaining any of the following degrees, namely:

(i) M.B.B.S. or any other degree equivalent thereto;

(ii) M.Sc. or Ph.D. in Biological Science or any other degree equivalent thereto;

(i) *"Pre-natal Diagnostic Procedures"* means all gynaecological or obstetrical or medical procedures such as foetoscopy, taking or removing samples of amniotic fluid, chorionic villi, blood or any tissue of a pregnant female for being sent to a genetic clinic or laboratory for pre-natal diagnostic test;

(j) *"Pre-natal Diagnostic Technique"* includes all pre-natal diagnostic procedures and pre-natal diagnostic tests;

(k) *"Pre-natal Diagnostic Test"* means any test or analysis of amniotic fluid, chorionic villi, blood or any tissue of a pregnant female carried out in a genetic clinic or laboratory in order to detect genetic or metabolic disorders or chromosomal abnormalities or certain congenital abnormalities or haemoglobinopathies or sex-linked diseases;

(l) "*Prescribed*" means prescribed by rules made under this Act;

(m) "*Registered Medical Practitioner*" means a medical practitioner who possesses any recognised medical qualification as defined in Clause (h) of Section 2 of the Indian Council Act, 1956, and whose name has been entered in the register prepared or deemed to be prepared and maintained under the Maharashtra Medical Council Act, 1965;

(n) "*State Vigilance Committee*" means the Committee appointed by the State Government under Section 13;

(o) "*Voluntary Organisation*" means the voluntary organisation working in the field of Health or Women Welfare or Human Rights.

CHAPTER II
REGULATION OF CENTRE, LABORATORY CLINIC AND PRE-NATAL DIAGNOSTIC PROCEDURE AND TECHNIQUE

3. *Regulation of centre and clinic:*

(1) No genetic centre, laboratory or clinic or place, unless registered under the Act, shall carry out or associate or help in carrying out activities relating to the pre-natal diagnostic techniques with the help of procedures such as amniocentasis, chorionic villi sampling or any other pre-natal diagnostic technique.

(2) No registered centre, laboratory or clinic shall employ or take services, whether honorary or on payment, from persons, including gynaecologists, who do not possess the prescribed qualifications.

(3) No medical geneticist or gynaecologist or medical practitioner or person shall carry out or help in carrying out or cause to carry out either himself or through his assistants, agents or associates, any pre-natal diagnostic technique at a place other than a genetic councelling centre, a genetic clinic or a genetic laboratory registered under this Act.

4. *Regulations of pre-natal diagnostic procedures and techniques:*

(1) No place including the registered Genetic Laboratory

shall be used and no person shall use or cause to be used the pre-natal diagnostic techniques except for the purposes specified in sub-sections (2) and (3).

(2) The pre-natal diagnostic technique shall not be used or carried out unless the person qualified to do so is satisfied that any one or more of the following conditions are fulfilled in each case, namely:

(i) age of the pregnant woman is about thirty-five years;
(ii) history of two or more abortions or foetal loss;
(iii) history of exposure to potentially teratogenic drugs, radiations, infections or hazardous chemicals;
(iv) family history of mental retardation or physical deformities such as spastic or deaf-mute child or any other genetic disease;
(v) any other condition as may be approved by the appropriate authority.

(3) The pre-natal diagnostic technique shall be carried out under this Act solely for the purpose of detection of any one or more of the following abnormalities namely:

(i) chromosomal abnormalities;
(ii) genetic metabolic diseases;
(iii) haemoglobinopathies;
(iv) sex-linked genetic diseases;
(v) congenital anomalies;
(vi) any other abnormalities or diseases as may be declared by the appropriate authority for the purpose of this sub-section.

(4) Before carrying out the pre-natal diagnostic procedures, the person qualified to do so shall obtain a written consent of the female-patient in the prescribed form after all possible side-effects of such procedures are clearly explained to her.

5. *Prohibition of pre-natal diagnostic techniques for certain purposes—on and from the date of commencement of the Act:*

(1) No genetic counselling centre, laboratory, clinic, gynaecologist, medical practitioner or any other person shall use or allow to be used the pre-natal diagnostic techniques including ultra-sonography for the purpose of indicating the sex of a foetus with or without the possible object of female foeticide.

(2) No centre, laboratory or clinic shall give advertisement in any manner regarding facilities of pre-natal prediction of sex available at the centre, laboratory or clinic.

(3) No person or members of family of a pregnant female shall seek to get the pre-natal diagnostic procedure done for a purpose other than those mentioned in sub-section (3) of Section 4.

CHAPTER III
STATE APPELLATE AUTHORITY

6. *Constitution of state appropriate authority:*

(1) On the commencement of this Act, or as soon thereafter as may be, the State Government shall, by a notification in the Official Gazette, constitute a State Appropriate Authority which shall consist of the following members, namely:

(i) the Director of Health Services, ex-officio Chairman;
(ii) the Joint Director of Health Services, ex-officio Secretary;
(iii) two representatives of voluntary organisation;
(iv) the Director of Medical Education and Research or his representative not below the rank of a Deputy Director;
(v) a Gynaecologist;
(vi) a Medical Geneticist;
(vii) a representative of the Indian Council of Medical Research.

The members referred to in clauses (ii), (iii), (v), (vi) and (vii) shall be nominated by the State Government.

(2) The Appropriate Authority may invite for its meeting the Civil Surgeon or Chief Medical Officer of the local area concerned as an Invitee Member whenever it thinks necessary.

7. *Meetings of authority:*

(1) The Appropriate Authority shall meet as and when necessary but not less than two meetings of the Committee shall be held every year. The Appropriate Authority may frame rules for conduct of its business.

(2) All decisions in the meetings of the Appropriate Authority shall be taken by a simple majority of members present at a meeting and the quorum for a meeting shall be of five members including the Chairman. The decisions of the Authority shall

not be vitiated or held as invalid only on the ground of vacancy or absence of any member:

(3) Any vacancy in the membership of the Authority on account of death, resignation or any other reason shall be filled expeditiously by the State Government and until the vacancy is so filled the remaining member shall continue to function as if no vacancy has fallen.

(4) The terms, conditions and duration of office of the non-official members shall be such as the State Government may, from time to time determine.

8. *Functions of authority:*

(1) The functions of the Appropriate Authority shall be as follows, namely:

(i) to advise Government on policy matters relating to use of pre-natal diagnostic techniques;

(ii) to recommend to Government changes necessary in the rules prescribed under the Act in keeping with progress in science, evolution of new procedures and techniques and in the light of the experience of the implementation of the Act;

(iii) to consider all applications made to it under Section 9 for grant, or section 10 for renewal, of registration to centres, laboratories and clinics;

(iv) to consider the complaints of breach of provisions of the Act and rules and to take action of suspension or cancellation of registration under Section 11;

(v) to prescribe guidelines about standards to be maintained by the registered centres, laboratories and clinics;

(vi) to supervise and monitor the performance of centres, laboratories or clinics;

(vii) to evolve a code of conduct for the persons who own, manage or run the centre, laboratory or clinic and for persons employed in such centre, laboratory or clinic;

(viii) to create public awareness against the practice of female foeticide which results in discrimination against women even from the pre-natal stage;

(ix) generally to supervise the implementation of the Act and rules made thereunder;

(x) to take such other action as the State Government may direct.

(2) In discharging its functions under this Act, the Appropriate Authority shall have all the powers of a Civil Court in respect of the follwoing matters under the Code of the Civil Procedure, 1908 in trying a suit:

(a) proof of facts by affidavit;
(b) summoning and enforcing the attendance of any person, and examining him on oath or affirmation;
(c) compelling the production of documents; and
(d) issuing commissions for the examination of witnesses.

CHAPTER IV
REGISTRATION OF CENTRE, LABORATORY OR CLINIC

9. *Registration of pre-natal diagnostic centres, laboratories or clinics:*

(1) Every genetic centre, laboratory or clinic engaged either partly or exclusively in pre-natal diagnostic techniques for any of the purposes mentioned in sub-section (3) of Section 4 of this Act shall apply for registration within sixty days from such date as the State Government may, by notification in the Official Gazette, appoint in this behalf, being a date not earlier than the date of constitution of the Appropriate Authority. Such application shall be made in such form and manner and shall be accompanied by such fees as may be prescribed.

(2) Subject to the provisions of Section 5, any centre, laboratory or clinic engaged in pre-natal diagnostic techniques for any of the purposes mentioned in sub-section (3) of Section 4 on the date appointed under sub-section (1) shall cease to carry out any pre-natal diagnostic technique on expiry of six months from such date unless such centre, laboratory or clinic has already made an application for registration and is so registered before that date under this Act.

(3) No person shall open a new genetic centre, laboratory or clinic after the commencement of this Act unless it is duly registered under this Act.

10. *Certificate of registration:*

(1) The Appropriate Authority shall, after holding an inquiry, if necessary, and after satisfying itself that the applicant has complied with all the requirements of this Act and the rules

made thereunder, grant a certificate of registration in the prescribed form to the centre, laboratory or clinic, as the case may be.

(2) If the applicant does not comply with the requirements of this Act and the rules the Appropriate Authority may give reasonable time to the applicant to effect such compliance. If, after the inquiry and giving an opportunity to the applicant of being heard, the Appropriate Authority is satisfied that the applicant has not complied with such requirements, it shall reject the application for registration after giving reasons therefore.

(3) Every certificate of registration shall be renewed in such manner and after such period and on payment of such fees as may be prescribed.

(4) The certificate of registration shall be displayed by the registered centre, laboratory or clinic in some conspicuous place in its office or place of business.

11. *Cancellation or suspension of registration:*

The Appropriate Authority may suo motu, or shall, on receipt of recommendation from the State Vigilance Committee or a Local Vigilance Committee issue a notice to the centre, laboratory or clinic to show cause why its registration should not be suspended or cancelled for the reasons mentioned in the notice. If after giving a reasonable opportunity to the centre, laboratory or clinic the Appropriate Authority is satisfied that there has been a breach of any of the provisions of this Act or rules, it may, without prejudice to any criminal action that it may take against the centre, laboratory or clinic, cancel or suspend its registration for such period as it may think fit.

12. *Appeal:*

(1) The centre, laboratory or clinic of which application for registration has been rejected or against which an order of suspension or cancellation of registration has been passed by the Appropriate Authority, may within thirty days from the date of receipt of the order, file an appeal to the State Government in the prescribed manner. The order of the State Government on appeal shall be final.

(2) If an appeal against the order of the Appropriate Authority directing suspension or cancellation of registration has

been filed or if the appeal so filed has been rejected by the State Government, the copy of the order of the Appropriate Authority or the State Government, as the case may be, shall be forwarded by the Appropriate Authority to the Maharashtra Medical Council for taking suitable action against the medical practitioner practising in such centre, laboratory or clinic and in respect of which such order has been passed.

CHAPTER V
VIGILANCE COMMITTEES

13. *State Vigilance Committee:*

On the commencement of this Act, or as soon thereafter as may be, the State Government shall appoint a State Vigilance Committee which shall consist of:

(i) Secretary of the Appropriate Authority as Chairman and Convener;
(ii) Two representatives of voluntary organisations;
(iii) The Director-General of Information and Public Relations or his representative;
(iv) A Gynaecologist;
(v) A Medical Geneticist;
(vi) A Civil Surgeon or Chief Medical Officer.

14. *Functions of State Vigilance Committee:*

The functions of the State Vigilance Committee shall be:

(a) to pay periodic and surprise visits to the centres, laboratories and clinics, with a view to check compliance of the provisions of the Act and the rules;

(b) to investigate complaints by members of public or other institutions or in the press about contravention of the provisions of this Act or the rules;

(c) to seize incriminating evidence or record for further administrative or legal action;

(d) to recommend to the Appropriate Authority, the cancellation or otherwise of registration of, or prosecution against a centre, laboratory or clinic;

(e) to check and prevent operation of unauthorised centres, laboratories or clinics;

(f) to take such other action as the Appropriate Authority or the State Government may direct.

15. *Meeting of State Vigilance Committee:*

(1) The State Vigilance Committee shall hold meetings as and when necessry to conduct business which may be placed before it. The Committee shall have powers to frame rules for conduct of its business.

(2) All decisions in the meeting of the State Vigilance Committee shall be taken by a simple majority of members present in the meeting. There shall be quorum of four members including the Chairman for a meeting.

(3) The decisions or any action of the State Vigilance Committee shall not be vitiated or held as invalid only on the ground of vacancy or absence of any member.

16. *Local Vigilance Committees:*

(1) There shall be a local Vigilance Committee for any such local area as the Appropriate Authority may specify. A local Vigilance Committee may consist of the following members, namely:

(i) deputy Director of Health Services of the region, ex-officio Chairman and Convener;
(ii) District Health Officer of the concerned district;
(iii) Civil Surgeon or Chief Medical Officer of the local area;
(iv) any officer not below the rank of a Tahsildar having the powers of an Executive Magistrate nominated by the Collector;
(v) a Gynaecologist;
(vi) a Medical Geneticist;
(vii) a representative of women's organisations;
(viii) a representative of any other voluntary organisations;

(2) The non-official members of the local Vigilance Committee shall be nominated by the Appropriate Authority.

17. *Meetings and Functiuons of Local Vigilance Committee:*

(1) All decisions in the meeting of local Vigilance Committee shall be taken by a simple majority of members present at the

meeting. There shall be a quorum of four members including the Chairman for a meeting.

(2) The decision or any action of a local Vigilance Committee shall not be vitiated or held as invalid only on the ground of a vacancy or absence of any member.

(3) All decisions and actions taken by a local Vigilance Committee shall be reported by it to the State Vigilance Committee in such manner and at such intervals as may be prescribed.

(4) The functions and powers of a local Vigilance Committee shall be the same as that of State Vigilance Committee which shall be discharged by it within its local area.

18. *Duration of appointment of non-official members and their allowances:*

(1) The non-official members of the State Vigilance Committee and a local Vigilance Committee shall be appointed for a period of three years and after expiry of the period of appointment they shall be eligible for re-appointment.

(2) The non-official members of these Committees shall be entitled to travelling, sitting and other allowances at such rates as the State Government may, from time to time determine.

CHAPTER VI
OFFENCES AND PENALTIES

19. *Offences and penalties:*

(1) Any Medical Geneticist, Gynaecologist, Registered Medical practitioner or any person who owns a centre, laboratory or a clinic or is employed in a centre, laboratory or a clinic or who gives his services to such a centre, laboratory or clinic, whether as an honorary or otherwise, and who contravenes any of the provisions of this Act or rules made thereunder shall, on conviction, be liable to be punished with rigorous imprisonment for a term which may extend to three years and with fine which may extend to rupees five thousand.

Provided that, in the case of every conviction the period of sentence shall not be less than one year and fine shall not be less than rupees one thousand.

Provided further that the name of Gynaecologist or Registered Medical Practitioner who has been convicted by Court shall be reported by the Appropriate Authority to the Maharashtra Medical Council for taking suitable action including that of suspension of his name from the register of the Council for a period of two years for the first offence and for permanent removal for subsequent offence.

(2) Any person who seeks the aid of a centre or laboratory or clinic or of a Medical Geneticist or a Gynaecologist or a Medical Practitioner for carrying out pre-natal diagnostic techniques on a pregnant female for any purpose other than these specified in sub-section (3) of Section 4 shall on conviction be liable to be punished with rigorous imprisonment for a term which may extend to three years and with fine which may extend to rupees three thousand.

Provided that, in the case of every conviction under this sub-section the period of sentence shall not be less than one year and fine shall not be less than rupees one thousand;

Provided further that the Court shall always presume, unless otherwise proved, that a woman who seeks such aid of pre-natal diagnostic procedures on herself has been compelled to do so by her husband or members of his family, who shall, on conviction, be liable to be punished for abetment of the offence under this sub-section for the same sentence and in that case the woman shall be liable to pay a fine of rupees fifty for each such offence.

(3) Whoever, contravenes any of the provisions of this Act or any rule or any direction issued thereunder, for which no penalty has been elsewhere provided in this Act, shall be punishable with imprisonment for a term which may extend to three months or with fine which may extend to one thousand rupees or with both, and in the case of continuing contravention with an additional fine which may extend to five hundred rupees for every day during which such contravention continues after convicting for the first such contravention.

20. *Offences to be cognizable etc.:*

Every offence punishable under sub-section (1) or (2) of Section 19 shall be cognizable, non-bailable and compoundable.

21. *Powers of court:*

(1) No court shall take cognizance of any offence under this Act except on a complaint made by:

(a) The Appropriate Authority, State or local Vigilance Committee or any officer authorised in this behalf by the State Government or the Appropriate Authority or the State or local Vigilance Committee.

(b) Any person who has given notice of not less than sixty days, in the manner prescribed, to the Appropriate Authority, any vigilance committee or an officer authorised as aforesaid of the alleged offence and of his intention to make a complaint to the Court, and no Court inferior to that of a Metropolitan Magistrate or a Judicial Magistrate of the first class shall try any offence punishable under this Act.

(2) Where a complaint has been made under clause (b) of sub-section (1), the Court may, on demand by such person, direct the Authortiy or Vigilance Committee to make available the relevant records in its possession to that person.

Provided that the Authority or Committee may refuse to make any such record available to such person if the same is, in its opinion against the public interest.

(3) The Court may, for adequate and special reasons to be recorded in judgement, impose a sentence less than the minimum sentence that can be imposed under this Act.

CHAPTER VII
MISCELLANEOUS

22. *Maintenance of records:*

(1) All records, charts, forms, consent letters and all other documents required to be maintained under this Act and the rules shall be preserved for a period of two years or such period as may be prescribed.

Provided that, if any criminal or other proceedings are instituted against any centre, laboratory or clinic, the records and all other documents of such centre, laboratory or clinic shall be preserved till the final disposal of such proceedings.

(2) All such records shall at all reasonable times be made available for inspection to the members of the Appropriate Authority or members of State or local Vigilance Committee or

to any other person as may be authorised by this State Government in this behalf.

23. *Power to seize records:*

(1) If the Appropriate Authority of the State or local Vigilance Committee has reason to believe that any breach of the provisions of this Act has been committed at any centre, laboratory or clinic or the pre-natal diagnostic procedures or techniques are used for prediction of sex, then the Chairman of the State or local Vigilance Committee shall have power to search the premises of such centre, laboratory or clinic and to seize such records and documents as may be necessary on granting a receipt for the same, and the records and documents so seized shall be retained by the Authority or the Committee for so long a period as may be necessary in connection with any proceeding or for a prosecution under this Act.

(2) The provisions of the Code of Criminal Procedure, 1973, shall apply to the proceedings taken under sub-section(1) and the person taking such proceeding shall take the assistance of a police officer of the nearest police station whenever necessary.

24. *Protection of action taken in good faith:*

No suit, prosecution or other legal proceeding shall lie against the State Government, the Appropriate Authority, State or local Vigilance Committee or any person acting under their authority for anything which is in good faith done or intended to be done under this Act.

25. *Exemption:*

The State Government may exempt a genetic centre, laboratory or clinic run by it or by any local authority from any or all of the provisions of this Act on recommendation by the Appropriate Authority that such exemption is in public interest.

Provided that such exemption is not made as regards minimum qualifications of persons, minimum equipment necessary, the standards to be maintained and the code of conduct of persons working at the genetic centre, laboratory or clinic.

26. *Powers to make rules*

(1) The State Government may, subject to the condition of

previous publication in the Official Gazette make rules for carrying out the purpose of this Act.

Provided that, if the State Government is satisfied that circumstances exist which render it necessary to take immediate action, it may dispense with the previous publication of any rule to be made under this Act.

(2) In particular and without prejudice to the generality of the foregoing power, such rules may provide for:

(i) the minimum qualifications of the persons employed at a registered centre or laboratory or clinic;

(ii) the form and manner of application for registration, records to be maintained, consent of a female patient to be obtained at regular centre or laboratory or clinic;

(iii) minimum equipments necessary at the centre or labortory or clinic;

(iv) the standards to be maintained by the centre or laboratory or clinic;

(v) the code of conduct of persons working at the centre or laboratory or clinic;

(vi) the manner in which an appeal may be filed to the State Government against the order of refusal, cancellation or suspension of registration;

(vii) the duration of validity of registration precedure of renewal of registration and fees to be charged for registration and renewal thereof;

(viii) manner of and intervals at which a local Vigilance Committee shall report its decisions and actions to the State Vigilance Committee;

(ix) the records, charts, reports and other documents to be maintained in centre, laboratory or clinic, period for which such records and documents shall be maintained and preserved; and

(x) any other matter that is required or may be prescribed under this Act.

(3) Every rule made under this section shall be laid as soon as may be after it is made before the expiry of the session or in two successive sessions and if, before the expiry of the session in which it is so laid or the session immediately following, both Houses agree in making any modification in the rule or both

Houses agree that the rule should not be made, and notify such decisions in the Official Gazette, the rule shall from the date of publication of such notification have effect only in such modified form or be of no effect, as the case may be; so, however, that any such modification or annulment shall be without prejudice to the validity of anything previously done or omitted to be done under that rule.

THE MEDICAL TERMINATION OF PREGNANCY ACT, 1971*

(No. 34 of 1971)

(10th August, 1971)

An Act to provide for the termination of certain pregnancies by registered medical practitioners and for matters connected therewith or incidental thereto.

Statement of objects and reasons:

(i) The provisions regarding the termination of pregnancy in the Indian Penal Code which was enacted in 1960 was drawn up in keeping with the then British Rule in India. Abortion was made a crime for which the abortionist as well as the woman were liable to be punished except under certain circumstances. It has been stated that this very strict law has been in breech of a large number of cases all over the country.

Furthermore, most of these mothers are married women, and are under no particular necessity to conceal their pregnancy.

(ii) In recent years, when health services have expanded and hospitals are availed of to the fullest extent by all classes of society, doctors have often been confronted gravely ill or dying pregnant woman whose uterus has been tampered with a view to causing an abortion and consequently suffered very severely.

(iii) There is thus avoidable wastage of the mother's health, strength and sometimes, life. The proposed measure which seeks to liberalise certain existing provisions relating to termination of pregnancy has been received;

(1) as a health measure—when there is a danger to the life or

---

* Received the assent of the President on August 10, 1971, and published in Gazette of India Extra Part II, Section I, dated 10th August 1971, pp. 237–240.

risk to physical or mental health of the woman,

(2) on humanitarian grounds—such as when pregnancy arises from a sex crime like rape or intercourse with a lunatic woman, etc., and

(3) eugenic grounds—when there is a substantial risk that the child, if born would suffer from deformities and disease.*

Be it enacted by Parliament in the Twenty-second year of the Republic of India as follows:

1. *Short title, extent and commencement:*

(1) This Act may be called the Medical Termination of Pregnancy Act, 1971.

(2) It extends to the whole of India except the State of Jammu and Kashmir.

(3) It shall come into force on such date as the Central Government, may, by notification, in the Official Gazette, appoint.

2. *Definitions:*

In this Act, unless the context otherwise requires;

(a) "*guardian*" means a person having the care of the person of a minor or a lunatic;

(b) "*lunatic*" has the meaning assigned to it in Section 3 of the Indian Lunacy Act, 1912, (4 of 1912);

(c) "*minor*" means a person who, under the provisions of the Indian Majority Act, 1875 (9 of 1875), is to be deemed not to have attained his majority;

(d) "*registered medical practitioner*" means a medical practitioner who possesses any recognised medical qualification as defined in clause (h) of Section 2 of the Indian Medical Council Act, 1956 (102 of 1956), whose name has been entered in a State Medical Register and who has such experience or training in gynaecology and obstetrics as may be prescribed by rules made under this Act.

---

* Gazette of India, Pt. II, Section 2, Extra., dt. Nov. '17 1969, pp. 880.

3. *When pregnancy may be terminated by registered medical practitioners:*

(1) Notwithstanding anything contained in the Indian Penal Code (45 of 1860), a registered medical practitioner shall not be guilty of an offence under that Code or under any other law for the time being in force, if any pregnancy is terminated by him in accordance with the provisions of this Act.

(2) Subject to the provisions of sub-section (4), a pregnancy may be terminated by a registered medical practitioner;

(a) where the length of the pregnancy does not exceed twelve weeks, if such medical practitioner is of the opinions mentioned in sub para (i) and (ii) below, or

(b) where the length of the pregnancy exceeds twelve weeks but does not exceed twenty weeks, if not less than two registered medical practitioners are, of opinion, formed in good faith, that:

(i) the continuance of the pregnancy would involve a risk to the life to the pregnant woman or of grave injury to her physical or mental health; or

(ii) there is a substantial risk that if the child were born, it would suffer from such physical or mental abnormalities as to be seriously handicapped.

Explanation I: Where any pregnancy is alleged by the pregnant woman to have been caused by rape, the anguish caused by such pregnancy shall be presumed to constitute a grave injury to the mental health of the pregnant woman.

Explanation II: Where any pregnancy occurs as a result of failure of any devise or method used by any married woman or her husband for the purpose of limiting the number of children, the anguish caused by such unwanted pregnancy may be presumed to constitute a grave injury to the mental health of the pregnant woman.

(3) In determining whether the continuance of a pregnancy would involve such risk of injury to the health as is mentioned in sub-section (2), account may be taken of the pregnant women's actual or reasonable foreseeable environment.

(4) (a) No pregnancy of a woman, who has not attained the age of eighteen years, or, who having attained the age of eigh-

teen year, is a lunatic, shall be terminated except with the consent in writing of her guardian.

(b) Save as otherwise provided in clause (a), no pregnancy shall be terminated except with the consent of the pregnant woman.

4. *Place where pregnancy may be terminated:*

No termination of pregnancy shall be made in accordance with this Act at any place other than;

(a) a hospital established or maintained by Government, or
(b) a place for the time being approved for the purpose of this Act by Government.

5. *Sections 3 and 4 when not to apply:*

(1) The provisions of Section 4, and so much of the provisions of sub-section (2) of Section 3 as relate to the length of the pregnancy and the opinion of not less than two registered medical practitioners, shall not apply to the termination of a pregnancy by a registered medical practitioner in a case where he is of opinion, formed in good faith, that the termination of such pregnancy is immediate necessity to save the life of the pregnant woman.

(2) Notwithstanding anything contained in the Indian Penal Code (45 of 1860), the termination of a pregnancy by a person who is not a registered medical practitioner, shall be an offence punishable under that Code, and that Code shall, to this extent, stand modified.

Explanation: For the purposes of this section, so much of the provisions of clause (d) of Section 2 as relate to the possession by a registered medical practitioner, of experience or training in gynaecology and obstetrics shall not apply.

6. *Power to make rules:*

(1) The Central Government may, by notification in the Official Gazette, make rules to carry out the provisions of this Act.

(2) In particular, and without prejudice to the generality of the foregoing power, such rules may provide for all or any of the following matters, namely:

(a) the experience or training, or both, which a registered medical practitioner shall have if he intends to terminate any pregnancy under this Act; and
(b) such other matters as are required to be or may be, provided by rules made under this Act.

(3) Every rule made by the Central Government under this Act shall be laid, as soon as may be after it is made, before each House of Parliament while it is in session for a total period of thirty days which may be comprised in one session in which it is so laid or the session immediately following, both Houses agree in making any modification in the rule or both Houses agree that the rule should not be made, the rule shall thereafter have effect only in such modified form or be of no effect, as the case may be; so, however, that any such modification or annulment shall be without prejudice to the validity of anything previously done under that rule.

7. *Power to make regulations:*

(1) The State Government may, by regulations:

(a) require any such opinion as is referred to in sub-section(2) of Section 3 to be certified by a registered medical practitioner or practitioners concerned, in such form and at such time as may be specified in such regulations, and the preservation or disposal of such certificates;
(b) require any medical practitioner, who terminates a pregnancy, to give intimation of such termination and such other information relating to the termination as may be specified in such regulations;
(c) prohibit the disclosure, except to such persons and for such purposes as may be specified in such regulations, of intimations given or information furnished in persuance of such regulations.

(2) The intimation given and the information furnished in persuance of regulations made by virtue of clause (b) of sub-section (1) shall be given or furnished, as the case may be, to the Chief Medical Officer of the State.

(3) Any person who wilfully contravenes or wilfully fails to comply with the requirements of any regulation made under

sub-section (1) shall be liable to be punished with the fine which may extend to one thousand rupees.

8. *Protection of action taken in good faith:*

No suit or other legal proceeding shall lie against any registereed medical practitioner for any damage caused or likely to be caused by anything which is in good faith done or intended to be done under this Act.

Notes:

"Good faith" is defined by Section 52 of the Indian Penal Code and runs as under:

"52. *Good faith*—Nothing is said to be done or believed in *"good faith"* which is done or believed without due care and attention."

Good faith includes element of 'due care and attention' and implies genuine effort to reach the truth.*

If the doctor is of opinion, on reasonable grounds, and with adequate knowledge, that the probable consequence of the continuance of the pregnancy will be to make the woman a physical or mental wreck, the court is entitled to take the view that the doctor who, under these circumstances and in that honest belief, operates, is operating for the purpose of preserving the life of the patient.**

---

* In re Ganapathia Pillai. AIR 1953 Mad. 9326.

** (1939) 1 KB 687.

Chapter 4

The Practice of Sati

4.01 Introduction

The incident of 'Sati' committed by Roop Kanwar on the 4th September 1987' at village Deorala in the district of Sikar (Rajasthan), who is reported to have voluntarily climbed the funeral pyre of her husband (Mal Singh deceased) attracted the attention of the press and the people of the country. She, by this act, is supposed to have set an example of love, sacrifice and devotion who did not hesitate to embrace death consequent upon the death of her husband.[1] This unfortunate incident took place after nine months of her marriage. After this incident Roop Kanwar distinguished herself as a living symbol of Hindu religion of a devoted wife. Linked with news was also the information that devotees and followers of Hindu religion in thousands, assembled at the spot and made offerings and that hundreds of Rajput youths armed with swords were protecting the area. A veil ceremony was going to be held and a sati temple was contemplated to be raised at the site.

Subsequently doubts were raised that the act of Roop Kanwar was not a voluntary one and she in fact was murdered by her in-laws. One Dr. Mangal Singh, her husband's family physician was reported to have given morphine injection presumably to make her insensitive to the horrors of burning.

According to the police report, Roop Kanwar had brought with her a dowry of 440 gms. of gold, a fixed deposit of Rs. 30,000, a colour television, cooking range and a refrigerator, which, according to the Rajput law should have gone to her parents after husband's death. This circumstance raised a sharp controversy whether Roop Kanwar voluntarily committed sati or was forced to climb her husband's funeral pyre.[2]

The observance of the practice of 'sati' by a young woman satisfies the male ego that there is someone who is ready to die for him or finds life meaningless without him.[3] The problem, however, is that given proper socio-economic status of women, at par or greater than the male counterpart, in this country can there be such a voluntary act? Whether the practice of sati is due to overt coercion? However, in a society where women are brain-washed from childhood that they are inferior to man, that marriage and service to husband and husband's family is the ultimate goal, that husband is god who must be obeyed and believed unquestioningly, how much freedom and independence of thought and action does an average woman can have? Added to this, are the countless fasts, worships and feasts to brahmins, which a woman has to observe for her husband's health, life and prosperity. Rajput women from childhood have to perform 'sati-puja' regularly which is extolled as the highest act of earthly devotion, that a woman can show. Our folk tales, stories and myths are full of praises for obedient women, who fulfilled all the wishes, both desirable and undesirable, of their husbands. This is the epitome of Indian womanhood.

When one considers the total impact of the brain-washing and romanticisation of the male-female roles on one hand and the plight of women, particularly widows on the other hand, one is satisfied that the number of 'sati' cases is disproportionately high. In the situation faced by women in general and widow in particular, surely it might be considered preferable to embrace a brief and painful death than face life-long insults, rebukes, contempt, insecurity and degradation and held responsible for the husband's death. The fact that more women do not take this way out is not any positive reflection on our society but due to the reason that even their married status is filled with drudgery, insults, beating, battering and total suppression of individuality.

This status of women is in sharp contrast to the position of women in Tribal Society because she is an economic asset and fetches a bride price. A young man in Bhil community prefers to marry a widow than an unmarried girl because she is supposed to have learnt the method of running a house and working in a field. If the woman is with a child, she further gains in the marriage market because her fertility stands proved. The whole plight, therefore, of the average woman in general and widows in particular as objects of economic and social exploitation is what deserves an anxious attention. An important aspect of this incident in village Deorala is that the whole village is minting money out of the death of Roop Kanwar. This is the third incident of sati in the village. Cards, talismans and booklets were selling like hot cakes and this leads to the vested interest of the whole village to keep the cult of Sati alive.

4.02. The Meaning of the Word 'Sati'

There is no text of Dharmshastra which has sanctioned the burning of widows. The expression 'Sati' in Sanskrit literature is a feminine noun of 'Sat' or truthfulness and honourable. Thus, as per ancient literatures, sati means a truthful woman who in course of time became synonym with devoted and faithful wife. But, there was no injunction in dharmshastra which permitted such a heinous crime against womenfolk. It came into practice during periods, when the women apprehending danger to their honour from the enemy in the event of defeat or the death of their husbands embraced voluntary death by jumping into fire and this was know as 'Jauhar'. This practice was most prevalent in Rajasthan as the people used to be warriors.

The term 'sati' is given not only to those women who immolated themselves on the husband's funeral pyre but also to those women who could die of shock on hearing of their husband's death. Both these types are given deification and both have their temples built to them so that they can be worshipped for their deep devotion to their husbands, bravery and courage.

4.03. Types of Sati[3]

Sati had two forms. One was the 'Sahmana' that is dying in company or 'Sanhgamana' which means cremation of the widow with the dead husband. The other was 'anumarna' or 'anugamana', that is: 'dying in accordance with.' The latter was the term used when her lord died and was burnt at a distance from her during a campaign perhaps or when her own death was postponed because she was pregnant. She was then burnt with something that belonged to and represented her husband, like turban, etc.

Filial love, it may seem strange, also led to Sati. Sometimes a grief-stricken mother committed sati on her son's pyre. It was known as 'Ma Sati'. The classical example of this type of 'Sati' was illustrated by the supreme sacrifice performed by Gajja. She was the mother of Ananda, the Minister of Harsha, of Kashmir (1089–1101) who was killed in a battle-field. In Central India, around 1880, James Malcolm records that the case of two mothers concremated themselves with their only sons consequent upon their deaths. One occurred at Amjhera near Bhopal and the other at Katkhorde. Sometimes sisters found solace in burning themselves on the funeral pyres of their brothers.

Even close relations and servants have climbed the funeral pyres of those whom they loved. Bana records that upon the death of Prabhakar-Vardhana, many of his favourite friends, ministers and servants plunged into the flames. Abu Zaid, the Arab traveller, who visited India during 916 A.D. records such incidents.

4.04. Sati Memorials[4]

The places where satis have taken place used to be memorialised by some shrines usually raised by stones. Usually, these were raised to inspire and induce others to make similar sacrifices. There are about one hundred temples in different States of the country. Of these forty are in Rajasthan and five are in Delhi.

There is one monument in Eran where a brief description is engraved on a pillar which is an account of 'sati' of Gopraja's wife. A number of such memorials called 'vikrals' have been raised at Hampi, the capital of Vijayanagar. Similar memorials raised in the countryside of Karnataka are called 'Mastikal' and 'Satikal'. The women, who committed 'sati' in Tamilnadu were called 'malaiyidu'. Malai means garland and since garlands were offered to their souls, they were called 'malaiyidu'.

The muslim invasion took place during the period from the middle of 14th century to mid 17th century, when the widows had been committing sati on a mind-boggling scale.

A study of the practice of Sati, however, presents a horrifying picture of sheer brutality. Even widows volunteering to commit 'sati' were likely to jump and recoil under intense agonies due to physical trauma resulting from the flames of the funeral pyre. Some had even attempted to jump out of the pyre. To avoid this, certain steps were taken, that is, they used to be tied to the log of wood or chained or the pyre was laid in a pit. The third alternative was, if the victim tried to escape, she used to be hit on her head. Before being laid on the funeral pyre, the women were drugged so that she became less sensitive to the pain or got incapacitated to jump out of the pyre.

Sati system had never been popular all the time with the widows but since refusal was considered a stigma to the personal conduct of the women, they did it. Jayamati, the queen of Uchchala, who died on December 8, 1111, bribed her minister with all her wealth to publicly dissuade her from her apparent resolve of committing sati. This would save her from embarrassment. The minister, however, delayed going to the cremation ground and she by that time was burnt down.

4.05. Sati During Muslim Period[5]

The sati was a common custom in the heyday of the Vijayanagara empire. According to Nicolo Conti (1420) and Durate Berbosa (1500–1516) a large number of widows and female slaves used to be concremated on the pyres of their husbands in the 15th, and the 16th Centuries. Any unwillingness on the part of the women deprived her of her right to property and possessions.

Sati was in common practice during the Mughal period. Even betrothed girls had to commit sati on the pyre of their would-be husbands. Abul Fazl, quotes Akbar as having once said, "It is a sad commentary on the magnanimity of men that they should seek their deliverance through the self sacrifice of their women." According to Akbar's biography Raja Man Singh had 1500 wives and sixty of them burnt themselves on his funeral pyre after his death in 1614.

Even the Muslim women are also recorded to have sacrificed themselves on the death of their husbands. A 12 year old muslim widow was buried alive along with her husband in the grave. Such practice was very common in Rajouri.

4.06. Post-Independence Era[6]

During the post-independence era, particularly in Rajasthan, the woman leaping unaided onto a four foot high pyre commands a minor relation of hers to light it. The police proceedings begin, the child, on account of his power of not understanding the consequences of the act is claimed an immunity from criminal liability or it is claimed that the pyre lit automatically. The woman's biography written by her interested relative would reveal that she was as pious as a child and she did not feel any pain as evidenced by her smiles. This is the plot of all the widow murders (37 cases since 1947 in Rajasthan) and the whole episode is described as divine miracle.

The community of the warrior class compensates loss of political and economic power by making 'sati' a matter of identity through an act of cowardice—burning an aggrieved, unarmed and helpless widow in an organised manner to the gaze of all in the name of 'Pati-Bhakti'. There is nothing as 'Patni-Bhakti'.

What once upon a time, a heritage of the Rajputs in Rajasthan extended to the entire Hindu community through an appeal to mobilise support for the October 8, 1987 rally to Jaipur in support of Deorala episode. This appeal also recorded the fact that in Rajasthan the practice of 'sati' has been voluntary. This claim can be falsified by a single example of the colonial records. It records the incident that when Mewar ruler died in 1861, who had the distinction of banning 'sati', all his queens refused to die on the funeral pyre of their husband. The situation was embarrassing for a ruler whose funeral pyre was going to be lit without a single woman being burnt with it. One Gopal Das finally succeeded in forcing a slave Aiza Bai on the pyre.

4.07. Preventive Measures[7,8,9]

No serious attempt was made to abolish 'sati' through legislation or through education in the past although there had been stray cases of rescue being attempted to retrieve unwilling women from committing 'sati'. The first rescue attempt is recorded to have been made by Akbar who succeeded in saving the daughter-in-law of the Raja of Jodhpur from burning against her will. In an attempt to suppress the act, Akbar, directed that no Hindu widow should be compelled to 'sati'. Aurangzeb also prohibited it but the efforts of the Muslim rulers were confined to a limited area in the periphery of Delhi.

The only Hindu principalities to attempt to prohibit the practice were the Maratha States of Tanjore and Savantwadi in early 19th Century.

The Portuguese, after capturing Goa, made a very determined attempt to abolish 'sati' in 1510. The Portuguese administration took stern action against all relatives and spectators of the 'sati' episode with the result that this evil practice soon died. The Danes at Serampur, the Dutch at Chinsura and the French at Chandannagore, prohibited it but their citizens made the regulations ineffective by arranging the cremation and immolation outside their territory.

Job Charnock, the founder of Calcutta in the year 1690, saved an unwilling young widow at the early age of 15 years from being burnt and dispersed the relatives, the priests and the crowd from the site. He, thereafter, married the widow. Her marriage lasted for another twenty-five years till her death.

The British adopted an ambiguous and ambivalent attitude. The British Government had given a clear understanding that they would preserve the existing laws of both the Hindus and Muslims and would protect them in the free exercise of their religion. The Government of Bengal, therefore, did not like to interfere, even they were strongly urged to do so by their own officials. This attitude was adopted by Madras Government too. The Bombay Government did not, at first tolerate this practice, but after the annexation of the Peshwa's dominions, adopted the attitude of neutrality and even passed a regulation holding the assistance at the rite of self-immolation, known as 'sati' was not murder.

Warren Hastings did not wish to interfere in the internal institutions of the Hindus and the Muslims. Lord Clive gave orders that no one should be allowed to interfere with the religious customs of the Hindus. To quote for instance, when asked by Diwan Naval Krishna, a senior member of the

Company's office to save the life of a widow who was going to be burnt with the dead body of her husband, Lord Wellesely advised "proper respect due to the pagoda."

Until 1812, the British Government did not lay down any policy on 'sati'. However, some courageous Britishers did not like this practice of burning alive widows. Sir John Astruther, Chief Justice of Supreme Court, banned sati in Calcutta on his own initiative, but the practice could not be stopped.

Advice was reluctantly given to officials in 1812 to prevent a widow from burning herself, if she was pregnant, pubertal, the mother of an infant or drugged by her relatives. The order, however, was not being observed. Thereupon Lord Hastings asked for stringent intervention by the local authorities through a circular issued in 1817. According to the circular only a legally wedded wife was permitted to commit 'sati' and not concubines.

Another circular was issued in 1915. This required the District Magistrate to file annual returns of 'satis' in Bengal. The relatives were asked to give prior notice of the impending immolation. This circular, however, helped to collect data and give an idea of the magnitude of live burning of widows. This gave a figure that in the year 1917-1918 out of a 839 'satis' in Bengal, 534 took place in Calcutta Division.

Year 1818 was the beginning of an epochal era for it heralded the advent of Raja Ram Mohan Roy and his massive movement for the modernisation of India. Side by side, the arrival of Lord William Bentinck was another important event in the history of India. He declared that on consideration of humanity, all those participating in 'sati' were guilty of little short of crime of multiple murder. Although Raja Ram Mohan Roy advised the Governor to go slow but he went ahead and abolished 'sati' by a regulation on December 4, 1829. The regulation declared that, "The practice of sati, burning or burying alive widows of Hindus, whether the sacrifice be voluntary in part or not, is illegal and punishable by the Criminal Courts."

Ram Mohan Roy's role in this whole affair was creating a climate in favour of abolition of 'sati'. Thus, when a number of Brahmins appealed against the regulations abolishing 'sati' and making it a penal offence, Ram Mohan Roy went to London and propagated against the appeal of the Brahmins. The appeal of the Brahmins, thus, was dismissed. This step prevented the large scale burning of women in the country, particularly in Bengal. Thus, the legend of sacrifice of women and children in the remote part was abhorrent to ancient sages also but was upheld by feudal ancestors, was stopped for ever.

4.08. Penal Provisions under the I.P.C.

The relevant penal provisions under the Penal Code are embodied in Section 306 and Section 309 of the Code.

Section 306: Abetment of Suicide

If any person commits suicide, whoever abets the commission of such suicide, shall be punished with imprisonment of either description for a term which may extend to ten years, and shall also be liable to fine.

Section 309: Attempt to Commit Suicide

Whoever attempts to commit suicide and does any act towards the commission of such offence, shall be punished with simple imprisonment for a term which may extend to due year, or with fine, or with both.

There are instances that convictions have taken place in some cases under Section 306 in such acts but the provisions made under Section 309, being against the intended victim, has been struck down. On December 13, 1984, Hon'ble Mr. Justice Sachchar, the Chief Justice of Delhi High Court quashed 119 cases of attempt to commit suicide pending before the Criminal Courts in Delhi and directed Delhi Administration and the police, not to prosecute such victims in future. He observed that the continuance of the Section "is an anachronism unworthy of a human society like ours."[10]

After Deorala incident, a countrywide stir made a significant impact in the various segments of the society and that led to the enactment of Rajasthan Sati (Prevention) Act, 1987.

The Rajasthan Government came out with the promulgation of an ordinance with effect from October 1, 1987. The action taken by the Governor and Speaker of Rajasthan Assembly in this context was the adjournment of the House to the promulgation of the ordinances on October 1, 1987. A Writ petition was filed against it, before the Rajasthan High Court challenging the Constitutional validity on the touch stone of Article 14 (equality before law) and Article 25 and 26 (relating to religious faith). Though under the Ordinance, provisions have been made to punish, attempts, abatement or glorification of the practice, the State Government has not exhibited any firmness to combat the evil. Besides this, clause 19 of the Ordinance says,

> "It is hereby declared that nothing in this ordinance shall affect any temple or other structure constructed for the glorification of the 'sati' and existence immediately before the commencement of the Ordinance or the continuance of any ceremonies in such temple or other structure in connection with such 'sati'.[11]

The Rajasthan Sati (Prevention) Ordinance was passed and got the final seal of authority with the President, Shri R. Venkatraman giving his assent to bring it on the Statute book.[12]

The Division Bench of Rajasthan High Court, ruled that the action taken by the Governor in proroguing the House and then promulgating the Ordinance was "legal and constitutional" and that of the Speaker's action in adjourning the House on September 30, 1987—a day before the promulgation of the Ordinance was neither malpractice nor unconstitutional.[13,14]

The Division Bench also struck down Section 19 of Rajasthan Sati (Prevention) Act, that banned all glorification of sati, but exempted existing temples from the purview of the law. The new law is now applicable to all temples glorifying widow burning. Moreover, the law has clearly defined what glorification amounts to. This includes any ceremony, procession, collection of funds or construction of a temple with a view to honouring a 'sati'.[15]

The judgement also dropped criminal proceedings against seventeen persons before a Special Judge (Sati) under Section 5 and Section 6(3) of the Act and ordered the release of 9 out of 17 accused persons who were refused bail earlier. The Supreme Court by its judgement dated December 18, 1987 ordered resumption of the trial under Rajasthan Sati (Prevention) Act, 1987.[16]

Following this, a bill was tabled in Lok Sabha, through which provisions were made to provide deterrent punishment to those who abet the evil practice of 'Sati'. The Statement in this connection is as given below[17]:

> "A general feeling has also grown in the country that the efforts put in by social reformers like Raja Ram Mohan Roy and others in the last century would be nullified by this single act in Rajasthan. The commission of sati in Deorala was also followed by a number of congregations, ceremonies and festivals and attempts were also made to collect funds for the construction of a temple at the site where 'sati' was committed.
>
> The place had also attracted larg e number of crowds and inspite of the various steps taken by the State Government of Rajasthan and order of the High Court of Rajasthan to prohibit any ceremony being conducted, it was feared that a temple would be constructed at the site to perpetuate the memory of the widow who committed 'sati'. These had evoked protests throughout the country and demands are being made by the Women's organisations and from persons inside and outside the parliament for the enactment of a strong and deterrent general law to provide for the more effective prevention of the commission of 'sati' and its glorification is not continued in states where there is no law for the prevention of glorification of 'sati'.
>
> Although the offence of attempt to commit suicide as contained in Section 309 of the Indian Penal Code has been held by various High Courts to include the commission of 'sati' punishable under the provision, the sentence provided in that Section was not deterrent enough to prevent the commission of such practice. Further, that Section also did not provide for the glorification of 'sati' subsequent to the commission of 'sati'.
>
> There are at present only three laws in force in the states, including the Rajasthan Sati (Prevention) Act, 1987. The other two enactments are the Bengal Sati Regulations".

THE COMMISSION OF SATI (PREVENTION) ACT, 1987*
(Act No. 3 of 1988) (3RD JANUARY, 1988)

An Act to provide for the more effective prevention of the commission of Sati and its glorification and for matters connected herewith or identical thereto;

Whereas sati or the burning or burying alive of widows or women is revolting to the feelings of human nature and is nowhere enjoined by any of the religions of India as an imperative duty;

And whereas it is necessary to take more effective measures to prevent the commission of sati and its glorification;

Be it enacted by Parliament in the Thirty-eighth Year of the Republic of India as follows:

PART I (PRELIMINARY)

1. *Short title, extent and commencement:*

(1) This Act may be called the Commission of Sati (Prevention) Act, 1987.

(2) It extends to the whole of India except the State of Jammu and Kashmir.

(3) It shall come into force in a state on such date as the Central Government may, by notification in the Official Gazette, appoint, and different dates may be appointed for different states.

2. *Definitions:*

(1) In this Act, unless the context otherwise requires:

(a) "*Code*" means the Code of Criminal Procedure, 1973 (of 1974);

(b) "*Glorification*", in relation to sati, whether such sati, was committed before or after the commencement of this Act, includes among other things:

(i) the observance of any ceremony or the taking out of a procession in connection with the commission of sati; or

(ii) the supporting, justifying or propagating the practice of sati in any manner; or

(iii) the arranging of any function to eulogise the person

* Received the assent of the President on January 3, 1988 and published in the Gazette of India, Part II, Section I, Dated 6th, January, 1988 pp. 1–7.

who has committed sati; or

(iv) the creation of a trust, or the collection of funds, or the construction of a temple or other structure or the carrying on of any form of worship or the performance of any ceremony thereat, with a view to perpetuate the honour of, or to preserve the memory of a person who has committed sati;

(c) "*Sati*" means the burning or burying alive of:

(i) any widow alongwith the body of her deceased husband or any other relative or with any article, object or thing associated with the husband or such relative; or

(ii) any woman along with the body of any of her relatives, irrespective of whether such burning or burying is claimed to be voluntary on the part of the widow or the women or otherwise;

(d) "*Special Court*" means a Special Court constituted under Section 9;

(e) "*Temple*" includes any building or other structure, whether roofed or not, constructed or made to preserve the memory of a person in respect of whom sati has been committed or used or intended to be used for the carrying on of any form of worship or for the observance of any ceremony in connection with such commission.

(2) Words and expressions used but not defined in this Act and defined in the Indian Penal Code (45 of 1860), or in the Code shall have the same meanings as are respectively assigned to them in the Indian Penal Code or the Code.

PART II
PUNISHMENTS FOR OFFENCES RELATING TO SATI

3. *Attempt to commit sati:*

Notwithstanding anything contained in the Indian Penal Code (45 of 1860), whoever attempts to commit sati and does any act towards such commission shall be punishable with imprisonment for a term which may extend to one year or with fine or with both.

Provided that the Special Court trying an offence under this section shall before convicting any person, take into consideration the circumstances leading to the commission of the offence, the act committed, the state of mind of the person charged of the offence at the time of the commission of the act and all other relevant factors.

Notes

This Section is analogous to Section 309 of Indian Penal Code which reads as follows-

309. Attempt to commit suicide: Whoever attempts to commit and does any act toward the commission of such offence, shall be punished with simple imprisonment for a term which may extend to one year, or with fine or with both.

In order to constitute an attempt, first, there must be an intention to commit a particular offence, second, some act must have been done towards the commission of the offence, and third, such act must be proximate to the intended result. The measure of opportunity is not relation to time and action but lies in relation to intention. In other words, the act must reveal, with reasonable certainty, in conjunction with other facts and circumstances and not necessarily in isolation, an intention, as distinguished from desire or object to commit the particular offence, though the act by itself may be merely suggestive or indicative of such intention, but that it must be indicative or suggestive of the intention. [*Malkiat Singh* Vs. *The State of Punjab*, (1969)1 SCC 157=(1969) 2SCR 663=1970 Cr. L.J. 750]

4. *Abetement of sati:*

(1) Notwithstanding anything contained in the Indian Penal Code (45 of 1860), if any person commits sati, whoever abets the commission of sati, either directly or indirectly, shall be punishable with death or imprisonment for life and shall also be liable to fine.

(2) If any person attempts to commit sati, whoever abets such attempt, either directly or indirectly, shall be punishable with imprisonment for life and shall also be liable to fine.

Explanation: For the purpose of this section, any of the following acts or the like shall also be deemed to be an abetment, namely:

(a) any inducement to a widow or woman to get her burnt or buried alive along with the body of her deceased husband or with any other relative or with any article, object or thing associated with the husband or such relative, irrespective of whether she is in a fit state of mind or is labouring under a state of intoxication or stupefaction or other cause impending the exercise of her free will;

(b) making a widow believe that the commission of sati would result in some spiritual benefit to her or her deceased husband or with any other relative or the general well being of the family;

(c) encouraging a widow or woman to remain fixed in her resolve to commit sati and thus instigating her to commit sati;

(d) participating in any procession in connection with the commission of sati or aiding the widow or woman in her decision to commit sati by taking her along with the body of her husband or relative to the cremation or burial ground;

(e) being present at the place where sati is committed as an active participant to such commission or to any ceremony concerned with it;

(f) preventing or obstructing the widow or woman from saving herself from being burnt or buried alive;

(g) obstructing or interfering with, the police in the discharge of its duties of taking any step to prevent the commission of sati.

Notes

Abetment has been defined in Section 107, I.P.C. as under:

"107. *Abetment of a thing:* A person abets the doing of a thing, who—

First—Instigates any person to do that thing; or

Secondly—Engages with one or more other person or persons in any conspiracy for the doing of that thing, if an act or illegal omission takes place in pursuance of that conspiracy, and in order to the doing of that thing; or

Thirdly—Intentionally aids, by any act or illegal omission, doing of that thing.

Explanation 1: A person who, by willful misrepresentation, or by willful concealment of a material fact which he is bound to disclose voluntarily causes or procures or attempts to cause or procure, a thing to be done, is said to instigate the doing of that thing.

Illustration

A, a public officer, is authorised by a warrant from a court of Justice to apprehend Z. B, knowing that fact and also that C is not Z, wilfully represents to A that C is Z, and thereby intentionally causes A to apprehend C. Here B abets by instigation the apprehension of C.

Explanation 2: Whoever, either prior to or at the time of the commission of an act, does anything in order to facilitate the commission of that act, and thereby facilitates the commission thereof, is said to aid the doing of that act.

"*109. Punishment of abetment if the act abetted is committed in consequence and where no express provision is made for its punishment:*

Whoever abets any offence shall, if the act is committed in consequence of the abetment, and no express provision is made by this Code, the punishment of such abetment, be punished with the punishment provided for the offence.

Explanation: An act or offence is said to be committed in consequence of abetment, when it is committed in consequence of the instigation, in pursuance of the conspiracy, or with the aid which constitutes the abetment.

Notes

In order to constitute the offence of abetment, the abetter must be shown to have intentionally aided the commission of the crime. Mere proof that the crime charged could not have been committed without the interposition of the alleged abettor, is not enough compliance with the requirements in respect of the ingredients of Section 107. A person may, for example, invite another person casually or for a friendly purpose that may facilitate the murder of the invitee. But unless the invitation was extended with intent to facilitate the commission of the murder, the person inviting cannot be said to have abetted the murder. Intentional aiding and, therefore, active complicity is the gist of the offence of abetment under the third paragraph of Section 107 I.P.C. [*Sia Ram* Vs. *The State of U.P.* AIR 1975 SC 175=1975 Cr. L.J. 240=1975 SCC (Cri) 87=(1975) 3 SCC 495]

5. *Punishment for glorification of sati:*

Whoever does any act for the glorification of sati shall be

punishable with imprisonment for a term which shall not be less than one year but which may extend to seven years and with fine which shall not be less than five thousand rupees but which may extend to thirty thousand rupees.

PART III
POWERS OF COLLECTOR OR DISTRICT MAGISTRATE TO PREVENT OFFENCES RELATING TO SATI

6. *Power to prohibit certain acts:*

(1) Where the Collector or the District Magistrate is of the opinion that sati or any abetment thereof is being, or is about to be committed, he may, by order, prohibit the doing of any act towards the commission of sati by any person in any area or areas specified in the order.

(2) The Collector or the District Magistrate may also, by order, prohibit in any manner the glorification of sati by any person in any area or areas specified in the order.

(3) Whoever, contravenes any order made under sub-section (1) or sub-section (2) shall, if such contravention is not punishable under any other provision of this Act, be punishable with imprisonment for a term which shall not be less than one year but which may extend to seven years and with fine which shall not be less than five thousand rupees but which may extend to thirty thousand rupees.

7 *Power to remove certain temples or other structures:*

(1) The State Government may, if it is satisfied that in any temple or other structure which has been in existence for not less than twenty years, any form of worship or the performance of any ceremony is carried on with a view to perpetuate the honour or to preserve the memory of, any person in respect of whom sati has been committed, by order, direct the removal of such temple or other structure.

(2) The Collector or the District Magistrate may, if, he is satisfied that in any temple or other structure, other than referred to in sub-section (1), any form of worship or the performance of any ceremony is carried on with a view to perpetuate the honour of, or to preserve the memory of, any person in respect of whom sati has been committed, by order, direct the removal of such temple or other structure.

(3) When any order under sub-section (1) or sub-section (2) is not complied with, the State Government or the collector or the District Magistrate, as the case may be, shall cause the temple or other structure to be removed through a police officer not below the rank of a Sub-Inspector at the cost of the defaulter.

8. *Power to seize certain properties:*

(1) When the Collector or the District Magistrate has reason to believe that any funds or property have been collected or acquired for the purpose of glorification of the commission of any sati or which may be found under circumstances which create suspicion of the commission of any offence under this Act, he may seize such funds or property.

(2) Every Collector or District Magistrate acting under sub-section (1) shall report the seizure to the Special Court, if any, constituted to try any offence in relation to which such funds or property were collected or acquired and shall await the orders of such Special Court as to the disposal of the same.

PART IV
SPECIAL COURTS

9. *Trial of offences under this Act:*

(1) Notwithstanding anything contained in the Code, all offences under this Act shall be triable only by a Special Court constituted under this section.

(2) The State Government shall by notification in the Official Gazette, constitute one or more Special Courts for the trial of offences under this Act and every Special Court shall exercise jurisdiction in respect of the whole or such part of the state as may be specified in the notification.

(3) A Special Court shall be presided over by a judge to be appointed by the State Government with the concurrence of the Chief Justice of the High Court.

(4) A person shall not be qualified for appointment as a judge of a Special Court unless he is, immediately before such appointment, a Sessions Judge or an Additional Sessions Judge.

10. *Special Public Prosecutors:*

(1) For every Special Court, the State Government shall appoint a person to be a Special Public Prosecutor.

(2) A person shall be eligible to be appointed as a Special Public Prosecutor under this section only if he has been in practice as an advocate for not less than seven years or has held, any post for a period of not less than seven years under the state requiring special knowledge of law.

(3) Every person appointed as a Special Public Prosecutor under this section shall be deemed to be a Public Prosecutor within the meaning of clause (u) of Section (2) of the Code shall have effect accordingly.

11. *Procedures and powers of Special Courts:*

(1) A Special Court may take cognizance of any offence, without the accused being committed to it for trial, upon receiving a complaint of facts which constitute such offence, or upon a police report of such facts.

(2) Subject to the other provisions of this Act, a Special Court shall, for the purpose of the trial of any offence have all the powers of a Court of Session and shall try such offences as if it were a Court of Sessions, so far as may be, in accordance with the procedure prescribed in the Code for trial before a Court of Session.

12. *Power of Special Court with respect to other offences:*

(1) When trying any offence under this Act, a Special Court may also try any other offence with which the accused may, under the Code, be charged at the same trial if the offence is connected with such other offence.

(2) If, in the course of any trial of any offence under this Act it is found that the accused person has committed any other offence under this Act or under any other law, a Special Court may convict such person also of such other offence and pass any sentence authorised by this Act or such other law for the punishment thereof.

(3) In every inquiry or trial, the proceeding shall be held as expeditiously as possible and, in particular, where the examination of witness has begun, the same shall be continued from day to day until all the witnesses in attendance have been examined, and if Special Court finds the adjournment of the same beyond, the following date to be necessary, it shall record its reasons for doing so.

13. Forfeiture of funds or property:

Where a person has been convicted of an offence under this Act, the Special Court trying such offence may, if it is considered necessary so to do, declare that any funds or property seized under Section 8 shall stand forfeited to the state.

14. Appeal:

Notwithstanding anything contained in the Code, an appeal shall lie as a matter of right from any judgement, sentence or order, not being an interlocutory order, of a Special Court to the High Court both on facts and on law.

(2) Every appeal under this section shall be preferred within a period of thirty days from the date of the judgement, sentence or order appealed from:

Provided that the High Court may entertain an appeal after the expiry of the said period of thirty days if it is satisfied that the applicant has sufficient cause for not preferring the appeal within the period of thirty days.

PART V
MISCELLANEOUS

15. Protection of action taken under this Act:

No suit, prosecution or other legal proceeding shall lie against the State Government or any officer or authority of the State Government for anything which is in good faith done or intended to be done in pursuance of this Act or any rules or orders made under this Act.

16. Burden of proof:

Where any person is prosecuted of an offence under Section 4, the burden of proving that he had not committed the offence under the said section shall be on him.

17. Obligation of certain persons to report about the commission of offence under this Act:

(1) All officers of the Government are hereby required and empowered to assist the police in the execution of the provisions of this Act or any rule or order made thereunder.

(2) All village officers and such other officers as may be

specified by the Collector or the District Magistrate in relation to any area and the inhabitants of such area shall, if they have reason to believe or have the knowledge that sati is about to be, or has been committed in the area shall forthwith report such fact to the nearest police station.

(3) Whoever contravenes the provisions of sub-section (1) or sub-section (2) shall be punishable with imprisonment of either description for a term which may extend to two years and shall also be liable to fine.

18. *Person convicted of an offence under Section 4 to be disqualified from inheriting certain properties:*

A person convicted of an offence under sub-section (1) of Section 4 in relation to the commission of sati shall be disqualified from inheriting the property of the person in respect of whom such sati has been committed or the property of other person which he would have been entitled to inherit on the death of the person in respect of whom such sati has been committed.

19. *Amendment of Act 43 of 1951:*

In the Representation of the People Act, 1951

(a) in Section 8, in sub-section (2), after the proviso, the following proviso shall be inserted, namely—

"Provided further that a person convicted by a Special Court for the contravention of any of the provisions of the Commission of Sati (Prevention) Act, 1987 shall be disqualified from the date of such conviction and shall continue to be disqualified for a further period of five years since his release."

(b) in Section 123, after Clause (3-A), the following clause shall be inserted, namely:

"(3-B) The propagation of the practice of the commission of sati or its glorification by a candidate or his agent or any other person with the consent of the candidate or his election agent for the furtherance of the prospects of the election of that candidate or for prejudicially affecting the election of any candidate.

Explanation: For the purposes of this clause, "Sati" and the "glorification" in relation to sati shall have the meaning respectively assigned to them in the Commission of Sati (Prevention) Act, 1987."

20. *Act to have overriding effect:*

The provisions of this Act or any rule or order made thereunder shall have effect notwithstanding anything inconsistent therewith contained in any enactment other than this Act or in any instrument having effect by virtue of any enactment other than this Act.

21. *Power to make rules:*

(1) The Central Government may, by notification in the Official Gazette, make rules for carrying out the provisions of this Act.

(2) Every rule made under this section shall be laid, as soon as may be after it is made, before each House of Parliament, while it is in session, for a total period of thirty days which may be comprised in one session or in two or more successive sessions, and if, before the expiry of the session immediately following the session or the successive sessions aforesaid, both Houses agree in making any modification in the rule or both Houses agree that the rule should not be made, the rule shall thereafter have effect only in such modified form or be of no effect, as the case may be; so, however, that any such modification or annulment shall be without prejudice to the validity of anything previously done under that rule.

22 *Repeal of existing laws:*

(1) All laws in force in any state immediately before the commencement of this Act in that state which provide for the prevention or the glorification of sati shall, on such commencement, shall be repealed.

(2) Notwithstanding such repeal, anything done or any action taken under any law repealed under sub-section (1) shall be deemed to have been done or taken under the corresponding provisions of this Act, and, in particular, any case taken cognizance of by a Special Court under the provisions of any law so repealed and pending before it immediately before the commencement of this Act in that state shall continue to be dealt with by that Special Court after such commencement as if such

Special Court had been constituted under Section 9 of this Act.

Flaws in the Act:

The Commission of Sati (Prevention) Act, 1987 suffers from the following flaws:

(i) The act of getting burnt voluntarily amounts to committing suicide and its attempt is 'attempt at committing suicide'. This is a penal offence as defined in Section 309 of the Indian Penal Code. The substitution of committing sati for suicide gives the act the colour of a religious sanction.

(ii) Whoever, creates conditions for committing sati or lights the funeral pyre has committed an offence of murder which is defined in Section 300 of the Indian Penal Code. The expression sati denotes that such person is doing some useful religious work.

(iii) The penal provisions made vide Section 3 of the Prevention of Sati Act in respect of the person rescued from accomplishing sati, will land her to a situation of criminal prosecution and conviction. The victim woman is rather an object of sympathy and not a criminal. The provisions of the Section 3 becomes redundant in the light of the judgement of two High Courts which have struck down the provisions of Section 309 I.P.C.

Section 15 of the Act is nothing but a duplication of effort. Similar provisions do exist in Section 197 of Cr. P.C. (Act 2 of 1974) detailed below:

197. Prosecution of judges and public servants:

(i) When any person who is or was a judge or magistrate or a public servant not removable from his office save by or with the sanction of the Government is accused of any offence alleged to have been committed by him while acting or purporting to act in the discharge of his official duty, no court shall take cognizance of such offence except with the previous sanction:

(a) in the case of a person who is employed or, as the case may be, was at the time of commission of the alleged offence employed, in connection with the affairs of the Union, of the Central Government.

(b) in the case of a person who is employed or, as the case may be, was at the time of commission of an alleged offence employed, in connection with the affairs of a state, of the State Government.

(ii) No court shall take cognizance, of an offence alleged to have been committed by any member of the Armed Forces of the Union while acting or purporting to act in the discharge of his official duty, except with the previous sanction of the Central Government.

(iii) The State Government may, by notification, direct that the provisions of sub-section (2) shall apply to such class or category of the members of the Forces charged with the maintenance of public order as may be specified therein, wherever they may be serving, and thereupon the provisions of that subsection will apply as if the expression "Central Government" occurring therein, the expression "State Government were substituted."

(iv) The Central Government, or the State Government, as the case may be, determine the person by whom, the manner in which, and the offence or offences for which, the prosecution of such judge, magistrate or public servant is to be conducted, and may specify the court before which the trial is to be held.

(v) Section 16 of the Act is on the question of burden of proof in respect of prosecution under Section 4 of the Act. The Act shifts the burden of proof on the accused. The ingredients of this Section do not confirm to notion of burden of proof in accordance with the provisions of Sections 101 to 114 in Chapter VII of the Evidence Act (1872).

(vi) Section 7(1) of the Act empowers State Government in respect of any temple or other structure which has been in existence for not less than twenty years and where any form of worship or the performance of any ceremony is carried out with a view to perpetuate the honour of, or to preserve the memory of, any person in respect of, in respect of whom sati has been committed, by order, direct the removal of such temple or other structure. If the object of the legislation is to ban glorification for a limited number of temples then it is alright but certainly the object is to ban glorification altogether.

(vii) Section 18 disqualifies persons, convicted of abetment, from inheriting the property of the person in respect of whom such sati has been committed or the property of any other person which he would have been entitled to on the death of the person in respect of whom such sati has been committed. This provision is liable to be struck down. While the powers given to the authorities (Section 8) to seize properties or funds which may have been collected or acquired for the purpose of glorification of the commission of any sati or which may be found under circumstances which create suspicion of commission of any offence under this Act makes sense, Section 18 does not. Assuming that the abettors are punished and awarded life imprisonment, he will be out after fourteen years. The property will still be there and he will be entitled to it under the normal inheritance laws. The provisions are in conflict with the law of inheritance and contravenes the provisions of Article 14 of the Constitution.[18]

What is needed is the plugging of loopholes in the provisions of the Act so that it becomes perfect.

REFERENCES

1. Inderjit Badhwar, "Sati—A Pagan Sacrifice", *India Today,* Oct. 15, 1987, pp. 98–105.
2. H.T. News Item, "Roop Kanwar ran for her life", *Hindustan Times,* dated October 21, 1987.
3. Sri Lata Swaminathan, "Satisfying the male ego", *Hindustan Times,* dated October 18, 1987.
4. Iqbal Kaul, "If a woman in her blindness climbed her dead lord's pyre, she goes to hell", *Times of India (Sunday Review),* dated December 27, 1987.
5. *Ibid.*
6. Iqbal Kaul, "Husband's right, wife's rite", *Times of India,* dated (Sunday) January 3, 1988.
7. Kumkum Sangri, "There is no such thing as Voluntary Sati", *Times of India (Sunday Review),* dated 25.10.1987.
8. Iqbal Kaul, "Husbands right, wife's rite", *The Times of India* (*Sunday*), January 3, 1988.
9. Iqbal Kaul, "Thirty-five Million Years of Heavenly Bliss", *The Times of India,* dated December 20, 1988.
10. V.N. Dutta, "Sati" (Manohar Book Service), Of guilt and goddesses'—Book Review by Mulk Raj Anand, *Times of India,* dated February 1, 1988.
11. Kumkum, "Anti Sati Measurers, Need for Central Law", *Hindustan Times,* dated November 12, 1987.
12. The Times of India News Service, "Rajasthan Sati Bill passed," *Times of India,* dated 28.11.1987
13. Kusum, "Anti Sati Measures—Need for Central Law," *The Hindustan Times,* dated Nov. 12, 1987.
14. News dated Nov. 28 of 1987, "Governor's action upheld in Sati Case," *Times of India,* dated November 29, 1987.

15. Pankan Pachauti, "Landmark Judgment—Anti Sati Law extended to all temples," *India Today*, December 31, 1987.
16. The Times of India Legal Correspondent, "Resumption of Sati case Trial ordered", *Times of India*, dated December 19, 1987.
17. The Times of India News Service, "Sati Bill tabled in Lok Sabha", *Times of India*, dated December 15, 1987.
18. Louise Fernandes, "A Burnt Out Case—A Need for Adequate Measures" *The Hindustan Times* (Delhi), Sunday Magazine, Sept. 4, 1988.

Chapter 5

Prostitution

5.01 Definition

The word 'prostitute' has been derived from the Latin word prostibula or proseda. The houses of ancient Greek harlots were allowed to be opened in the afternoon. The girl stood or sat before the lupanaria to attract and entice passers-by. Therefore, they were called prostibula or proseda.[1]

The dictionary meaning of the word 'prostitute' is the act or practice of engaging in sexual intercourse for money and the word 'prostitute' connotes a person, usually a woman who engages in sexual intercourse for money.[2]

The Suppression of Immoral Traffic in Women and Girls Act (1956) defines 'prostitute' as a female who offers her body for promiscuous sexual intercourse for hire, whether in money or in kind; and 'prostitution' means the act of a female offering her body for promiscuous sexual intercourse for hire, whether in money or in kind.[3] The act was amended in 1978,[4] wherein the definition of the word 'prostitute' was omitted and the expression 'prostitution' was redefined as the act of a female offering her body for promiscuous sexual intercourse for hire, whether in money or in kind, and whether offered immediately or otherwise and the expression 'prostitute' shall be construed accordingly.

Mamoria,[5] defined prostitution as a sexual union by a woman with a person who is not her husband, for some consideration in cash or kind and prostitute is a woman who sells her sexual favours indiscriminately and takes money or other valuables for each act of intercourse; and who has no psychic involvement.

The gist of the problem is that "it is more or less a promiscuous sexual intercourse" that is; all women who are guilty of intercourse outside the marriage state may be regarded as prostitutes. The important ingredients of prostitution, according to Weaver, are:[6]

(i) Promiscuity, barter and emotional indifference;
(ii) It is different from the broader concept of sexual immorality due to the commercial nature of the relationship, and
(iii) It is distinguished from illegitimacy, which invariably involves an illicit sex relationship but refers particularly to the production of a child outside the socially approved reproduction.

5.02 Types of Prostitution

1. *Common prostitutes:*

These comprise of the unfortunate women and girls who are recruited through pimps and procurers who have been sold or landed in brothels and vice-dens maintained by old prostitutes or men. Their induction into the trade is through poverty, allurement, misguidance, neglect and kidnapping and abduction from their homes. Sister Rozario of Joint Women's Programme (JWP), an organisation working for the upliftment of women has conducted a study for four years and interviewed three thousand prostitutes in fourteen states and two union territories and brought out pathetic tales of their induction into the trade. Some of these are enumerated below:[7,8]

(i) Several young women got into prostitution because they were raped and neither their family nor society was willing to accept them. For example K who, today is a street walker in Karnataka was raped by her brother's friend; a teenager of 17, who visited her home. She got the impression that he was in love with her because he carried her to shops and brought her sweets and coloured ribbons. When she attained puberty at the age of 12, he said that he wanted to marry her and on that pretext he took her from home and lodged her in a rented room. He stayed with her for a few days then went back to his house leaving her some money for her needs. Every time, he visited her she reminded him of his promise to marry her. He continued making excuses and one day stopped going to her. Today, the boy is happily married to a girl and the girl with whom he eloped has become a prostitute. As a matter of fact, the man should have been prosecuted under various sections of the Indian Penal Code and Suppression of Immoral Traffic Act and Prevention of Immoral Traffic Act but inspite of these provisions, there is nobody to take appropriate action in the matter.

(ii) Pimps are constantly on the look-out for destitutes willing to sell their children. The JWP has now the proof of the fact that girls are sold by near relations on account of acute poverty. Nearly one third of the total population of the prostitutes come from this source. In Raichur district of Karnataka, a poor couple with three daughters sold his one teenaged girl for Rs. 5000 only so that others could survive. In another case, a girl was sold for Rs. 10,000 only by her parents so that her elder sister could be married. The girl now works hard as a maid servant during day so that she can raise Rs. 10,000 and earn her freedom. Rama Kumari (31) was an orphan and at the age of 13 years was sold by a person to a hotel owner, who in turn sold her to a theatre owner in Salem. She is now a prostitute, who claims to have respectable persons including MLAs as her clients and their respectability remains untouched even after their association with a degraded person like her. A mother, in lieu of a sari, dedicated the child in her womb to Goddess Yellamma, should the child so born is a female one and thus condemned her to a life of shame even before her birth. A bridegroom has sold his newly wedded wife to a brothel and young children have been raped by the people they trusted. Sister Rita Rozario interviewed a girl from Bihar who was sold just for one thousand rupees because she was raped and the family did not want to keep a girl in the house with a stigma of having been raped. Naseema was raped by her own father at the age of 13 and sold to a brothel.[9]

(iii) Importing of girls from foreign country, buying and selling minors for the purpose of prostitution are punishable offences under Section 366-B, Section 371 and Section 372 of the Penal Code but these continue, inspite of the legal provisions in this respect. According to Mrs. Jyotsna Chatterji, at any time some twenty thousand girls are being transported from one end of the country to another for prostitution. Neither the law on immoral trafficking nor the greater awareness about the women's right have changed the lot of the poor women. The network of traffickers and pimps, engaged in this trade is well organised. Girls procured in one state are auctioned and sold like cattles in transit centres, which are invariably outside the big cities and after being sold they are sent to red light areas. In every state, there are three towns which form a triangle and act as the nodal area for sale of girls. The network is so well organised that girls from Bangladesh are taken through India and sold in Pakistan. The route is very often the same as used by drug traffickers. The participants to the auction are drawn from pimps and merchants of the flesh trade, industrialists and rich persons. According to Sister Rita Rozario, a Bombay industrialist paid Rs. 70,000 for a girl at an auction just outside the city.

(2) *Hereditary prostitutes:*

Hereditary prostitutes are a class in themselves, who have a heritage from the Mughal period. They are drawn both from the Hindu and Muslim community. In them, the prostitution is handed down from mother to daughter as a profession with no stigma attached to a life of immorality. They are trained in the art of singing and dancing and the girls in the family are trained in this art from early age. As a matter of fact, a large number of them have acquired an excellence in the rendering of classical and semi-classical music so much so that they have earned a place of pride and respect among the knowledgeable persons. Looking to their past life, it has been known that they have maintained contact with only one man and cannot, therefore, be classed as prostitutes in strict sense.

(3) *Traditional prostitutes:*

This class of prostitutes comprised of beautiful women and girls who were raised by the Rajas, Maharajas and Jagirdars. They were well trained in the art of singing and dancing and were required to render special services for the rulers at the time of festivals to entertain audiences and guests. Sometimes, they had to enter into competitions with similar artists from outside and their excellence and performance had a bearing on the prestige of darbar. They were known as 'Kalavanthis', 'Mangalmukhis', and 'Nrityamangalis'. Seeing their face in the morning and at the commencement of a journey was considered auspicious. They had to become the paramours of princes or sardars or important courtiers of the state. Young men from the royal families used to visit them for learning the art of manners and behaviours and lessons on sex education. Their descendents are still found.

(4) *Hotel prostitutes:*

Some hotel managements maintain their contact with society girls belonging to the elite or upper middle class families, who live in private houses, are educated and gainfully employed. They are well dressed, well mannered and enter into the trade not on account of any compulsion or financial constraints but for fun and extra income needed for meeting the expense of their luxurious life. They are called 'call girls' and are classed among voluntary prostitutes.[10]

(5) *Temple prostitutes:*[11]

Temple prostitutes are known by different names, e.g., Devadasis, Khudikar, Murli, Basavi, Bhavin, Devali, Naikin and Jogins in different parts of the country.

Though the term 'devadasi' did not figure earlier than Chola times (850 A.D to 1280 A.D.), the cult of devadasi is closely associated with the cultural life of the people in the South. The devadasi is a semiotic unit within the sacred play of Hindu rituals. Her duties comprise of a combination of (a) propitiatory, (b) ritual and (c) entertainment to assert positive fertility and prosperity. She is expected to carry out these functions through her female sexuality which is identified/ritually merged with the goddess, through her act. Thus she has functioned variously as the 'matangi', the virali (female bard), the rajdasi and devadasi acquiring along the way ever-sophisticated rituals and artistic accomplishments. They, on account of being married to god or goddesses, such as 'Yellamma' or 'Mathamma', were called 'Nitya-sumangali'.

In the early period, devadasis enjoyed a place of honour in the society. Even now, at some places, they perform certain rituals during fairs and festivals. In the by-gone days, temple dancers were the only women in India who could, sing, dance and recite before the deity.

The custom of dedicating girls to Gods is believed to have evolved in the 3rd Century A.D.. At that time, they used to be drawn from among the prostitutes to serve as temple dancers and courtesans. In some cases, the temple priests brought good-looking girls from poor parents and converted them into devadasis. At times, superstitious parents presented their first born female child to the temple under the belief that offering of the female child would bring prosperity for the family and the community. This system still continues in parts of Karnataka and Goa.

In course of time, the system has developed to the level of prostitution. To a great extent, the victim falls prey to superstitious beliefs and traditional customs which not only hampers progress but ruins innocent lives. Once a devadasi, the woman ends up living miserable life of a prostitute or a beggar.

The prevalence of jogins/basavis/parvatis, an offshoot of Devadasi system continues in large part of the State of Andhra Pradesh in the districts of Adilabad, Nizamabad, Medak, Warangal and Hyderabad districts. They are called jogins in Karimnagar district and at other places as parvatis and in Rayalseema districts in areas bordering Karnataka as basavis and in other districts such as Nellore, Chittoor, they are known as mathamma and theyamma.[12]

Under the prevailing custom, a young girl or woman is dedicated to the service of god/goddess, such as Yellamma. Poleramma etc. on some auspicious day by Dasaries, Jagnams, Ayyavarnulu or Potharaju. After the dedication, the dedicated women/girls have to recite certain mantra, and to beg on specific days a week. The girl is not allowed to marry as by marrying a deity she has attained the status of a 'Sumangali'.

Most of the jogins belong to Mala, Madiga and Dommara communities and they end up in prostitution. In Nizamabad area, the system of jogin is prevalent in Bodhan, Banswada, Armoor, Nizamabad, Yellareddy and Madnoor. There are nearly five thousand jogins in nearly four hundred villages in the district and most of them hail from Bodhan area.

To quote for instance, Ganga, a schedule caste girl, was initiated as a jogin around the year 1960 at the age of six years. After eight years of initiation, at the age of fourteen, Dora, a local Zamindar came and took her away at night and in a span of a few years burdened her with a couple of children and paid a paltry sum of Rs. two hundred to her father by way of compensation and maintenance. After that she was passed on from one landlord to another till she died at the early age of thirty years. The children left by Ganga are begging and the landlord has taken another jogin. There are about ten thousand jogins in the area.

Among the Bajgi community in Purola region, its occupation in service of the temple may be closely connected with the large number of women who are made to adopt this trade. Although devadasi system as such does not exist, certain class of people closely connected with the work of the temple are more prone to prostitution. They come from landless families and up to 75 per cent bonded for life to upper caste moneylenders. Many persons in this community practice polyandry due to high bride price. Women generally occupy a very low social position and labour ceaselessly in fields or in homes once they are bought or sold. Trafficking is on increase in these regions and sometimes powerful men or higher caste people act as agents and are in liasion with procurers and brothel keepers for inducting girls into prostitution.[13]

Inspite of all these odds, the devadasi system has made a definite contribution to growth of refinement in classical dances like Bharat Natyam, Mohini- Attam, Kuchipudi, Kathakali in the South, Odissi in Orissa and Kathak style in the North.

(6) *Prostitutes belonging to backward tribes:*

Another group of prostitutes are drawn from the scheduled castes and backward criminal tribes, scattered all over the country distributed mostly in the northern and central part of the country. These are Berias, Dhairs, Kanjars, Sansis in the North and Basavis, Koyis, Bediyas, Kolhatis, Harnis, Baradas, Mang, Garudus, Dombars etc., in the South.[14]

Large hordes of Nuts, Chandravedis and others do not hesitate to claim that no stigma is attached to the trade of prostitution. They openly seduce girls. Males contract marriages and have a progeny to please their patrons. They believe in the theory that it is better to prostitution than to starve or beg. They have a custom to dedicate girls to prostitution and in the tribe these girls are not looked down upon.[15] The following are quoted by way of illustration.

(i) The road from Neemuch to Mandsaur in Madhya Pradesh, are dotted with houses that are spread over some distance form one another. The young women of these houses sit under a tree close to their houses to solicit customers. These women belong to Basadi tribe and earn through prostitution. This suits the members of the tribe as well, who instead of roaming from one place to another prefer to settle at one place and carry on this trade.

The menfolk of this tribe live at places located at some distance from them and work as labourer during day and commit various forms of crimes like thefts, robberies and dacoities during night.

Prostitution among the members of this tribe is a way of life. If a girl, who is not beautiful wants to lead a normal married life, she is permitted to do so. On the other hand, if a beautiful girl wishes to keep herself out of the profession and lead a normal married life, she is first persuaded against this idea and if she does not agree, she is repeatedly raped and ravished by the members of the community and thus is forced to adopt this trade.

Basadi's are believed to have originated from the criminal tribe of Kanjars and they have spread out to the neighbouring areas and preferred to remain near the borders of the earstwhile Princely Estates, as this used to be the most convenient method for them to commit crimes in one territory and escape to another territory. It is believed, that in the 19th Century, the then ruler of Gwalior ordered the shifting of 'Basadis' by the sides of those roads, that were generally used by the British troops during their movements.

Naseerabad, Neenuch and Mhow being Army Cantonments, the roads connecting these areas were frequented by the members of the troops. Since there were allegations of molestation of village women by the members of the troops, the Maharaja ordered the rehabilitation of the members of 'Basadi' tribe as their women practiced prostitution.[16]

(ii) Wadia is a small hamlet in Tharad Taluka of Banskantha District in North Gujrat which is inhabited by nearly sixty families of a Denotified Tribe (DNT) called as 'Saraniya'. This is a baster tribe living solely on the earnings of the women by prostituion. According to the history, around the middle of the 17th Century, the birth rate among the Rajputs suddenly fell which was taken as the fall in vitality of its male members. Thus a new system known as 'Goda' was introduced.

Godas were well bodied healthy persons who were also called 'Saand' (Ox) and had been given by the society the right to have sex with a childless woman. The Godas, used to wear a special type of Nagra shoe, which when kept outside a woman's bedroom was a signal to her husband to keep himself away. Unfortunately the offspring of 'Godas' were not acceptable to the families and were regarded as illegitimate while the male child remained in the family to run the family tree the female child being of illegitimate origin were unable to secure husbands and finally landed as concubines of Jagirdars and Zamindars.

After the partition of the country and abolition of Zamindari system, the female members have now taken to prostituion. The clientele are mainly from Ahmedabad, Baroda and Bombay. But Saraniya women also go to nearly places like Palanpur, Mahsana, Disa and Sabarkantha. For them summer is the best season to visit a hill station because many Saraniya women visit Mount Abu during their holidays instead of coming to Wadia. But it is in later part of autumn, when the festive season starts and Deepavali is round the corner that Wadia gets the best business of the year.

An outsider can marry a Saraniya woman by paying the necessary price which is not more than Rs. 500 but the bride has to stay with the clan. If the husband chooses, he can stay away from his wife and visit her once in a while. The woman can continue with her trade but they are never forced to do so once they are married.[17]

(iii) The Banchchara community living in the Western Madhya Pradesh area was, once a time, a notified criminal tribe. The members belonging to this community speak a language which is a mixture of Gujrati, Rajasthani and Malvi. The custom among this community is that the eldest daughter in the family must take to prostitution to support the family.[18] The population of this community in the locality is nearly five thousand and prostitution is socially sanctioned. Every fifth woman in the community is a 'Khilwadi' (a nomenclature for prostitute). No stigma is attached to a woman who is 'khilwadi'. Once a 'khilwadi', the woman is not allowed to marry in the community nor any man in the community can take sex favours from a 'khilwadi'. It is said that Banchcharas belonged predominantly to the community of farm labourers and their womenfolk were forced to become 'khilwadi' to cater to the sexual advances of their feudal masters. The efforts of the State Government to rehabiltate them proved unsuccessful.

(iv) The Sansis are concentrated in three villages—Kadia, Gulkhedi and Hulkhedi, a place about 60 kms from Bhopal. They number about two thousand. Most of the residents own agricultural lands but they do not know farming and so indulge in criminal activities like house-breaking, dacoity and illicit liquor brewing. Many sansi women have been sold by their parents to agents who in turn sold them to the brothel keepers in the city.[19]

It was in 1965, that the exploitation of sansi girls began by outsiders. It began with the visits to the area by a retired police official of Uttar Pradesh who developed a relationship with a beautiful woman named Vaijanthi, daughter of Kishan Tikliya. Vaijanthi was lured away to Agra where she landed in a brothel. When Vaijanthi started sending large sums of money to her father, the father sold her two other daughters for Rs. 5000 and Rs. 10,000. Eventually Vaijanthi's father Kishan allegedly became king-pin of the flesh trade in the area.

Within years, number of girls took to prostitution. While some were forced into it, others joined it on their own to earn a living.

5.03 Other Forms of Sexploitation

(a) The Mondapatta tribals in pockets of Ganjam district in Orissa are selling their wives to stave off their hunger. Although this practice has the sanction of the tribal society, only in recent years this phenomenon has increased due to abject poverty.

Monapattas are basically a nomadic tribe but some of them have now taken to settled life and are residing on the outskirts of the village in the areas around Aska, Bhanjnagar, Chitki and Rambha.

Recently a news appeared in Indian Express,[20] narrating the incident of Panchu Patra; living below the mountains near Kendrabali village in Namina Panchayat, about 11 kms from Aska, buying his fourth wife, a young girl named Kantha around the close of the year 1987, from a village near Rambha in Ganjam district for an amount as low as rupees seventy only. When asked from Kantha as to how long she was going to stay with her husband, she only smiled but Panchu Patra told that he sold his first wife to his own tribesman in Andhra Pradesh for a sum of Rs. 110 only. His second wife was taken away by his own parents near Digapahandi. His own daughter was sold to one Sanya Patra for Rs. 300 only. The price of the woman in such deals vary between rupees sixty to three hundred.

The sanctioned custom of mortgaging women folk has given place to direct sale of wives as the person mortgaging his wife often fails to collect the amount needed for the recovery from the bondage of mortgage. Thus a woman is not more than a saleable commodity. This phenomenon is a crime against the dignity of womanhood.

(b) Miraj Tehsil, in Sangli district in Maharashtra, developed as a Medical city after Sir William Wanless Mission Hospital was set up in 1896. On account of its good climate and the standard of treatment, it, now attracts patients from Arab countries. This has not only come to exert a stranglehold on Miraj's economy but has adversely affected the ethics of medical profession. Another disquieting feature of the visits by the Arabian clientele is the flourishing flesh trade. This is in the form of availability of a convenient bride for a couple of months or so during which an Arabian stays, whom he divorces before flying back. The good time is provided by the large number of prostitutes who have now flocked to Miraj. There are about four hundred 'tabaks' mainly Muslims, who were originally Bidi-makers, but as soon as Arabs arrive, these persons become their cooks and domestic servants and many them become their temporary concubines. They are given temporary rooms outside their hotels where they cook on kerosene stoves for Rs. ten per day plus their meals. The cause of the sexploitation is poverty as morality cannot be preached on an empty stomach.[21]

(c) Among the muslims of Hyderabad, there exists a custom known as 'Parwardah' system where impecunious people with large family give away their children to the wealthy for a consideration, relinquishing all rights over them and requiring no obligations to be fulfilled by them with regard to their education, health, training or living conditions. These children are used as domestic servants by their patrons and as the girls grow to maturity they are sexually exploited by the male members of the family.[22]

(d) There is a system among certain Bengali communities whereby widows are taken to the Vishwanath temple in Varanasi and left there to spend the rest of their lives to prayer and meditation. Large number of such widows often find themselves in the brothels of Banaras.[23]

(e) In Kumari—a young girl, worshipped as the principal goddess of Nepal—superstition, religion and primitivism combine to give a faith of uniqueness of dimension in Durbar Square in Kathmandu.

Kumari is supposed to be the living incarnation of goddess Taleju temporarily. There is a legend that in the 17th century, King Jai Prakash Malla, while playing a game of dice with goddess Taleju could not refrain from having amorous thoughts about her. Reading his mind, the goddess in anger cursed that henceforth he would never see her in person and he must worship her in the body of a young virgin girl of low caste. Since then, Kumari worship is prevalent in Nepal. For this purpose, a girl of seven years of age is selected and initiated as a deity. The reigning king seeks blessings from her annually.

Her cries and laughs are interpreted as omens and her powers considered as supreme. This belief is strengthened by an incident that in 1955, the goddess placed a 'Tikka' on the forehead of the crown prince instead of the king—eight months later, the king died and was succeeded by the crown prince. This episode is interpreted as a strong proof of Kumari's powers to anticipate future events.

The selection of Kumari is made from the Buddhist Sakya Tribe and she is also worshipped as Vajrayana deity. The selection is made from a chosen set of young girls who should be unblemished and should not have lost even one tooth. She continues to remain a Kumari deity till she attains puberty.

The child is put through various tests culminating in the final test of courage. She is thus made to walk among several slaughtered goats and buffaloes in the temple of Taleju for secret initiation rites. After having done this, she has to wear a permanent top-knot, have red-painted toes, wear heavy black eye make up, red clothes and sport a painted third eye on her forehead.

The 'Kumari' is then isolated. She is not allowed to mix with any other girl of her age and then deprived of the natural desire to have the company of a play-mate at her age. She does not receive any education and is not allowed to step out of her room where she continues to receive her devotees only. She is taken out of her room only once in a year during 'Indra Yatra' which takes place in September-October in a chariot and is never allowed to touch the bare earth, lest she will be defiled.

To mark the beginning of the procession, a goat is sacrificed at the yoke of the chariot. On the final day of the festival, 108 goats and buffaloes are sacrificed at the Taleju temple. The 'Kumari' walks on a red cloth from the nearby temple to the 'Taleju' temple where she undergoes secret rites for the annual replenishment of the godly powers from the 'Taleju' deity. She is then worshipped by the king and commoners follow him in worship.

The misfortune of the 'Kumari' starts as soon as she attains puberty. Once worshipped as a goddess she is discarded and replaced by a substitute. No body marries her under the supposed belief that whoever will marry her will be short-lived. She has not learnt anything and thus after being dethroned, she is thrown to prostitution.[24]

5.04 Prostitution as an International Problem

The commercialisation of sex is not confined to India only but has existed and is existing in some form or the other throughout the world. It is recognised internationally as a social evil which has not only given a stigma to the society but has brought out great harm to the individual, family and the society. Prostitution not only brings about personal and family disorganisation by wrecking the personality, marital relations, family life and communication of disease and, therefore, it must be uprooted from the society. Suppression of trafficking in women and girls has been adopted by legislation of almost all the countries.

5.05 International Instruments[25]

The League of Nations in 1937, through a draft resolution took up this issue. A convention to suppress the traffic in persons and against the practice of prostitution was signed at New York (U.S.A.) by several nations including India on May 9, 1950. The International Instruments are as follows:

(1) International Agreement of 18th May, 1904 for the Suppression of White Slave Traffic, as amended by the Protocol approved by the General Assembly of the United Nations on the 3rd December, 1948.
(2) International Convention of the 4th May, 1910 for the Suppression of White Slave Traffic, as amended by the above-mentioned Protocol.
(3) International Convention of 30th September, 1921, for the Suppression of the Traffic in Women and Children, as amended by the Protocol approved by the General Assembly of the United Nations 20th October, 1947.
(4) International Convention of 11th October, 1933 for the Suppression of Traffic in Women of Full Age, as amended by the aforesaid Protocol.

The objects and reasons of the Suppression of Immoral Traffic in Women and Girls Bill No. 58 of 1954 were published in Government of India, Extraordinary, Part II, Section 2 dated December 20, 1954. The same is reproduced below:

(1) In 1930, the Government of India ratified an International Convention for the suppression of Immoral Traffic in persons and the exploitation of the prostitution of others. Under Article 23 of the Convention, traffic in human beings is prohibited and any contravention of the prohibition is an offence punishable by law. Under Article 35, such a law has to be passed by Parliament as soon as may be, after the commencement of the Constitution.
(2) Legislation on the subject of Suppression of Immoral Traffic does exist in a few states but the laws are neither uniform nor do they go far enough. In the remaining states there is no bar on the subject at all.
(3) In the circumstances, it is necessary and desirable that Central Law should be passed which will not only secure uniformity but would be sufficiently deterrent for the purpose. But a special feature of the Bill is that it provides that no person or authority other than the State Government shall establish or maintain any protective home except under a licence issued by the State Government. This will check the establishment of homes which are really dens for prostitution.

5.06 Legal Aspects of Prostitution

In pursuance of the International Convention for the Suppression of Immoral Traffic in Women and Girls, signed in 1950, the Suppression of Immoral Traffic in Women and Girls Act (1956) was enacted vide Act No. 104 of 1956 and in the next twenty-two years, the Act was amended vide Act No. 46 of 1978. The 1978 amendment was made to make good some inadequacies in the implementation of the provisions of the Act in the light of the experience gained in its implementation. Hence the Act was further amended in 1986 vide Act No. 44 of 1986 with effect from 26.1.1987. In the re-amended Act the emphasis was on prevention and the title of the Act was changed to "The Immoral Traffic (Prevention) Act, 1956.

5.07 Salient Features of the Amended Act of 1978

The Act envisages to fulfil twin objectives, viz; (a) upholding public morality and (b) protecting women and girls who are the

Section	Specific Offence	Sentence of Imprisonment Minimum	Maximum	Fine
3.	Punishment for keeping a brothel or allowing premises to be used as a brothel			
	(i) First conviction	R.I. for one year	R.I. for three years	Rs. 2000
	(ii) Subsequent conviction	R.I. for two years	R.I. for five years	-do-
4.	Living on the earnings of prostitution	—	Imprisonment for two years	Rs. 1000
5.	Procuring, inducing or taking woman or girl for the sake of prostitution			
	(i) First conviction	R.I. for one year	R.I. for two years	Rs. 2000
	(ii) Subsequent conviction	R.I. for two years	R.I. for five years	-do-
6.	Detaining a woman or girl in premises where prostitution is carried on			
	(i) First conviction	R.I. for one year	R.I. for two years	Rs. 2000
	(ii) Second or subsequent conviction	R.I. for two years	R.I. for five years	Rs. 2000
7.	Prostitution in the vicinity of public places			
	(i) First conviction	Imprisonment for three months		Rs. 200
	(ii) Subsequent conviction	Imprisonment for six months		-do-
8.	Seduction or soliciting for purpose of prostitution			
	(i) First conviction	Imprisonment for six months		Rs. 500
	(ii) Second conviction	Imprisonment for one year		-do-
9.	Seduction of a woman or girl in custody			
	(i) First conviction	R.I. for one year	R.I. for three years	Rs. 1000
	(ii) Subsequent conviction	R.I. upto five years		-do-

victims of the acts of prostitution. The penal provisions of the Act are as given in the table.

5.08 Amendment vide Act No. 44 of 1986

In accordance with the provisions of Article 23 of the Constitution, traffic in human beings is prohibited. Under Article 35, such a law has to be passed by the Parliament after the commencement of the Constitution. The International Convention also refers to traffic in human beings which includes both the sexes. Thus the amending Act of 44 of 1986 which has its effect from 26.1.1987, the title of the Act has been changed from "Suppression of Immoral Traffic in Women and Girls Act" to "Immoral Traffic (Prevention) Act" and for the expressions "women and girls" and "women or girls" wherever they occur, the words "person" and "persons" have been substituted. Now the Act prohibits traffic in human beings and not traffic in women and girls alone. In the amended Act (44 of 1986) emphasis is on prevention instead of suppression of the previous Act (No. 104 of 1956 as amended by Act. No. 46 of 1978). In this Act, the scope of the Act has been enlarged to cover all persons belonging to both the sexes. The salient features of the amended Act are as under:

(i) In order to cover persons belonging to both sexes, whether male of female who are sexually exploited for commercial purposes the Act has been renamed as "Immoral Traffic (Prevention) Act".

(ii) Punishments for offences against children and minors have been enhanced and thus such punishments have been made more stiff.

(iii) Trafficking police officers appointed under the Act have been empowered to investigate offences having inter-state ramification.

(iv) Licensing authorities have been empowered to suspend licences of hotels where children or minors are detected to be used for purposes of prostitution.

(v) In case of seduction of any person in custody, the punishment has been enhanced and has been prescribed which is at par with rape in accordance with the provisions of Indian Penal Code.

(vi) Section 10, which provided for release on probation of good conduct or after due admonition of a person convicted for the first time, and Section 12, which makes provision of security for good behaviour from habitual offenders have been omitted from the Act.

(vii) Provision has been made under Section 15(5-A) for the medical examination of persons removed from a brothel in persuance of a search made under Section 15 of the Act.

(viii) While making search in persuance of this Section, the Special Police Officer or the Trafficking Officer shall be accompanied by at least two women police officers and in the event of the removal of a girl or woman, the interrogation if required to be done, shall be taken up by a woman police officer and if no women police officer is available in the presence of a lady member of recognised welfare institution or organisation.

(ix) Section 22-AA has been inserted to enable the Central Government to set up special courts with jurisdiction to try offences which have inter-state ramifications.

5.09 Other Acts in force in the States

(1) The Bombay Prevention of Prostitution Act XI of 1923.
(2) The U.P. Minor Girls Protection Act VIII of 1929.
(3) Madras Suppression of Immoral Traffic Act VI of 1930.
(4) Bengal Suppression of Immoral Traffic Act VI of 1933.
(5) U.P. Suppression of Immoral Traffic Act VIII of 1933.
(6) The Bombay Devadasi Protection Act X of 1934.
(7) The Punjab Suppression of Immoral Traffic Act IV of 1935.
(8) The Mysore Suppression of Immoral Traffic Act VI of 1936.
(9) The Madras Devadasi Prevention of Dedication Act XXXI of 1947.
(10) The Bihar Suppression of Immoral Traffic Act III of 1948.
(11) The U.P. Naik Girls Protection Act VII of 1950.
(12) Hyderabad Suppression of Immoral Traffic Act of 1952.
(13) The Saurashtra Prevention of Prostitution Act VIII of 1952.
(14) The M.P. Suppression of Immoral Traffic Act of 1953.

The Immoral Traffic (Prevention) Act 1956 as amended up to Act No. 44 of 1986 is as under:

THE IMMORAL TRAFFIC (PREVENTION)+ ACT, 1956

(Act. No. 104 of 1956 as amended up to by Act No. 44[1] of 1986).

An Act to provide in persuance of the International Convention signed at New York on the 9th of May, 1950, for *(the prevention of immoral traffic)

Be it enacted by Parliament in the Seventh Year of the Republic of India as follows:

1. *Short title, extent and commencement:*

(1) This Act may be called *the Immoral Traffic (Prevention) Act, 1953.

(2) It extends to the whole of India.#

(3) This Section shall come into force at once, and the remaining provisions of this Act shall come into force on such date as the Central Government may by notification in the official Gazette, appoint.†

2. *Definitions:*

In this Act, unless the context otherwise requires:

(a) "brothel" includes any house, room, @[conveyance] or place or any portion of any house, room, @[conveyance], or place, which is used for purpose @[of sexual exploitation or abuse] for the gain of another person or for the mutual gain of two or more prostitutes;

¢(aa) "child" means a person who has not completed the age of sixteen years;

§[(b) "corrective institution" means an institution, by whatever name called (being an institution established or licensed as such under Section 21), **(persons) who are in need of correc-

---

1. The provisions of the amending Act are to be enforced w.e.f. 26.1.1987.

+ The title of the Act has been substituted by Act No. 44 of 1986 w.e.f Jan, 26. 1987.

* Subs. by Act No. 44 of 1986, w.e.f. 26.1.1987.

Extended to Pondicherry by Act 26 of 1968 and to Goa, Daman and Diu by Regulation II of 1963 and Dadra and Nagar Haveli by regulation 6 of 1963 and Sikkim on Sept. 15, 1984.

† May 1, 1958

@ Ins. by Act No. 46 of 1978.

¢ Ins. by Act 44 of 1946, w.e.f. 26.1.1987

§ Old Clause (aa) renumbered as Clause (b) and the old Clause (b) omitted by Act 44 of 1986, w.e.f. 26.1.1987.

** Subs. by Act No. 44 of 1986, w.e.f. 26.1.1987.

tion, may be detained under this Act, and includes a shelter where §(undertrials) may be kept in pursuance of this Act.

+[(c) "magistrate" means a magistrate specified in the second column of the Schedule as being competent to exercise the powers conferred by the section in which the expression occurs and which is specified in the first column of the Schedule;]

#[(ca) "major" means a person who has completed the age of eighteen years;

(cb) " minor" means a person who has completed the age of sixteen years but has not completed the age of eighteen years;

(d) "prescribed" means prescribed by rules made under this Act;

(e) †[x x x x x]

@(f) "prostitute" means the sexual exploitation or abuse of persons for commercial purposes and the expression "prostitute" shall be construed accordingly;]

(g) "protective home" means an institution, by whatever name called (being an institution established or licensed as such under Section 21), in which *(persons), who are in need of care and protection, may be kept under this Act #(and where appropriate technically qualified persons, equipment and other facilities have been provided), but does not include:

(i) a shelter where *(undertrials) may be kept in persuance of this Act; or

(ii) a corrective institution;

(h) "public place" means any place intended for use by, or accessible to, the public and includes any public conveyance;

(i) "special police officer" means a police officer appointed by or on behalf of the State Government to be incharge of police duties with a specified area for the purpose of this Act;

*[(j) "trafficking police officer" means a police officer appointed by the Central Government under sub-section (4) of section 13.]

#[2-A. *Rule of construction regarding enactments not extending to Jammu and Kashmir:*

---

§ Subs. by Act No. 44 of 1986, w.e.f. 26.1.1987.

+ Subs. by Act No. 46 of 1978.

Ins. by Act 44 of 1986, w.e.f. 26.1.1987.

† Omitted by Act No. 46 of 1978.

@ Subs. by Act No. of 1986, w.e.f. 26.1.1978.

* Subs. by Act No. 44 of 1986, w.e.f. 26.1.1987.

Any reference in this Act to a law which is not in force in the State of Jammu and Kashmir shall, in relation to that State, be construed as a reference to the corresponding law, if any, in force in that State.]

3. *Punishment for keeping a brothel or allowing premises to be used as a brothel:*

(1) Any person who keeps or manages, or acts or assists in the keeping or management of, a brothel, shall be punishable on first conviction with rigorous imprisonment for a term of not less than one year and not more than three years and also with fine which may extend to two thousand rupees and in the event of a second or subsequent conviction, with rigorous imprisonment for a term of not less than two years and not more than five years and also with fine which may extend to two thousand rupees.

(2) Any person who:

(a) being the tenant, lessee, occupier or person in charge of any premises, uses, or knowingly allows any other person to use, such premises or any part thereof as a brothel, or

(b) being the owner, lessor or landlord of any premises or the agent of such owner, lessor or landlord, lets the same or any part thereof with the knowledge that the same or any part thereof is intended to be used as a brothel, or wilfully a party to the use of such premises or any part thereof as a brothel,

shall be punishable on first conviction with imprisonment for a term which may extend to two years and with fine which may extend to two thousand rupees and in the event of a second or subsequent conviction, with rigorous imprisonment for a term which may extend to five years and also with fine.

¢[(2-A) For the purpose of sub-section (2), it shall be presumed, until the contrary is proved, that any person referred to clause (a) or clause (b) of that sub-section is knowingly allowing the premises or any part thereof to be used as a brothel or, as the case may be, has knowledge that the premises or any part thereof are being used as a brothel, if:

¢ Ins by Act No. 46 of 1978.

(a) a report is published in a newspaper having circulation in the area in which such person resides to the effect that the premises or any part thereof have been found to be used for prostitution as a result of a search made under this Act; or

(b) a copy of the list of all things found during the search referred to in clause (a) is given to such person.]

(3) Notwithstanding anything contained in any other law for the time being in force, on conviction of any person referred to in clause (a) or clause (b) of sub-section (2) of any offence under that sub-section in respect of any premises or any part thereof, any lease or agreement under which such premises have been leased out or are held or occupied at the time of the commission of the offence, shall become void and inoperative with effect from the date of the said conviction.

4. *Punishment for living on the earnings of prostitution:*

(1) Any person over the age of eighteen years who knowingly lives, wholly or in part, on the earnings of the prostitution of *(any other person) shall be punishable with imprisonment for a term which may extend to two years, or with fine which may extend to one thousand rupees, or with both †(and where such earnings relate to the prostitution of a child or minor, shall be punishable with imprisonment for a term of not less than seven years and not more than ten years).

+[(2) where any person over the age of eighteen years is proved:

(a) to be living with or to be habitually in the company of, a prostitute; or

(b) to have exercised control, direction or influence over the movements of a prostitute in such a manner as to show that such person is aiding, abetting or compelling his prostitution; or

(c) to be acting as a tout or pimp on behalf of a prostitute, it shall be presumed, until the contrary is proved that such person is knowingly living on the earnings of prostitution of another person within the meaning of sub-section (1).]

---

* Subs. by Act No. 44 of 1986, w.e.f. 26.1.1987.

† Added by Act No. 44 of 1986, w.e.f. 26.1.1987.

\+ Subs. by U.P. Act Act No. 46 of 1986.

5. *Procuring, inducing or taking *(persons) for the sake of prostitution:*

(1) Any person who:

(a) procures or attempts to procure a *(person) whether with or without his consent, for the purpose of prostitution; or

(b) induces a *(person) to go from any place, with the intent that he may for the purpose of prostitution become the inmate of, or frequent a brothel; or

(c) takes or attempts to take a *(person), or causes a *(person) to be taken, from one place to another with a view to his carrying on, or being brought up to carry on prostitution; or

(d) causes or induces a *(person) to carry on prostitution;

*[shall be punishable on conviction with rigorous imprisonment for a term of not less than three years and not more than seven years and also with fine which may extend to two thousand rupees, and if any offence under this sub-section is committed against the will of any person, the punishment of imprisonment for a term of seven years shall extend to imprisonment for a term of fourteen years.

Provided that if the person in respect of whom an offence committed under this sub-section:

(i) is a child, the punishment provided under this sub-section shall extend to rigorous imprisonment for a term of not less than seven years but may extend to life;

(ii) is a minor, the punishment provided under this sub-section shall extend to rigorous imprisonment for a term of not less than seven years and not more than fourteen years.]

(2) †[... ... ...]

(3) An offence under this section shall be triable:

(a) in the place from which a *(person) is procured, induced to go, taken or caused to be taken or from which an attempt to procure or take such *(person) is made; or

(b) in the place to which he may have gone as a result of the inducement or to which he is taken or caused to be taken or an attempt to take him is made.

---

* Subs. by Act No. 44 of 1986, w.e.f. 26.1.1987.

† Sub-section (2) omitted by Act No. of 1986, w.e.f. 26.1.1987.

6. *Detaining a *(Person) in premises where prostitution is carried on.*

(1) Any person who detains *(any other person, whether with or without consent),

(a) in any brothel, or
(b) in or upon any premises with intent *(that such person may have sexual intercourse with a person who is not the spouse of such person)

shall be punishable *(on conviction, with imprisonment of either description for a term which shall not be less than seven years but which may be for life or for a term which may extend to ten years and shall also be liable to fine.

Provided that the court may, for adequate and special reasons to be mentioned in the judgement, impose a sentence of imprisonment for a term of less than seven years.)

*[(2) Where any person is found with a child in a brothel, it shall be presumed, unless the contrary is proved, that he has committed an offence under sub-section (1).

(2-A) where a child or minor is found in a brothel, is, on medical examination, detected to have been sexually abused, it shall be presumed, unless the contrary is proved, that the child or minor has been detained for purposes of prostitution or, as the case may be, has been sexually exploited for commercial purposes.]

(3) A person shall be presumed to detain a woman or girl in a brothel or in or upon any premises for the purpose of sexual intercourse with a man other than her lawful husband, if such person, with intent to compel or induce her to remain there:

(a) Withholds from her any jewellery, wearing apparel, money or other property belonging to her; or
(b) threatens her with legal proceedings if she takes away with her any jewellery, wearing apparel, money or other property lent or supplied to her by the direction of such person.

(4) Notwithstanding any law to the contrary, no suit, prosecution or other legal proceeding shall lie against such woman

* Subs. by Act No. 44 of 1986, w.e.f. 26.1.1987.

or girl at the instance of the person by whom she has been detained, for the recovery of any jewellery, wearing apparel or other property alleged to have been lent or supplied to or for such woman or girl or to have been pledged by such woman or girl or for the recovery of any money alleged to be payable by such woman or girl.

7. *Prostitution in or in the vicinity of public places:*

*[(1) Any †(person), who carries on prostitution and the person with whom such prostitution is carried on, in any premises:

(a) which are within the area or areas, notified under sub-section (3); or

(b) which are within a distance of two hundred metres of any place of public religious worship, educational institution, hostel, hospital, nursing home or such other public place of any kind as may be notified in this behalf by the Commissioner of Police or Magistrate in the manner prescribed, shall be punishable with imprisonment for a term which may extend to three months.]

+[(1-A) Where an offence committed under sub-section (1) is in respect of a child or minor, the person committing the offence shall be punishable with imprisonment of either description for a term which shall not be less than seven years but which may be for life or for a term which may extend to ten years and shall also be liable to fine.

Provided that the court may, for adequate and special reasons to be mentioned in the judgement, impose a sentence of imprisonment for a term of less than seven years.]

(2) Any person who:

(a) being the keeper of any place knowingly permits prostitutes for purpose of their trade to resort to or remain in such place; or

---

* Subs. by Act No. 46 of 1978.

† Subs. by Act No. 44 of 1986, w.e.f 26.1.1987.

\+ Ins. by Act No. 44 of 1986, w.e.f 26.1.1987.

(b) being the tenant, lessor, occupier or person in charge of any premises referred to in sub-section (1) knowingly permits the same or any part thereof to be used for prostitution; or

(c) being the owner, lessor or landlord of any premises referred to in sub-section (1), or the agent of such owner, lessor or landlord, lets the same or any part thereof with the knowledge that the same or any part thereof may be used for prostitution, or is wilfully a party to such use,

shall be punishable on first conviction with imprisonment for a term which may extend to three months, or with fine which may extend to two hundred rupees, or with both, and in the event of a second or subsequent conviction with imprisonment for a term which may extend to six months and also with fine *[which may extend to two hundred rupees, and if the public place or premises happen to be a hotel, the licence for carrying on the business of such hotel under any law for the time being in force shall also be liable to be suspended for a period of not less than three months but which may extend to one year.

Provided that if an offence committed under this sub-section is in respect of a child or minor in a hotel, such licence shall also be liable to be cancelled.

Explanation: For the purpose of this sub-section, "hotel" shall have the meaning as in clause (6) of Section 2 of the Hotel-Receipts Tax Act, 1980. (54 of 1980).]

+[(3) The State Government may, having regard to the kinds of persons frequenting any area or areas in the state, the nature and the density of population in the Official Gazette, direct that prostitution shall not be carried on in such area or areas as may be specified in the notification.

(4) Where a notification is issued under sub-section (3) in respect of any area or areas, the State Government shall define the limits of such area or areas in the notification with reasonable certainty.

(5) No such notification shall be issued so as to have effect from a date earlier than the expiry of a period of ninety days after the date on which it is issued.

---

* Subs. by Act No. 44 of 1986, w.e.f. 26.1.1987.

\+ Ins. by Act No. 46 of 1978.

8. *Seducing or soliciting for purpose of prostitution*

Whoever, in any public place or within sight of, and in such manner as to be seen or heard from, any public place, whether from within any building or house or not:

(a) by words, gestures, wilful exposure of his person (whether by sitting by a window or in the balcony of a building or house or in any other way), or otherwise tempts or endeavours to tempt, or attracts or endeavours to attract the attention of, any person for the purpose of prostitution; or

(b) solicits or molests any person, or loiters, or acts in such manner as to cause obstruction or annoyance to persons residing nearby or passing by such public place or to offend against public decency, for the purpose of prostitution,

shall be punishable on first conviction with imprisonment for a term which may extend to six months, or with fine which may extent to five hundred rupees, or with both, and in the event of a second or subsequent conviction, with imprisonment for a term which may extend to one year, and also with fine, which may extend to five hundred rupees.

*[Provided that where an offence under this section is committed by a man, he shall be punishable with imprisonment for a period of not less than seven days but which may extend to three months.]

9. *Seduction of a *(person) in custody*

†(* * *)Any *person who +[having the custody, charge or care of any of, or a position of authority over, any *(person)] causes or aids or abets the seduction of prostitution of that *(person) *(shall be punishable on conviction with imprisonment of either description for a term which shall not be less than seven years but which may be for life or for a term which may extend to ten years and shall also be liable to fine.

Provided that the court may, for adequate and special reasons to be mentioned in the judgement, impose a sentence of imprisonment for a term of less than seven years.

---

* Ins. by Act No. 44 of 1986, w.e.f. 26.1.1987.

† Sub-section (2) omitted Act No. 44 of 1986, with effect from 26.1.1987 and so "(1)" also omitted.

+ Subs. by Act No. 46 of 1978.

(2) §[* * *]

10. *Release on probation of good conduct or after due admonition:* ¢[* * *]

#[10-A. Detention in a corrective institution. Where:

(a) a female offender is found guilty of an offence under Section 7 or Section 8, @[* * *]; and

(b) the character, state of health and mental condition of the offender and the other circumstances of the case are such that it is expedient that she should be subject to detention for such term and such instruction and discipline as are conducive to her correction,

it shall be lawful for the court to pass, in lieu of a sentence of imprisonment, an order for detention in corrective institution for such term, not being less than two years and not being more than five years, as the court thinks fit.

Provided that before passing such an order:

(i) the court shall give an opportunity to the offender to be heard and shall also consider any representation which the offender may make to the court as to the suitability of the case for treatment in such an institution, as also the report of the probation officer appointed under the Probation of Offenders Act, 1958 (20 of 1958); and

(ii) the court shall record that it is satisfied that the character, state of health and mental condition of the offender and other circumstances of the case are such that the offender is likely to benefit by such instruction and discipline as aforesaid.

(2) Subject to the provisions of sub-section (3), the provisions of the Code of Criminal Procedure, 1973 (2 of 1974), relating to appeal, reference and revision, and to the Limitation Act, 1963 (36 of 1963), as to the period within which an appeal shall be filed, shall apply in relation to an order of detention under sub-section (1) as if the order had been a sentence of imprison-

---

§ Omitted by Act No. 44 of 1986, w.e.f. 26.1.1987.

¢ Subs. by Act No. 46 of 1978 and omitted by Act No. 44 of 1987, w.e.f. 26.1.1987.

Ins. by Act No. 46 of 1978.

@ Omitted by Act No. 44 of 1986, w.e.f. 26.1.1987.

ment for the same period as the period for which the detention was ordered.

(3) Subject to such rules as may be made in this behalf, the State Government or authority authorised in this behalf may, at anytime after the expiration of six months from the date of an order for detention in a corrective institution, if it is satisfied that there is a reasonable probability that the offender will lead a useful and industrious life, discharge her from such an institution, without condition or with such conditions as may be considered fit, and grant her a written licence in such form as may be prescribed.

(4) The conditions on which an offender is discharged under sub-section (3), may include requirements relating to residence of the offender and supervision over offender's activities and movements.]

11. *Notification of address of previously convicted offender:*

(1) When any person having been convicted

(a) by a court in India of an offence punishable under this Act or punishable under Section 363, Section 365, Section 366, Section 366-A, Section 366-B, Section 367, Section 368, Section 370, Section 371, Section 372 or Section 373 of the Indian Penal Code (45 of 1960), with imprisonment for a term of two years or upwards; or

(b) by a court or tribunal in any other country of an offence which would, if committed in India, have been punishable under this Act or under any of the aforesaid sections with imprisonment for a like term,

is within a period of five years release from prison, again convicted of any offence punishable under this Act or under any of those sections with imprisonment for a term of two years or upwards by a court, such court may, if it thinks fit, at the time of passing the sentence of imprisonment on such person, also order that his residence, and any change of, or absence from such residence, after release be notified according to rules made under Section 23 for a period not exceeding five years from the date of expiration of that sentence.

(2) If such conviction is set aside on appeal or otherwise, such order shall become void.

(3) An order under this section may also be made by an Appellate Court or by the High Court when exercising its power of revision.

(4) Any person charged with a breech of any rule referred to in sub-section (1) may be tried by a magistrate of competent jurisdiction in the district in which the place last notified as his residence is situated.

12. *Security for good behaviour from habitual offenders.* +(- -|-):

13. *Special police officer and advisory body:*

(1) There shall be for each area to be specified by the State Government in this behalf a Special Police Officer appointed or on behalf of that Government for dealing with offences under this Act in that area.

#[(2) The special police officer shall not be below the rank of an Inspector of Police.

(2-A) The District Magistrate may, if he considers it necessary or expedient so to do, confer upon any retired police or military officer all or any of the powers conferred by or under this Act on a special police officer, with respect to particular cases or classes of cases or to cases generally:

Provided that no such power shall be conferred on

(a) a retired police officer unless such officer, at the time of his retirement, was holding a post not below the rank of an inspector;

(b) a retired military officer unless such officer, at the time of his retirement was holding a post not below the rank of a commissioned officer.]

(3) For the efficient discharge of his functions in relation to offences under this Act:

(a) the special police officer of an area shall be assisted by such number of subordinate police officers (including women

---

\+ Omitted by Act No. 44 of 1986, w.e.f 26.1.1987.

\# Subs. by Act No. 46 of 1978.

police officer wherever practicable) as the State Government may think fit; and

(b) the State Government may associate with the Special Police officer, a non-official advisory body consisting of notmore than five leading social welfare workers of that area (including women social workers wherever practicable) to advice him on questions of general importance regarding the working of this Act.

*[(4) The Central Government may, for the purpose of investigating any offence under this Act or under any other law for the time being in force dealing with sexual exploitation of persons and committed in more than one state, appoint such number of police officers as trafficking police officers and they shall exercise all the powers and discharge all the functions as are exercisable by special police officers under this Act with the modification that they shall exercise such powers and discharge such functions in relation to the whole of India.]

14. *Offences to be cognizable:*

Notwithstanding anything contained in the §[Code of Criminal Procedure, 1973 (2 of 1974)], any offence punishable under this Act shall be deemed to be cognizable offence within the meaning of that Code.

Provided that, notwithstanding anything contained in that Code:

(i) arrest without warrant may be made only by the special police officer or under his direction or guidance, or subject to his prior approval;

(ii) when the special police officer requires any officer subordinate to him to arrest without warrant otherwise than in his presence any person for an offence under this Act, he shall give the subordinate officer an order in writing, specifying the person to be arrested and the offence for which the arrest is being made and the latter officer before arresting

---

* Ins. by Act No. 44 of 1986, w.e.f 26.1.1987.

§ Subs. by Act No. of 1978.

the person shall inform him of the substance of the order and, on being required by such person, show him the order.

(iii) Any police officer, not below the rank of †sub-inspector specially authorised by the special police officer may, if has reason to believe that on account of delay involved in obtaining the order of special police officer, any valuable evidence relating to any offence under this Act is likely to be destroyed or concealed, or the person who has committed or is suspected to have committed the offence is likely to escape, or if the name and address of such a person is unknown or there is reason to suspect that a false name and address has been given, arrest the person concerned without such order, but in such a case he shall report, as soon as may be to the special police officer the arrest and the circumstances in which the arrest was made.

15. *Search without warrant:*

(1) Notwithstanding anything contained in any other law for the time being in force, whenever the special police officer *[or the trafficking police officer, as the case may be] has reasonable grounds for believing that an offence punishable under this Act has been or is being committed in respect of a +(person) living in any premises and that search of the premises with warrant cannot be made without undue delay, such officer may, after recording the grounds of his belief, enter and search such premises without a warrant.

(2) Before making a search under sub-section (1), the special police officer *[or the trafficking police officer, as the case may be], shall call upon two or more respectable inhabitants (at least one of whom shall be a woman), of the locality in which the place to be searched is situated, to attend and witness the search and may issue an order in writing to them or any of them so to do:

†[Provided that the requirement as to the respectable inhabitant being from the locality in which the place to be searched

---

† Subs. by Act No. 46 of 1978.

* Ins. by Act No. 44 of 1986, w.e.f. 26.1.1987.

\+ Subs. by Act No. 44 of 1986 w.e.f. 26.1.1987.

† Ins. by Act No. 46 of 1978.

is situated, shall not apply to a woman required to attend and witness the search].

(3) Any person who, without reasonable cause refuses or neglects, to attend and witness a search under this section, when called upon to do so by an order in writing delivered or tendered to him, shall be deemed to have committed an offence under Section 187 of the Indian Penal Code (45 of 1860).

+[(4) The special police officer or the trafficking police officer, as the case may be,entering any premises under sub-section (1) shall be entitled to remove therefrom all the persons found therein.]

(5) The special police officer *(or the trafficking police officer, as the case may be), after removing the +(person) under sub-section (4) shall forthwith produce him before the appropriate magistrate.

*[5-A] Any person who is produced before a magistrate under sub-section (5), shall be examined by a registered medical practitioner for the purposes of determination of the age of such person, or for the detection of any injuries as a result of sexual abuse or the presence of any sexually transmitted diseases.

Explanation: In this sub-section "registered medical practitioner' has the same meaning as in the Indian Medical Council Act, 1956 (102 of 1956)].

(6) The special police officer *(or the trafficking police officer, as the case may be), and other persons taking part in, or attending, and witnessing a search shall not be liable to any civil or criminal proceeding against them in respect of anything lawfully done in connection with, or for the purpose of the search.

*[(6-A) The special police officer or the trafficking police officer, as the case may be, making a search under this section shall be accompanied by at least two women police officers, and where any women or girl removed under sub-section (4) is required to be interrogated, it shall be done by a woman police officer and if no woman police officer is available, the interrogation shall be done only in the presence of a lady member of a recognised welfare institution or organisation.

\+ Subs. by Act No. 44 of 1986, w.e.f. 26.1.1987.

* Ins. by Act No. 44 of 1986, w.e.f. 26.1.1987.

Explanation: For the purposes of this sub-section and Section 17-A, "recognised welfare institution or organisation" means such institution or organisation as may be recognised in this behalf by the State Government.]

†[(7) The provisions of the Code of Criminal Procedure, 1973 (2 of 1974), shall, so far as may be, apply to any search under this Section as they apply to any search made under the authority of a warrant issued under Section 94 of the said Code.]

@16. *Rescue of* +*(persons):*

(1) Where a magistrate has reason to believe from information received from the police or any other person authorised by the State Government in this behalf otherwise, that +[any person is living, or carrying on, or is being made to carry on, prostitution in a brothel], he may direct a police officer not below the rank of a sub-inspector to enter such brothel, and to remove therefrom such @(person) and produce him before him.

(2) The police officer, after removing the +(person) shall forthwith produce him before the magistrate issuing the order.

17. *Intermediate custody of* +*(persons) removed under Section 15 or rescued under Section 16:*

(1) When the special police officer removing a +(person) under sub-section (4) of Section 15 or a police officer rescuing a +(person) under sub-section (1) of Section 16, is for any reason unable to produce him before the appropriate magistrate as required by sub-section (5) of Section 15, or before the magistrate issuing the order under sub-section (2) of Section 16, he shall forthwith produce him before the nearest magistrate of any class, who shall pass such orders as he deems proper for his safe custody until he is produced before the appropriate magistrate, or, as the case may be, the magistrate issuing the order.

Provided that no #(person) shall be

(i) detained in custody under this sub-section for a period exceeding ten days from the date of the order under this subsection; or

† Ins. by Act No. 46 of 1978.

@ Subs. by Act No. 46 of 1978.

+ Subs. by Act No. 44 of 1986, w.e.f. 26.1.1987.

Subs. by Act No. 44 of 1986, w.e.f. 26.1.1987.

(ii) restored to or placed in the custody of a person who may exercise a harmful influence over him.

(2) When the +(person) is produced before the appropriate magistrate under sub-section (5) of Section 15 or the magistrate under sub-section (2) of 16, he shall, after giving him an opportunity of being heard, cause an enquiry to be made as to the correctness of the information received under sub-section (1) of Section 16, the age, character and antecedents of the +(person) and the suitability of his parents, guardian or husband for taking charge of him and the nature of the influence which the conditions in his home are likely to have on him if he is sent home, and, for this purpose, he may direct a probation officer appointed under the Probation of Offenders Act, 1958 (20 of 1958), to enquire into the above circumstances and into the personality of the +(person) and the prospects of his rehabilitation.

(3) The magistrate may, while an enquiry is made into a case under sub-section (2), pass such orders as he deems proper for the safe custody of the +(person).

+[Provided that where a person rescued under Section 16 is a child or minor, it shall be open to the magistrate to place such child or minor in any institution established or recognised under any Children Act for the time being in force in any state for the safe custody of children.

Provided further that] no +(person) shall be kept in custody for this purpose for a period exceeding three weeks from the date of such an order, and no +(person) shall be kept in the custody of a person likely to have a harmful influence over him.

(4) Where a magistrate is satisfied, after making an inquiry as required under sub-section (2):

(a) that the information received is correct; and
(b) that he is in need of care and protection,

he may, subject to the provisions of sub-section (5), make an order that such +(person) be detained for such period, being not less than one year and not more than three years, as may be specified in the order, in a protective home, or in such other

---

\+ Subs. by Act No. 44 of 1986, w.e.f. 26.1.1987.

custody as he shall, for reasons to be recorded in writing, consider suitable.

Provided that such custody shall not be that of a person or body of persons of a religious persuasion different from that of the [+](person) and that those entrusted with the custody of the [+](person), including the person in charge of a protective home, may be required to enter into a bond which may, where necessary and feasible, contain undertakings based on directions relating to the proper care, guardianship, education, training and medical and psychiatric treatment of the [+](person) as well as supervision by a person appointed by the court, which will be in force for a period exceeding three years.

(5) In discharging his function under sub-section (2), a magistrate may summon a panel of five respectable persons, three of whom shall, wherever practicable, be women, to assist him; and may, for this purpose, keep a list of experienced social welfare workers, particularly women social welfare workers, in the field of suppression of immoral traffic in [+](person).

(6) An appeal against an order made under sub-section (4) shall lie to the Court of Sessions whose decision on such appeal shall be final.

*[17-A. *Conditions to be observed before placing persons rescued under Section 16 to parents or guardians:*

Notwithstanding anything contained in sub-section (2) of Section 17, the magistrate making an inquiry under Section 17 may, before passing an order for handing over any person rescued under Section 16 to the parents, guardian or husband, satisfy himself about the capacity or genuineness of the parents, guardian or husband to keep such person by causing an investigation to be made by a recognised welfare institution or organisation.]

18. *Closure of brothel and eviction of offenders from the premises:*

(1) A magistrate may, on receipt of information from the police or otherwise, that any house, room, place or any portion

---

[+] Subs. by Act No. 44 of 1986, w.e.f. 26.1.1987.

* Ins. by Act No. 44 of 1986, w.e.f. 26.1.1987.

thereof within a distance of *(two hundred metres) of any public place referred to in sub-section (1) of Section 7, is being run or used as a brothel by any person, or is being used by prostitutes for carrying on their trade, issue notice on the owner, lessor or landlord of such house, room, place or portion or the agent of the owner, lessor or landlord or on the tenant, lessee, occupier of, or any other portion in charge of such house, room, place or portion, to show cause within seven days of the receipt of the notice why the same should not be attached for improper user thereof; and if, after hearing the person concerned, the magistrate is satisfied that the house, room, place or portion is used as a brothel or for carrying on prostitution, then the magistrate may pass orders:

(a) directing eviction of the occupier within seven days of the passing of the order from the house, room, place or portion:

(b) directing that before letting it out during the period of one year, +(or in a case where a child or minor has been found in such house, room, place or portion during a search under Section 15, during the period of three years}, immediately after the passing of the order, the owner, lessor or landlord or the agent of the owner, lessor, or landlord shall obtain the approval of the magistrate.

Provided that, if the magistrate finds that the owner, lessor, or landlord as well as the agent of the owner, lessor or landlord, was the innocent of the improper user of the house, room, place or portion, he may cause the same to be restored to the owner, lessor or landlord, or the agent of the owner, lessor or landlord, with a direction that the house, room, place or portion shall not be leased out, or otherwise given permission of, to or for the benefit of the person who was allowing the improper user therein.

(2) A court convicting a person of any offence under section 3 or Section 7 may pass orders under sub-section (1), without further notice to such person to show cause as required in that sub-section.

(3) Orders passed by the magistrate or court under sub-section (1) or sub-section (2) shall be subject to appeal and shall not be stayed or set aside by the order of any court, civil or

* Subs. by Act No. 46 of 1978.
+ Ins. by Act No. 44 of 1986, w.e.f. 26.1.1987.

criminal, and the said order shall cease to have validity after the +(expiry of one year or three years as the case may be).

Provided that where a conviction under Section 3 or Section 7 is set aside in appeal on the ground that such house, room, place or any portion thereof is not being run or used as a brothel, or is not being used by prostitutes for carrying on their trade, any order passed by the trial court under sub-section (1) shall also be set aside.

(4) Notwithstanding anything contained in any other law for the time being in force, when a magistrate passes an order under sub-section (1), or a court passes an order under sub-section (2), any lease or agreement under which the house, room, place or portion is occupied at the time shall become void and inoperative.

(5) When an owner, lessor or landlord, or the agent of such owner, lessor or landlord fails to comply with a direction given under clause (b) of sub-section (1), he shall be punishable with fine which may extend to five hundred rupees or when he fails to comply with a direction under the proviso to that sub-section, he shall be deemed to have committed an offence under clause (b) of sub-section (2) of Section 3 or clause (c) of sub-section (2) of Section 7, as the case may be, and punished accordingly.

*19. *Application for being kept in a protective home or provided care and protection by court:*

(1) A +(person) who is carrying on, or is being made to carry on, prostitution, may make an application, to the magistrate within the local limits of whose jurisdiction he is carrying on, or is being made to carry on, prostitution, for an order that he may be:

(a) kept in a protective home, or
(b) provided care and protection by the court in the manner specified in sub-section (3).

(2) The magistrate may, pending inquiry under sub-section (3), direct that the +(person) be kept in such custody as he may consider proper, having regard to the circumstances of the case.

+ Subs. by Act No. 44 of 1986, w.e.f. 26.1.1987.

* Subs. by Act No. 46 of 1978.

(3) If the magistrate, after hearing the applicant and making such inquiry as he may consider necessary, including an inquiry by a probation officer appointed under the Probation of Offenders Act, 1958 (20 of 1958), into the personality, conditions of home and prospects of rehabilitation of the applicant, is satisfied that an order should be made under this section, he shall, for reasons to be recorded, make an order that the applicant be kept:

(i) in a protective home, or

(ii) in a corrective institution, or

(iii) under the supervision of a person appointed by the magistrate,

for such period as may be specified in the order.]

20. *Removal of prostitute from any place:*

(1) A magistrate on receiving information that any †(person) residing in or frequenting any place within the local limits of his jurisdiction is a prostitute, may record the substance of the information received and issue a notice to such †(person) requiring him to appear before the magistrate and show cause why he should not be required to remove himself from the place and be prohibited from re-entering it.

(2) Every notice issued under sub-section (1) shall be accompanied by a copy of the record aforesaid, and the copy shall be served along with the notice on the †(person) against whom the notice is issued.

(3) The magistrate shall, after the service of the notice referred to in sub-section (2), proceed to enquire into the truth of the information received, after giving the †(person) an opportunity of adducing evidence, take such further evidence as he thinks fit, and if upon such inquiry it appears to him that such †(person) is a prostitute and that it is necessary in the interests of the general public that such †(person) should be required to remove himself therefrom and be prohibited from re-entering the same, the magistrate shall, by order in writing communicate to the †(person) in the manner specified therein, require him after a date (to be specified in the order) which shall not be less than seven days from the date of the order, to remove himself

† Subs. by Act No. 44 of 1986, w.e.f. 26.1.1987..

from the place to such place whether within or without the local limits of his jurisdiction, by such route or routes and within such time as may be specified in the order and also prohibit from re-entering the place without the permission in writing of the magistrate having jurisdiction over such place.

(4) Whoever

(a) fails to comply with an order issued under this section, within the period specified therein, or whilst an order prohibiting him from re-entering a place without permission is in force, re-enters the place without, such permission, or

(b) knowing that any †(person) has, under this section, been required to remove himself from the place and has not obtained the requisite permission to re-enter it, harbours or conceals such †(person) in the place,

shall be punishable with fine which may extend to two hundred rupees and in the case of continuing offence with an additional fine which may extend to twenty rupees for every day after the first during which she or he has persisted in the offence.

21. *Protective homes:*

(1) The State Government may in its discretion establish *(as many protective homes and corrective institutions under this Act as it thinks fit and such homes and institutions) when established, shall be maintained in such manner as may be prescribed.

(2) No person or no authority other than the State Government shall after the commencement of this Act, establish or maintain any +(protective home or corrective institution) except under and in accordance with the conditions of, a licence issued under this section by the State Government.

(3) The State Government may, on application made to it in this behalf by a person or authority, issue to such person or authority a licence in a prescribed form for establishing and maintaining or as the case may be, for maintaining a *(protec-

---

† Subs. by Act No. 44 of 1986, w.e.f. 26.1.87.

* Subs. by Act No. 46 of 1978.

\+ Subs. by Act No. 46 of 1978.

tive home or corrective institution) and a licence so issued may contain such conditions as the State Government may think fit to impose in accordance with the rules made under this Act.

Provided that any such condition may require that the management of the *(protective home or corrective institution) shall, wherever practicable, be entrusted to women.

Provided further that a person or authority maintaining any protective home at the commencement of this Act shall be allowed a period of six months from such commencement to make an application for such licence.

*[Provided also that a person or authority maintaining any corrective institution at the commencement of the Suppression of Immoral Traffic in Women and Girls (Amendment) Act, 1978 (46 of 1978), shall be allowed a period of six months from such commencement to make an application for such licence.]

(4) Before issuing a licence the State Government may require such officer or authority as it may appoint for the purpose, to make a full and complete investigation in respect of the application received in this behalf and report to it the result of such investigation and in making any investigation the officer or authority shall follow procedure as may be prescribed.

(5) A licence, unless sooner revoked, shall remain in force for such period as may be specified in the licence and may, on application made in this behalf at least thirty days before the date of its expiration, be renewed for a like period.

(6) No licence issued or renewed under this Act shall be transferable.

(7) Where any person or authority to whom a licence has been granted under this Act or any agent or servant of such person or authority commits a breach of any of the conditions thereof or any of the provisions of this Act, or where the State Government is not satisfied with the condition, management or superintendence of any *(protective home or corrective institution) the State Government may, without prejudice to any other penalty which may have been incurred under this Act, for reasons to be recorded, revoke the licence by order in writing.

* Subs. by Act No. 46 of 1978.

Provided that no such order shall be made until an opportunity is given to the holder of the licence to show cause why the licence shall not be revoked.

(8) Where a licence in respect of a *(protective home or corrective institution) has been revoked under the foregoing sub-section such *(protective home or corrective institution) shall cease to function from the date of such revocation.

(9) Subject to any rules that may be made in this behalf, the State Government may also vary or amend any licence issued or renewed under this Act.

*[(9-A) The State Government or any authority authorised by it in this behalf may, subject to any rules that may be made in this behalf, transfer an inmate of a protective home to another protective home or to a corrective institution or an inmate of a corrective institution to another corrective institution or to a protective home, where such transfer is considered desirable having regard to the conduct of the person to be transferred, the kind of training to be imparted and other circumstances of the case.

Provided that:

(a) no †(person) who is transferred under this sub-section shall be required to stay in the home or institution to which he is transferred for a period longer than he was required to stay in the home or institution from which he was transferred;

(b) reasons shall be recorded for every order of transfer under this sub-section.]

(10) whoever establishes or maintains a *(protective home or corrective institution) except in accordance with the provisions of this Section, shall be punishable in the case of a first offence with fine which may extend to one thousand rupees and in the case of second or subsequent offence with imprisonment for a term which may extend to one year, or with fine which may extend to two thousand rupees, or with both.

---

* Subs. by Act No. 46 of 1978.

† Ins. by Act No. 44 of 1986, w.e.f. 26.1.1987.

+[21.A *Production of records:*

Every person or authority who is licensed under sub-section (3) of Section 21 to establish or maintain, or, as the case may be, for maintaining, a protective home or corrective institution shall whenever required by a court, produce the records and other documents maintained by such home or institution before such court.]

22. *Trials:*

No court, inferior to that of *(Metropolitan Magistrate or a Judicial Magistrate of the first class) shall try any offence under Section 3, Section 4, Section 5, Section 6, Section 7 or Section 8.

#[22-A. *Power to establish Special Courts:* (1) If the State Government is satisfied that it is necessary for the purpose of providing for speedy trial of offences under this Act in any district or metropolitan area, it may, by notification in the official Gazette and after consultation with the High Court, establish one or more courts of Judicial Magistrates of the first class, or, as the case may be, Metropolitan Magistrates, in such district or metropolitan area.

(2) Unless otherwise directed by the High Court, a court established under sub-section (1) shall exercise jurisdiction only in respect of cases under this Act.

(3) Subject to the provisions of the sub-section (2), the jurisdiction and powers of the presiding officer of a court established under sub-section (1) in any district or metropolitan area shall extend throughout the district or the metropolitan area, as the case may be.

(4) Subject to the foregoing provisions of the section, a court established under sub-section (1) in any district or metropolitan area shall be deemed to be a court established under sub-section (1) of Section 11, or, as the case may be, sub-section (1) of Section 16, of the Code of Criminal Procedure 1873 (2 of 1974) and the provisions of that Code shall apply accordingly in relation to such courts.

+ Ins. by Act No. 44 of 1986, w.e.f. 26.1.1987.

* Subs. by Act No. 46 of 1978.

Ins. by Act No. 44 of 1986, w.e.f. 26.1.1987.

Explanation: In this section, "High Court" has the same meaning as the clause (e) of Section 2 of the Code of Criminal Procedure, 1973 (2 of 1974).

+[22-AA. *Power of central government to establish special courts:* (1) If the Central Government is satisfied that it is necessary for the purpose of, providing for speedy trial of offences under this Act and committed in more than one state, it may, by notification in the official gazette and after consultation with the High Court concerned, establish one or more courts of Judicial Magistrates of the first class or Metropolitan Magistrates for the trial of such offences.

(2) The provisions of Section 22-A shall, so far as may be, apply to the courts established under sub-section (1), as they apply to courts established under that section.]

#[22-B. *Power of court to try cases summarily*: Notwithstanding anything contained in the Code of Criminal Procedure, 1973 (2 of 1974)., the State Government may, if it considers it necessary so to do, direct that offences under this Act shall be tried in a summary way by a magistrate [including the presiding officer of a court established under sub-section (1) of Section 22-A] and the provisions of Section 262 to 265 (both inclusive) of the said Code, shall, as far as may be, apply to such trial.

Provided that in the case of any conviction in a summary trial under this section, it shall be lawful for the Magistrate to pass a sentence of imprisonment for a term not exceeding one year.

Provided further that when at the commencement of, or in the course of, a summary trial under this section, it appears to the magistrate that the nature of the case is such that a sentence of imprisonment for a term exceeding one year may have to be passed or that it is for any other reason, undesirable to try the case summarily, the magistrate shall, after the parties record an order to the effect and thereafter recall any witness, who may have been examined and proceed to hear or rehear the case in the manner, provided by the said Code.]

23. *Power to make rules:*

(1) The State Government may, by notification in the official Gazette, make rules for carrying on the purposes of this Act.

+ Ins. by Act No. 44 of 1986, w.e.f. 26.1.1987.

Ins. by Act No. 46 of 1978.

(2) In particular, and without prejudice to the generality of the foregoing powers, such rules may provide for:

(a) the notification of any place as a public place;

†[(b) the placing in custody of person for whose safe custody orders have been passed under sub-section (1) of Section 17 and their maintenance:

*[(bb) the discharge of an offender under sub-section (3) of Section 10-A from a corrective institution and the form of licence to be granted to such offender;]

+[(c) the detention and keeping in protective homes, or, as the case may be, in corrective institutions of †(Persons) under this Act and their maintenance;]

(d) the carrying out of the provisions of Section 11 regarding notification of residence or change of or absence from residence by released convicts;

(e) the delegation of authority to appoint the special police officer under sub-section (1) of Section 13;

(f) the carrying into effect of the provisions of Section 18;

+(g) (i) the establishment, maintenance, management and superintendence of protective homes and corrective institutions under Section 21 and the appointment, powers and duties of persons employed in such homes or institutions;

(ii) the form in which an application for a licence may be made and the particulars to be contained in such application;

(iii) the procedure for the issue or renewal of a licence, the time within which such licence shall be issued or renewed and the procedure to be followed in making a full and complete investigation in respect of an application for a licence;

(iv) the form of a licence and the conditions to be specified therein;

(v) the manner in which the accounts of a protective home and a corrective institution shall be maintained and audited;

(vi) the maintenance of registers and statements by a licence and the form of such registers and statements;

(vii) the care, treatment, maintenance, training, instruction, control and discipline of the inmates of protective homes and corrective institutions;

---

† Subs. by Act No. 44 of 1986, w.e.f. 26.1.1987.

* Ins. by Act No. 46 of 1978.

\+ Subs. by Act No. 46 of 1978.

(viii) the visits to and communication with such inmates;

(ix) the temporary detention of †(persons) sentenced to detention in protective homes or in corrective institutions until arrangements are made for sending them to such homes or institutions;

(x) the transfer of an inmate from:

(a) one protective home to another or to a corrective institution,

(b) one corrective institution to another or to a protective home under sub-section (9-A) of Section 21;

(xi) the transfer in persuance of an order of the court from a protective home or a corrective institution to a prison of a †(person) found to be incorrigible or exercising bad influence upon other inmates of the protective home or the corrective institution and the period of his detention in such prison;

(xii) the transfer to a protective home or corrective institution of †(persons) sentenced under Section 7 or Section 8 and the period of their detention in such home or institution;

(xiii) the discharge of inmates from a protective home or corrective institution either absolutely or subject to conditions, and their arrest in the event of breach of such conditions;

(xiv) the grant of permission to inmates to absent themselves for short period;

(xv) the inspection of protective home and corrective institutions and other institutions in which †(persons) may be kept, detained and maintained;]

(h) any other matter which has to be, or may be, prescribed.

(3) In making any rule under clause (d) or clause (g) of sub-section (2), the State Government may provide that a breach thereof shall be punishable with fine which may extend to two hundred and fifty rupees.

(4) All rules made under this Act shall, as soon as after they are made, may be laid before the State Legislature.

24. *Act not to in derogation of certain other Acts:*

Nothing in this Act shall be construed to be in derogation of provisions of the Reformatory Schools Act, 1897 (8 of 1897)

† Subs. by Act No. 44 of 1986, w.e.f. 26.1.1987.

or any State Act enacted in modification of the said Act or otherwise, relating to juvenile offenders.

25. *Repeal and savings:*

(1) As from the date of the coming into force in any state of the provisions other than Section 1 of this Act, all State Acts relating to suppression of immoral traffic in †(persons) or to the prevention of prostitution, in force in that State immediately before such date shall stand repealed.

(2) Notwithstanding the repeal by this Act of any State Act referred to in sub-section (1), anything done or action taken (including any direction given, any register, rule or order made, any restriction imposed) under the provision of such State Act shall in so far as such thing or action is not in consistent with the provisions of this Act be deemed to have been done or taken under the provisions of this Act as if the said provisions were in force when such thing was done or such action was taken and shall continue in force accordingly until superseded by any thing done or any action taken under this Act.

Explanation: In this section the expression "State Act" includes a "Provincial Act".

† Subs. by Act No. 44 of 1986, w.e.f. 26.1.1987.

*THE SCHEDULE
See Section 2(c)

Section	Magistrate competent to exercise the powers
7(1)	District Magistrate
11(4)	Metropolitan Magistrate or Judicial Magistrate of the First Class
+[x x x x x x x x x x x x x x x x x]	
15(5)	Metropolitan Magistrate, Judicial Magistrate of the First Class, District Magistrate or Sub-Divisional Magistrate
16	Metropolitan Magistrate, Judicial Magistrate of the First Class, District Magistrate or Sub-Divisional Magistrate
18	District Magistrate or Sub-Divisional Magistrate.
19	Metropolitan Magistrate, Judicial Magistrate of the First Class, District Magistrate or Sub-Divisional Magistrate
20	District Magistrate, Sub-Divisional Magistrate or any Executive Magistrate, specially empowered by the State Government
22(B)	Metropolitan Magistrate, Judicial Magistrate of the First Class

* Ins. by Act No. 46 of 1978.

\+ 12(4) and matter connected therewith, omitted by Act 44 of 1986, w.e.f. 26.1.1987.

5.10. Extracts from U.P. and A.P. Suppression of Immoral Traffic in Women and Girls Rules, 1961

In accordance with the provisions of Section 17(4) a person can be ordered to be kept in a protective home. Section 21 of the Act, provided necessary regulations for establishment of protective homes and the various states Rules regulate the function of such homes. Important provisions of the U.P. Rules are given below:

R.4. *Placing of girls in safe custody:*

(1) Where a responsible and trustworthy person belonging to the same religious persuasion as that of a girl produced before a Magistrate under sub-section (1) of Section 17 is willing to take charge of the girl and the Magistrate, acting under sub-section (1) or sub-section (2) of that section passes an order placing the girl in the safe charge of that person, such person shall execute before the Magistrate an undertaking in Form I.

(2) If the person in whose custody the girl is placed is no longer willing to fulfil the conditions of the undertaking, he may apply to the Magistrate for releasing him from the obligation to keep the girl in his custody.

R.5. *Detention of women and girls in protective homes:*

Where, in persuance of sub-section (2) of Section 19, a Magistrate passes an order directing that a woman or girl be detained in a protective home, warrant of detention in Form III shall be prepared in duplicate and shall be forwarded to the Superintendent of the Protective Home who shall retain one copy and return the other two to the Magistrate after making an endorsement thereon that the woman or girl referred to in the warrant has been duly taken in his charge.

R.7. *Licensing of protective home:*

(1) Application for a licence sub-section (3) of Section 21(3) shall be made in Form III to the State Government.

(2) On receipt of an application for a licence, the State Government shall before issuing the licence cause full and complete investigation to be made through an officer or authority appointed in this behalf. The said officer or authority before

reporting on the application to the State Government shall report the statements of the applicant or applicants and the Special Police Officer appointed for the area. In addition, he may make enquiries for such social welfare worker or respectable persons of the locality as he may deem necessary. The State Government, if satisfied, that the applicant or applicants is or are fit person or persons to whom a licence may be issued, may issue a licence in Form IV which if issued will remain in force for a period of one year.

(3) An application for the renewal of a licence shall be made in Form VI at least thirty days before the date of its expiry. The licence may thereupon be renewed for a like period.

(4) No licence issued or renewed under this Rule shall be transferable.

(5) The management of every licenced protective home shall, wherever practicable, be entrusted to women.

(6) The licensee shall comply all the conditions of the licence and the provisions of the Act and shall maintain all registers and accounts in the manner hereinafter laid down and shall submit all statements and returns as prescribed in the rules.

R.8. *Admission into protective home:*

On the admission of a woman or a girl into a protective home under the provisions of the Act, she shall be examined by the Superintendent who shall record in the Inmate's Register in Form VI the particulars required to be shown in that register.

(2) The woman or girl admitted into a protective home shall then be supplied with a new set of clothes and the clothes worn by her at the time of admission shall be destroyed, if they are in rags or in filthy or in verminous condition. The clothing of every woman and girl to be detained for a period of two years or more shall, if they are not liable to be destroyed, be sold and the proceeds credited to the personal account of the woman or girl. In all other cases, the clothings of a woman or girl shall be returned to the parents/guardians or relatives of the woman or girl and if it is not possible to do so, shall be washed, tied up in a bundle and stored and returned to the woman or girl on her discharge. She shall be given a bath, which shall be of a disinfection nature.

(3) The Superintendent or some other official of the protective home considered suitable by such Superintendent, shall

then take the woman or girl to the nearest hospital for examination. If there is no hospital within a reasonable distance, the medical examination of the woman or girl shall be conducted by the nearest qualified lady doctor.

(4) Women or girls found from any veneral diseases shall be kept, as far as possible, separate from the other inmates of the protective home. Women or girls suffering from minor ailments shall be treated by the Medical Officer of the protective home. If the woman or girl is suffering from serious illness, she shall be taken to the nearest hospital for admission and a report shall immediately be sent to the Commissioner of Police and/or to the nearest Magistrate. A copy of the report shall be simultaneously sent to the Chief Inspector.

R.9. *Admission of children accompanying inmates into protective homes:*

(1) A child below seven years of age in the care of its mother who is detained or ordered to be kept in the protective home may also be admitted to the home along with her, if it cannot be placed with its relative or otherwise properly provided for. If any question arises as to whether a child is below seven years of age or not, such question shall be determined by the Superintendent.

(2) A child born in the home after the admission of the inmate into the protective home may remain with her mother.

(3) No child shall be kept in the protective home if it has completed the age of seven years. On a child completing such age, the Superintendent shall intimate the fact to the Chief Inspector with a view to make arrangements, if possible, to place the child with its relatives.

(4) A child kept in the protective home shall be allowed such diet and clothing as the Medical Officer attached to the protective home may think fit.

R.10. *History ticket:*

A record hereinafter referred to as history ticket shall be maintained in respect of each inmate in Form VII.

R.11. *Medical examination:*

Every inmate shall be medically examined and weighed

once in every month and the result of such examination and weighment shall be recorded in the history ticket of the inmate. A statement in Form VIII shall be submitted before the 10th of every month to the Chief Inspector showing the weighment statistics of the protective home.

R.15. *Weekly inspection:*

(1) On one morning in every week, which shall usually be Monday, the Superintendent shall hold an inspection parade of all the inmates to which the Medical Officer shall also be present. At each such parade, the Superintendent shall satisfy himself/herself:

(a) that every inmate is provided with proper clothing and bedding;
(b) that they are clean and tidy;
(c) that the rules and orders applicable to inmates are being duly carried out.

(2) The Superintendent shall carry such parade, hear and enquire into the complaints and requests that the inmates may wish to make. It shall be his/her duty to hear the complaints, and requests of inmates patiently and to afford them reasonable facilities for making such complaints and requests.

(3) Nothing in this rule shall debar any inmate from making a complaint or request to the Superintendent at other times than at the weekly parade, and it shall be the duty of every member of the staff to produce before the Superintendent without delay any inmate desiring to see him/her.

R.19. *Duties of the Medical Officers of protective homes:*

In addition to such other duties as may be assigned to the Medical Officer of a protective home by the State Government from time to time in consultation with the Chief Inspector, the Medical Officer shall visit the protective home every day except on Sunday and other holidays also, when necessary. He/she shall attend to the health and cleanliness of the inmates, the treatment of the sick, the sanitation of the protective home, general inspection and supervision of food and all other matters connected directly or indirectly with the health of the staff and inmates of the home.

(2) On each visit to the protective home, the Medical Officer shall enter his/her remarks in the register in Form IX.

(3) The Medical Officer shall accompany the Chief Inspector during his/her inspection of the protective home.

(4) During the absence of the Superintendent on short leave (other than casual leave) or during a vacancy in the post of the Superintendent for a short period, the Medical Officer, with the previous approval of the Chief Inspector, may act as the Superintendent, in addition to his/her own duties.

R.20. *Educational and vocational training of the inmates of protective homes:*

(1) Provision may be made for general education in all protective homes. Besides general education, each protective home shall, as far as possible, provide for the vocational training of the inmates, the wishes of each inmate being consulted, as far as possible, as to the particular training she shall undergo. Suitable employment, which shall include house work, sewing, weaving, spinning and the like may be provided. All courses of training shall be approved by the Chief Inspector.

(2) Teachers shall be engaged for imparting general education and instructors appointed for giving vocational training to the inmates. In an emergency, the Superintendent may direct such teachers and instructors to attend to executive duties.

Rule 21 prescribes the 'daily routine of protective homes', Rule 22 with diet to inmates; Rule 23 with clothing to inmates, Rule-24 makes provision for living space (usually 8 ft x 5 ft) per bed, Rule 25 deals with religious and moral instructions and Rule 26 prescribes that every protective home shall be provided with a library.

R.27. *Attendance of the inmates of protective homes before Police or Magistrates:*

Any inmate whose attendance is required before the police or before a court shall be permitted to leave the protective home for the purpose, only on receipt of a written requisition signed by a police officer not below the rank of a Deputy Superintendent of Police or of a summons issued by the court of competent jurisdiction. The inmate shall in such cases be accompanied by the Superintendent or by any other member of the staff considered suitable by the Superintendent.

R.31. *Visits to and communications with the inmates of protective homes:*

(1) No inmate shall be allowed to see visitors or receive letters without the express permission of the Superintendent and no male visitor shall be permitted to interview any of the inmates except in the presence of the Superintendent or any other member of the staff of the home so authorised by the Superintendent in this behalf.

(2) Every inmate newly admitted to a protective home shall be allowed reasonable facilities for seeing or communicating with her relatives, friends, or legal adviser with a view to the preparation of an appeal.

(3) Parents and guardians may visit inmates of protective homes on Saturdays and Sundays between 4 P.M. and 6 P.M. For very urgent reasons, visitors may be allowed on other days at other times with the special permission of the Superintendent. The privilege of receiving visitors may be refused on the orders of the Superintendent as a punishment for misconduct by the inmate, or if it is used to introduce any prohibited article in to the home or of the parent or guardian has or is likely to have in the opinion of the Superintendent, a bad influence on an inmate or inmates or for any other sufficient cause. The Superintendent shall record his/her reason for such refusal in the office journal.

(4) Every inmate shall be allowed to write or receive a letter once a month during the period of her detention or stay in the home, subject to the condition of good conduct.

(5) If the address of the parents or guardians is known they shall be given notice of any serious illness of the inmate and the Superintendent shall answer any reasonable enquiries made by the parents or guardians.

(6) Inmate shall be allowed, if they so desire, special letter in order to inform the parents or guardians of their transfer from one protective home to another. This shall not be counted as a letter for the purpose of sub-rule (4).

(7) No letter shall be delivered to or sent by an inmate unless the Superintendent has satisfied himself/herself that its transmission is unobjectionable.

(8) The Superintendent may at his/her discretion grant interviews or allow the despatch on receipt of letters at short

intervals than those provided in sub-rule (4) in spite of the inmate's misconduct, if he/she considers that special or urgent grounds exist for such concession.

(9) A register shall be maintained by the Superintendent for recording the visits of parents or guardians of the inmates of the home. Cases of refusal to permit visits shall be recorded in this register with reasons.

(10) A register of correspondence between the inmates and their parents and guardians shall be maintained.

R.33. *Discipline and punishments:*

The following acts are forbidden in a protective home and every inmate who wilfully commits any of these shall be deemed to have wilfully disobeyed the regulations of the protective home:

(a) quarrelling with any other inmate;
(b) any assault or use of criminal force;
(c) use of insulting, obscene or threatening language;
(d) immoral or indecent or disorderly behaviour;
(e) wilfully disabling herself for labour;
(f) continuously refusing to work;
(g) wilful idleness and negligence at work;
(h) wilful damage to the property of protective home;
(i) wilful mismanagement of work;
(j) tampering with or defacing history tickets, records, documents or tools;
(k) receiving, possessing or transferring any objectionable articles;
(l) feigning illness;
(m) wilfully bringing a false accusation against official or inmate;
[(n) omitting or refusing to report—as soon as it comes to the knowledge of the inmate, the occurence of any fire, any plot or conspiracy, any escape, attempt or preparation or any attack upon any inmate or official of the protective house;
(o) conspiring to escape or to assist in escaping;
(p) answering untruthfully any question put by an officer of the protective home or a visitor;
(q) refusing to eat food or wilfully destroying food;
(r) committing a nuisance in any part of the protective home.

(2) The Superintendent may award any of the following punishments for the act or acts specified in sub-rule(1).

(a) deprivation of play hours;
(b) temporary cessation of visits from parents or guardians; and
(c) change to labour of severe nature for a period not exceeding one month.

(3) A punishment book shall be maintained by the Superintendent who shall record full particulars of the punishment inflicted by his/her together with the nature of breach of discipline, the nature of the persons committing such breaches of discpline and the number of previous punishments awarded to them.

(4) An extract from the punishment book shall be sent by the Superintendent to the Chief Inspector before 10th of every month.

R.33. *Prohibited articles:*

Liquor, intoxicating drugs including opium and ganja shall be prohibited articles and shall not be introduced, received, possessed or transferred to the protective home.

R.38. *Marriage of inmates of protective home:*

(1) The Superintendent may, if possible, arrange for the marriage of an inmate with a man of her own religion, provided that her previous consent in writing and that of her parent or guardian, if she has not attained the age of 18 years, is obtained and provided that no monetary consideration is accepted to whom the inmate is married or from any person interested in him. In case, there is no parent or guardian living, the consent of the nearest relation should be obtained. The wishes of the inmate shall in every case be considered.

(2) No such marriage shall be performed without the permission of the District Magistrate.

Thus it can be inferred that the provision of protective homes and corrective institutions has been made in this Act by way of a welfare scheme of the Government and is required to be run under strict rules which have been framed meticulously and contains every details. But inspite of all these, the protective homes, in some States, are not properly managed. In a case filed by Dr. Upendra Baxi[+] in respect of the mismanagement and deplorable condition of Agra Protective Home, the Supreme Court of India ordered the State Government of U.P. to carry out the following directions:[27]

(1) The approach road to the new building shall be made into a pucca or semi-pucca road so that it does not get blocked or waterlogged by rain. This shall be done within three months from today.

(2) The big hall as also the three class rooms and the kitchen shall be provided with cross ventilation by putting up sufficient number of windows so as to ensure passage of air in and out of the rooms. The District Judge or the Addl. District Judge nominated by him shall determine how many windows are necessary to be constructed for this purpose.

(3) Exhaust fans shall be provided in the big hall, three class rooms, kitchen and offices.

(4) The State Government shall provide police protection throughout day and night for the inmates of the protective home in the new building.

(5) The State Government shall either provide accommodation to the staff of the protective home in or near the new building or provide conveyance to the members of the staff for coming to the Protective Home and going back to their respective homes unless public transport is available in the immediate vicinity of the protective home.

(6) We are informed that mosquito nets have been provided by the State Government to each and every inmate as also to the members of the staff staying in the Protective Home but if that has not yet been done, the State Government shall immediately take steps to provide mosquito nets to each and every inmate and members of the staff staying in the Protective Home.

(7) The State Government shall provide a conveyance for taking the inmates to the court and bringing them back to the Protective Home and similarly, conveyance shall also be provided to the District Judge or Additional District Judge inspecting the Protective Home.

(8) The District Manager (Telephones), Agra shall immediately shift the telephone to the new building and whatever steps

+ Director, Indian Law Institute, Bhagwan Das Road, New Delhi-110001.

are necessary for this purpose shall be taken by the State Government without any delay.

(9) The State Government shall immediately provide cooking gas in the kitchen so that it is not necessary to use wood for cooking which may emit a lot of smoke and lead to discomfort and suffocation on account of lack of ventilation.

(10) The State Government shall immediately proceed to carry out rewiring as also to instal the electric meter in a safe place where there is no dampness. We find from the latest Inspection Report of the Additional District Judge dated June 30, 1986 that the electric meter has been shifted to the chamber of the Superintendent. We hope and trust that the new place to which it is shifted is not damp so as to imperil the safety of the inmates. That is a matter which would have to be looked into by the District Judge or the Additional District Judge when he goes for inspection. But we also think it is necessary to direct that since the electric line is of 440 voltage and not of 220 voltage and would, therefore, be dangerous for the inmates, the State Government shall without any undue delay proceed to take the necessary steps to instal a generator so that the safety of the inmates is not jeopardised.

(11) The State Government was further directed to set up, within a period of two weeks from the receipt of this order, a Board of Visitors on which there shall be at least three social activists working in the field of welfare of women and two persons to be nominated by the District Judge Agra shall also be included in the Board of Visitors within two weeks from today.

(12) The Superintendent of Protective Home was directed to take to see that no woman or girl is detained in the protective home without due authority and process of law. The District Judge Agra, who carries out monthly inspection of the protective home shall verify during every visit that no woman or girl is detained except under the authority of law, he shall take steps to see that she is released and repatriated to her parents or husband or other proper authority.

(13) The District Judge, Agra was directed to nominate two socially committed advocates who would by turns visit the Protective Home once in a fortnight and enquire from the

inmates in regard to their needs and requirements and provide them legal aids and assistance, where required. Each of the advocates visiting the protective home persuant to this direction shall be paid by the State Government an honorarium of Rs. 50 per visit plus out of pocket expenses.

(14) The Supreme Court further stressed that the inmates must be given vocational training and guidance by way of rehabilitation as it is absolutely essential that the inmates in the Protective Home should be provided a proper rehabilitation programme so that after coming out of the Protective Home they can look after themselves and do not slide into prostitution on account of financial needs.

In an earlier judgement,[28] the Supreme Court passed the following orders in respect of (a) discharge of inmates, (b) admission of minor girls and (c) compliance of rules:

(a) Rule 37 requires that the State Government may at any time order any inmate of the protective home to be discharged either absolutely or on such conditions as they approve and it would be seen that only when an appropriate order is made by the State Government that an inmate can be discharged from Home.

Whenever an inmate of the protective home is to be discharged it shall be done in accordance with the procedure and provisions as laid down in Rule 37 and information of the intended discharge shall be given by the Superintendent of the protective home to the Chief Judicial Magistrate at least five days in advance. The whole object of this direction was that the Chief Judicial Magistrate should be able to satisfy himself that the inmates in protective home were not being sent out without any justification and without complying with the requirements of Rule 37 and taking care to see whether they had any alternative place where they could go.

While discharging the inmates, the Superintendent of the protective home should enquire of them as to where they propose to go and they should be supplied with railway tickets as contemplated under sub-rule (4) of Rule 37, even though that rule may not be strictly applicable. If not under the rules, at least on humanitarian grounds, it should be enquired of them whether they have money for the railway ticket and their own subsistence and how they propose to look after themselves. The Superintendent can,. if necessary obtain orders from the authorities for the purpose of supplying them with railway tickets at the time of discharge.

(b) It is not at all desirable that minor girls between the ages of 7 and 18 should be allowed to remain in the protective home in the company of hardened prostitutes or women who have been rescued from the brothels and also women suffering from diseases. Their proper place would be only in Children's Homes.

(c) When a woman or girl is admitted to the Home under the orders of the Additional District Magistrate (city), the Superintendent should comply with all the provisions of the Rules in regard to the treatment to be meted out to a woman or girl, even though she may not have been admitted under the provisions of the Act. The provisions in the Rules such as Rules 8, 11, 19, 20, 22, 23, 24 26, 31, 34 and 35 in regard to the treatment to be meted out to the woman or girl admitted to the Home, are provisions laying down humane conditions ensuring the right to live with human dignity and they must therefore, be scrupulously followed by the Superintendent even in regard to women and girls admitted otherwise than under the provisions of the Act.

Patna Care Home:[29,30,31]

A practising advocate of Sasaram, who is also a member of Yuva Adhivakta Kalyan Samity addressed a letter to the Supreme Court in respect of poor and inhuman living conditions and exploitation of the inmates of the Home for Destitute Women in Patna where inmates numbering 100, were said to be exploited sexually by the staff and the management. Even the outsiders and the anti-social elements visited the Home. It was alleged that some of the inmates used to be sent outside the Care Home to extract money from "Customers" and in the event of their resistance to it, they were brutally assaulted and starved for a day or two by way of punishment. Other allegations were the very low quality of food, only one toilet without roof and doors for 100 persons and no bath room. The female inmates had to take bath in presence of male staff. The medical facility was extremely poor. A seven year girl, Alka, died and at last twenty-five inmates including one M.A. student Megha Varma went mad. The said letter, which was sent by the Advocate after talking to a young girl who fled from there to save her life and womanhood, was treated by the Supreme Court as a Writ Petition and was taken up by the Free Legal Aid Committee.

In persuance of the orders of the Supreme Court, the Patna District Judge visited the Care Home and reported that the living condition was deplorable and pathetic. According to the report, there were ninety-five inmates, twelve had been transferred to the Lunatic Asylum Ranchi, eleven children had been transferred to Bal Bhawan in Deoghar and thirty of them had escaped. Majority of the inmates were major in age and were kept in "Protective Custody" under the orders of Judicial Officers. In the opinion of the District Judge, the inmates detention was unwarranted as a majority of them were not minors and only a few were held as accused persons. Ever since they were brought to the Home, the authorities never produced them before concerned magistrate.

On the living conditions, the District Judge found that the Care Home had five damp dirty rooms with no windows which could hardly accommodate twenty-five persons. The other seventy had to sleep on verandah for throughout the year. Not all the inmates were provided with cots and blankets. They were made to sleep on broken floors without any sheet of cloth to cover their bodies. They are not provided with any woollen clothes, soap or oil. The provision of diet worth only Rs. 5 was hardly adequate to sustain them.[32,33]

Living amid acute water shortage, the inmates told the Judge that they had three lavatories which are in dilapidated condition and located far from the building. The inmates did not confirm allegations about sexual abuse by the Staff members or outsiders.

Describing the Care Home, Patna, as a crowded hovel in which a large number of human beings have been thrown together and thus compelled to subsist in conditions of animal survival, the Supreme Court directed the State Government of Bihar, to take immediate steps to comply with the various directions given by the court for the welfare of the inmates of the Care Home. The court also made it clear that in the event of a no, or insufficient compliance being made with the directions, it would be open in the case for such further steps as may be necessary for enforcing the directions.[33a]

Survey by Joint Women Programme (JWP):

In a survey committed by the Joint Women Programme (JWP), an organisation, working for the upliftment of women in which, 1,100 case studies by a nun Sister Rita Rozario were made, it has been revealed that six percent of women interviewed were sold into prostitution by Nari Niketan, other protective homes and social workers. A couple of girls from Andhra Pradesh said that they had been pushed into the trade by the village Gram Sevika and Bal-Sevikas.

The JWP has evidence of sale of girls by the Nari Niketan in Lilowah, Kanpur and Banaras.

The establishment of Women's and Children's Institutions are controlled by the Act titled as "The Women's and Children's Institutions (Licensing) Act, 1956 (Annexed) but inspite of it, for want of effective and efficient vigilance, the purpose of this enactment gets defeated.

THE WOMEN'S AND CHILDREN'S INSTITUTION (LICENSING) ACT, 1956 (No. 105 of 1956)

(30th December, 1956)

An Act to provide the licensing of institutions for women and children and for matters incidental thereto.

Be it enacted by Parliament in the Seventh Year of the Republic of India as follows:-

1. *Short title, extent and commencement:*

(1) This Act may be called the Women's and Children's Institutions (Licensing) Act, 1956.

(2) It extends to the whole of India except the State of Jammu and Kashmir.

(3) It shall come into force in a state on such date as the State Government may, by notification in the Official Gazette, appoint.

2. *Definitions:*

In this Act, unless the context otherwise requires:

(a) "child" means a boy or girl who has not completed the age of eighteen years;
(b) "institution" means an institution established and maintained for the reception, care, protection and welfare of women or children;
(c) "licensing authority" means the State Government or such officer or authority as may be prescribed;
(d) "prescribed" means prescribed by rules made by the State Government under this Act;
(e) "woman" means a female who has completed the age of eighteen years.

3. *Licensing of institutions:*

After the commencement of this Act, no person shall establish or maintain an institution except under and in accordance with the conditions of a licence granted under this Act.

4. *Application for licence:*

Every person desiring to establish an institution shall make an application to the licensing authority in such form and containing such particulars as may be prescribed.

Provided that a person maintaining an institution at the commencement of this Act shall be allowed a period of three months from such commencement to make an application for a licence.

5. *Grant of licence:*

(1) On receipt of an application under Section 4, the licensing authority, after making such inquiry as it considers necessary, shall, by order in writing, either grant the licence or refuse to grant it.

(2) Where a licence is refused, the grounds for such refusal shall be communicated to the applicant in the prescribed manner.

(3) A licence, unless sooner revoked, shall remain in force for such period as may be specified in the licence and may, on application made in this behalf sixty days before the date of

expiration, be renewed for such period as the licensing authority may deem proper.

Provided that a licence may be renewed on an application made within sixty days before the date of its expiration if the licensing authority is satisfied that there was sufficient cause for not making the application earlier.

(4) Every licence granted under this Act, shall be in the prescribed form and shall be subject to such conditions as may be prescribed.

Provided that any such condition may require that the management of an institution shall, wherever practicable, entrusted to women.

(5) No fee shall be charged for the grant of a licence under this Act.

6. *Licence not transferable:*

A licence granted under this Act shall not be transferable.

7. *Revocation of licence:*

(1) Where any person to whom a licence has been granted under this Act, or any agent or servant of such person commits a breach of any of the conditions thereof, or any of the provisions of this Act, or any of the rules made thereunder, or where the licensing authority is not satisfied with the condition, management or superintendence of an institution, the licensing authority may, without prejudice to any other penalty which may have been incurred under this Act, for reasons to be recorded, revoke the licence by order in writing.

Provided that no such order shall be made until an opportunity is given to the holder of the licence to show cause why the licence should not be revoked.

(2) Where a licence in respect of an institution has been revoked under the foregoing sub-section, such institution shall cease to function:

(a) where no such appeal has been preferred, immediately on the expiration of the period prescribed for the filing of such appeal;

(b) where such appeal has been preferred but the order of revocation has been upheld, from the date of the appellate order.

(3) On the revocation of a license in respect of an institution the licensing authority may direct that any woman or child who is an inmate of such institution on the date of such revocation shall be:

(a) restored to the custody of her or his parent, husband or lawful guardian, as the case may be; or
(b) transferred to another institution.

8. *Appeals:*

(1) Where the licensing authority is other than the State Government, any person aggrieved by an order of the licensing authority refusing to grant a licence or revoking a licence may within such period as may be prescribed, prefer an appeal to the State Government against such refusal or revocation.

(2) The order of the State Government on such appeal and subject only to such order, the order of the licensing authority shall be final.

9. *Penalty:*

Any person who contravenes any of the provisions of this Act or of any rule made thereunder, or any of the conditions of a licence shall be punishable with imprisonment for a term which may extend to three months, or with fine which may extend to two hundred and fifty rupees, or with both.

10. *Act not to apply to certain institution.*

Nothing in this Act shall apply to:

(a) hostels, or boarding houses attached to, or controlled or recognised by educational institutions; or
(b) any protective home established under the Suppression of Immoral Traffic in Women and Girls Act, 1956.

11. *Power to make rules:*

(1) The State Government may, by notification in the Official Gazette, make rules for carrying out the purposes of this Act.

(2) In particular and without prejudice to the generality of the foregoing power, such rules may provide for:

(a) the form of application for licence and the particulars to be contained therein;

(b) the form of licence and the conditions subject to which such licence may be granted;

(c) the management of institutions;

(d) the reception, care, protection and welfare of women and children institution, including all matters relating to their diet, clothing, accommodation, training and general conduct;

(e) the inspection of institution;

(f) the maintenance of registers and account and submission of returns and audit of such accounts;

(g) the discharge from institutions of women and children and their transfer from one institution to another;

(h) the manner of filing appeals under this Act and the time within which such appeal shall be filed;

(i) the manner of service of orders and notices under this Act;

(j) any other matter which is to be or may be prescribed.

12. *Repeal and savings:*

(1) As from the date of commencement in any state of this Act, any State Act corresponding to this Act in force in that State immediately before such commencement shall stand repealed.

(2) Notwithstanding the repeal by this Act of any State Act referred to in sub-section (1), anything done or any action taken (including any direction given, any register, rule or order made or any restriction imposed) under the provisions of such State Act shall in so far such thing or action is not inconsistent with the provisions of this Act be deemed to have been done or taken under the provisions of this Act as if the said provisions were in force when such thing was done or such action was taken and shall continue in force accordingly until superseded by anything done or any action taken under this Act.

Explanation: In this Section, the expression "State Act" includes a "Provincial Act".

The vice of prostitution has two aspects, viz; prevention and rehabilitation. For the purpose of prevention, the Act suffers from one possible drawback in the provisions itself, that is; a prostitute can be punished when she carries on prostitution within a distance of 200 yards of any place of public, religious worship, educational institution, hostel, hospital, nursing home etc., in accordance with the provisions of Section 7 of the Act.

Another practical difficulty arises due to the provisions made in Section 15(2) of the Act which lays down that Special Police Officer or the trafficking police officer, as the case may be, shall call upon two or more respectable inhabitants, at least one of whom shall be a woman, of the locality in which the place is situated to attend and witness the search. This provision has been made to see that exploitation of the women is prevented and avoid false implication by the police and the search and raids are not testified by stock witnesses. But this has another aspect as well in view of the existing social condition where no respectable man or woman will be willing to get involved in any way in sex offences. Besides this frequent summoning in the police station at the cost of the witness him/herself and several visits to the court in evidence without even a reasonable compensation for the time and money spent for such attendance. The witness has to face harassment not on account of lengthy cross-examination only but by threat by the criminals to the life, honour and property.

The problem of rehabilitation is linked with creating a condition in which the rescued women do not return to the same profession from which they have come. The law makes a provision for grant of bail and the persons who stand as bailers are usually the procurers or brothel keepers. Instead of sending the women to jail they are sent to the protective homes as it has been said the living conditions in protective home, Nari Niketans are not so encouraging. According to reports, women have been sent to prostitution from protective homes and Nari Niketans as well. Unless these institutions are manned by truly dedicated persons, situations are not going to improve. In respect of rehabilitation the Rama Rau Committee (1954) has said that the after care homes are not adequate and they should be associated with some programmes to help rehabilitation. Those who are detained under the Act require long-term treatment for rehabilitation. Special counselling service is required to be provided. The children of prostitutes should be prevented from entering the prostitution. The present position with respect to these problems are not at all encouraging with the result prostitutes living in G.B. Road flats of Delhi feel almost unanimously that the life they are leading is "dignified and respectful" as disclosed in personal enquiries by police. According to one Deputy Commissioner of Police, Delhi, each one of these girls and women has a misery back home, in their families, and are unwilling to go back.[34] They feel that they will not be accepted and that their present way of life is better.

Majority of the women and girls were completely uprooted from their families and homes and for them the red light areas have become real homes albeit forced. According to the police official rarely do voluntary social and women's organisations come forward to join hands with the police or offer their services to conduct any systematic and indepth study on the lives of inmates of these flats (numbering about twenty houses, having nearly 1200 women and girls) to help the unwilling inmates move away from a decandant life and rehabilitate them.

Children's Education:

With regard to the education of those children whose mothers are prostitutes in a red light area in Delhi, the children have been denied admission in a school simply because they could not fill up the column requiring the father's name in the application form. The relevant provisions of the Constitution and also of International Conventions of Human Rights have a bearing on this issue.

Under the Universal Declaration of Human rights (1948), Article 25(2) states, "Motherhood and Children are entitled to special care assistance. All children born, whether in or out of wedlock, shall enjoy the same social protection."

Under Article 26(1) "everyone has the right to education. Education shall be free at least in the fundamental and elementary stages. Elementary education shall be compulsory...."

Article 26(2) contemplates that "Education shall be directed to the full development of the human personality and to the strengthening of respect for human rights and the fundamental freedoms...."

Article 10(3) of the International Covenant on Economic, Social and Cultural Rights mentions: "Special measures of the protection and assistance should be taken on behalf of all children and young persons without any discrimination for reasons of parentage or other conditions".

Article 24(1) of the International Covenant on Civil and Political Rights(1966) says: "Every child has, without any discrimination as to race, colour, sex, language, religion, national or social origin, property or birth, the right to such measures of protection as are required by his status as a minor, on the part of his family, society and the State".

Constitution of India provides for necessary protection to safeguard the interests of certain sections of the people. Amongst such provisions, a reference is made to the provisions of Article 39 of the Constitution which runs as under:

"The State shall, in particular, direct its policy towards securing:

(e) that the health and strength of workers, men and women, and the tender age of children are not abused and that citizens are not forced by economic necessity to enter advocations unsuited to their age or strength:

(f) that children are given opportunities and facilities to develop in a healthy manner and in conditions of freedom and dignity and that childhood and youth are protected against exploitation and against moral and material abandonment."

Article 46 envisages that the State shall promote with special care the educational and economic interests of the weaker section of the people, and, in particular, of the Scheduled Castes and the Schedule Tribes, and shall protect them from social injustice and all forms of exploitation.

Needless to emphasise that children including those whose paternity is not known, would be covered by this clause. Unfortunately filling up the column meant for the father is insisted upon even in those cases where mother is the sole guardian. It is a fact that paternity is pre-emption, whereas maternity is a fact which cannot be doubted.

The matter of denial of admission of prostitutes' children has thus been brought to the notice of the Supreme Court of India, through a Writ Petition filed under Article 32 of Constitution against which the Supreme Court has issued notice to the concerned authorities.[35] The centre, following the petition filed by the Patita Udhar Samity in the Supreme Court, has asked the educational institutions not to ask these children to give their father's name.[36]

On account of these hurdles and their isolation from their fellow class-mates in a large number of cases, some children have been withdrawn from their schools. In such a situation, the children may grow up in an unhealthy atmosphere with the result that boys will become criminal and drug addict and girls take to prostitution.

The mere enactment of (Prevention) of Immoral Traffic Act is not enough for the benefit of society, instead resources should be mobilised to provide rescue homes for women and training to equip them for job if the society wants to win the moral war against commercialised promiscuity.[37]

REFRENCES

1. Varma, P. "Sex Offences in India and Abroad: A Sociological Study" (1979) B.R. Publishing Corporation, Delhi, pp. 119.
2. The Random House Dictionary of the English Languages (College Edition) Allied Publishers Pvt. Ltd. pp. 1063, Col. 1.
3. Vide Section 2(e) and (f) of Supression of Immoral Traffic in Women and Girls Act (1956).
4. Vide Section 2(f) of Suppression of Immoral Traffic in Women and Girls Act (Act No. 46 of 1978).
5. Mamoria C.B., 'Social Problems and Social Disorganisation in India' (1981) Kitab Mahal, Allahabad, pp. 754.
6. Weaver, W.Wallace, Social Problems, The Dryden Press, New York (1956) pp. 332.
7. Rai, Usha; 'Distress Sale of Girls by Families', *The Times of India*, dated May 4, 1987.
8. Rai, Logan; 'Each Night is Torture', *The Times of India* (Sunday), Sept. 13, 1987.
9. Gandhey, S., 'Why are we not shocked by Crimes against Women' *The Illustrated Weekly of India*, July 31-Aug, 6. 1988, pp. 8–15.
10. Kapoor, (Dr.) P. The Life and World of Call Girls in India, (1978) Vikas Publishing House, Shahibabad, pp. 30–31.
11. Karsenboom, Saskia C. 'Nityasumangali, Devadasi Traditions in South India,' Motilal Banarsi Das.
12. 'Condemned to a life of Shame' Hindustan Times Correspondent (News Item) *Hindustan Times* (Delhi), dated 17.2.1987.
13. 'Towards Equality'—Report of Committee on the Status of Women in India, Government of India, Department of Social Welfare, Ministry of Education and Social Welfare (December 1974), pp. 93.
14. Mamoria C.B., "Social Problems and Social Disorganisation in India, (1981) Kitab mahal, Allahabad, pp. 754.
15. *Ibid.*, pp. 754.
16. Natha Nael (1987) "Where Flesh Trade is a Tradition", *The Hindustan Times* (Delhi Edition), Sunday Magazine Section, July 12, 1987.

17. Mitra Anirudhya, "Where Prostitution is the only way of life" *The Hindustan Times*, Sunday Magazine, Dec 14, 1986.
18. Singh N.K., Rushkarna, P. "Madhya Pradesh—Cursed by Custom", *India Today*, Jan 31, 1988, pp. 124–127.
19. Varma S., Madhya Pradesh—Sansi Women, Still on Sale, *The Hindustan times*, Sunday Magazine, July 12, 1987.
20. Express News Service; "Selling Wives to Stave off Hunger", *The Indian Express* (Delhi Edition), dated May 31, 1988.
21. Kumar, Ajay; "Miraj Arabian Nights", *India Today*, August 31, 1986. pp. 151–53.
22. Mamoria C.B.; "Social Problems and Social Disorganisation in India" Kitab Mahal, Allahabad (2nd Edition 1981), pp. 964.
23. *Ibid.*
24. Joshi Rita, "From Adulation to Abuse", *The Hindustan Times* (Delhi Edition), Feb. 8, 1987.
25. Gupta R.L., "Medicolegal Aspects of Sexual Offences" (2nd Edition 1981) Eastern Book Company, Lucknow, pp. 315–317.
26. Vide State Rules framed by several State Governments in exercise of the powers conferred under Section 23 of Suppression of Immoral Traffic in Women and Girls (Act No. 104 of 1956).
27. *Upendra Bakshi* Vs. *The State of Uttar Pradesh*, (1986) 4 SCC, 106(113) = AIR 1987 SC 191.
28. *Upendra Baxi* Vs. *The State of U.P.* (1983) 2 SCC 308 = 1983 SC.
29. Legal Correspondent "Supreme Court Notice on abuse of women", *Times of India* (Delhi Edition), dated 19.11.1987.
30. Legal Correspondent, "Patna Care Home for Women, not safe" *The Hindustan Times*, dated 29.1.1988.
31. Legal Coresspondent, "Care Home Condition Pathetic, Miserable" *Times of India*, dated 29.3.1988.
32. *Ibid.*
33. *Id.*

33a. *Vikramdeo Singh Tomar* Vs. *State of Bihar*, AIR 1988 SC 1782.

34 News Item—"Prostitution happy the way they are" Disclosed by A.K. Kanth, Deputy Commissioner of Police (Crime) in a recent Seminar on Social Audit of Immoral Traffic (Prevention) Act, *Hindustan Times*, dated 18.7.1988.

35. Kusum, "Why Father's Name?" *The Hindustan Times*, dated 12.4.1988.
36. Kamaljeet Rattan (Cal.) David Devadas (Delhi), S.H. Venkataraman (Madras) and Salil Tripathi (Bombay); "A Red Light Trap", *India Today*, July 31, 1988 pp. 106–107.
37. H.T. Correspondent, "Fallen women need shelter, jobs," *Hindustan Times*, dated Feb. 7, 1988.

Chapter 6

Obscenity and the Law

6.01 Introduction

In the third quarter of the year 1993, a case came up before Delhi Court praying for banning of the film titled "Khalnayak" directed by Subhash Ghai on the ground that the film contained an obscene song whose first line was "Choli ke picchey kya hai", inspite of the fact that the film was granted a certificate under Section 6 of the Cinematographic Act. The defence plea was that the song was a piece of art and based on the folk song of Rajasthan. The court accepted the defence plea and dismissed the petition for banning the same.

The term "obscene" or "obscenity" has not been defined under Section 292 of the I.P.C[1] except that what obscenity amounts to, has been described under this Section.

The expression "obscenity" in legal sense is generally referred to the portrayals of such conduct in publications and other representations.[2] The dictionary meaning of this expression is character of being obscene. "Obscene" means (1) offensive to modesty or decency; (2) causing or intended to cause sexual excitement or lust; (3) abominable or disgusting; repulsive on obscene exhibition of public discourtesy.[3]

Section 292, Sec. 293 and Sec. 294 deal with various aspects of this subject. The three Sections are reproduced below:

292. Sale, etc. of obscene books, etc.:[4]

[(1) For the purpose of sub-section (2), book, pamphlet, paper, writing, drawing, painting, representation, figure or any other object, shall be deemed to be obscene if it is lascivious or appeals to the prurient interest or if its effect, or (where it comprises two or more distinct items) the effect of any one of its items, is, if taken as a whole, such as to tend to deprave and corrupt persons who are likely, having regard to all relevant circumstances, to read, see or hear the matter contained or embodied in it.]

[5][(2) Whoever:

(a) sells, lets to hire, distributes, publicly exhibits or in any manner puts into circulation, or for purpose of sale, hire, distribution, public exhibition or circulation, makes, produces or has in possession any obscene book, pamphlet, paper, drawing, painting, representation or figure or any other obscene object whatever, or

(b) imports, exports or conveys any obscene object for any of the purposes aforesaid, or knowing or having reason to believe that such object will be sold, let to hire, distributed or publicly exhibited or in any manner put into circulation, or

(c) takes part in or receives profits from any business in the course of which he knows or has reasons to believe that any such obscene objects are, for any of the purposes aforesaid, made, produced, purchased, kept, imported, exported, conveyed, publicly exhibited or in any manner put into circulation, or

(d) advertises or makes known by any means, whatsoever, that any person is engaged or is ready to engage in any act which is an offence under this Section, or that any such obscene object can be procured from or through any person, or

(e) offers or attempts to do any act which is an offence under this section,

shall be punished [6][on first conviction with imprisonment of either description for a term which may extend to two years, and with fine which may extend to two thousand rupees, and, in the event of a second or subsequent conviction, with imprisonment of either description for a term which may extend to five years, and also with fine which may extend to five thousand rupees.]

[7][*Exception:* This section does not extend to:

(a) any book, pamphlet, paper, writing, drawing, painting, representation or figure:

(i) the publication of which is proved to be justified as being for the public good on the ground that such book, pamphlet, paper, writing, drawing, painting, representation or figure is in the interest of science, literature, art or learning or other objects of general concern, or

(ii) which is kept or used bona fide for religious purposes:

(b) any representation sculptured, engraved, painted or otherwise represented on or in:

(i) any ancient monument within the meaning of the Ancient Monuments and Archaeological Sites and Remains Act,1958 (24 of 1958), or

(ii) any temple, or on any car used for the conveyance of idols, or kept or used for any religious purpose.]

Local Amendments:

ORISSA: Amended by Orissa Act 13 of 1962 [same as that of Tamil Nadu].

TAMIL NADU: [Amended by Tamil Nadu Act 25 of 1960.] In its application to the whole of the State of Tamil Nadu, in Section 292 the words "shall be punished with imprisonment of either description for a term which may extend to three months or with fine or with both" substitute the following, namely:

"shall be punished with imprisonment of either description for a term which may extend to two years or with fine or with both:

Provided that for a second or any subsequent offence under this section, he shall be punished with imprisonment of either description for a term which shall not be less than six months and not more than two years and with fine."

Local Amendments

SECTION 292-A

ORISSA: Amended by Orissa Act 13 of 1962 [same as that of Tamil Nadu].

TAMIL NADU: [Amended by Tamil Nadu Act 25 of 1960.] In its application to the whole of the State of Tamil Nadu, after Section 292 insert the following new section namely,

"292-A" Printing etc. of grossly indecent or scurrilous matter or matter intended for blackmail.

Whoever

(a) prints or causes to be printed in any newspaper, periodical or circular, or exhibits or causes to be exhibited, to public view or distributes or causes to be distributed or in any manner puts into circulation any picture or any printed or written document which is grossly indecent, or is scurrilous or intended for blackmail, or

(b) sells or lets for hire, or for purpose of sale or hire makes, produces or has in his possession, any picture or any printed or written document which is grossly indecent or is scurrilous or intended for blackmail, or

(c) conveys any picture or any printed or written document which is grossly indecent or is scurrilous or intended for blackmail knowing or having reason to believe that such picture or document will be printed, sold, let for hire, distributed or publicly exhibited or in any manner put into circulation, or

(d) takes part in, or receives profits from, any business in the course of which he knows or has reason to believe that any such newspaper, periodical, circular, picture or other printed or written document is printed, exhibited, distributed, circulated, sold, let for hire, made, produced, kept, conveyed or purchased, or

(e) advertises or makes known by means whatsoever that any person is engaged or is ready to engage in any act which is an offence under this section, or that any such newspaper, periodical, circular, picture or other printed or written document which is grossly indecent or is scurrilous or intended for blackmail can be procured from or through any person, or

(f) offers or attempts to do any act which is an offence under this section, shall be punished with imprisonment of either description for a term which may extend to two years, or with fine, or with both.

Provided that for a second or any subsequent offence under this section, he shall be punished with imprisonment of either description for a term which shall not be less than six months and not more than two years and with fine.

Explanation I: For the purpose of this section, the word 'scurrilous' shall be deemed to include any matter which is likely to be injurious to morality or is calculated to injure any person.

Provided that it is not scurrilous to express in good faith anything whatever respecting the conduct of:

(i) a public servant in the discharge of his public functions or respecting his character so far as his character appears in that conduct and no further; or

(ii) any person touching any public question, and respecting his character, so far as his character appears in that conduct and no further.

Explanation II: In deciding whether any person has committed an offence under this section, the court shall have regard, inter alia, to the following considerations:

(a) the general character of the person charged, and where relevant, the nature of his business;

(b) the general character and dominant effect of the matter alleged to be grossly indecent or scurrilous or intended for blackmail;

(c) any evidence offered or called by or on behalf of the accused person as to his intention in committing any of the acts specified in this section.

293. Sale, etc., of obscene objects to young person:

Whoever sells, lets to hire, distributes, exhibits or circulates to any person under the age of twenty years any such obscene object as it is referred to in the last preceding section, or offers or attempts so to do, shall be punished.[8]

On first conviction with imprisonment of either description for a term which may extend to three years, and with fine which may extend to two thousand rupees, and, in the event of a second or subsequent conviction, with imprisonment of either description for a term which may extend to seven years, and also with fine which may extend to five thousand rupees.]

Local Amendments:

ORISSA: Amended by Orissa Act 13 of 1962 (same as that of TAMIL NADU Act.)

TAMIL NADU: Amended by Tamil Nadu Act 25 of 1960.] In its application to the whole of the state of Tamil Nadu in Section 293:

(a) for the words "any such obscene object as is referred to in the last preceding section" substitute the words, figures and letter, "any such obscene object as is referred to in Section 292 or any such newspaper, periodical, circular, picture or other printed or written document as is referred to in Section 292-A."
(b) for the words "which may extend to six months" substitute the words "which may extend to three years".
(c) in the marginal note, after the words "obscene objects "insert the words "and grossly indecent or scurrilous matter intended for blackmail".

294. *Obscene acts and songs:*

Whoever, to the annoyance of other,

(a) does any obscene act in any public place; or
(b) sings, recites or utters any obscene songs, ballad or words, in or near any public place.

shall be punished with imprisonment of either description for a term which may extend to three months, or with fine, or with both.

Notes on Sec. 292–294:

The various aspects of obscenity have elaborately been discussed by the Hon'ble High Court (Orissa) in case *Ramchandra alias Ramanandan Sahu* Vs. *Niranjan Rout & Another*[9]. The facts of this case was that the accused Police Officer, took work of removal of logs from two labourers. Considering the amount of remuneration paid at the rate of Rs. 4 each, the labourers demanded more. Instead of paying their legitimate dues, Opposite Party No. 2, then posted as officer-in-charge Champua Outpost, lost his temper and asked him to go out of the Out Post. The labourers approached the local MLA. The MLA came in company of a few more persons. The Officer-in-charge abused the MLA and others. When one Kogalhari Dehwey requested him not to do so, Opposite Party No.1 gave him a kick blow and made him sit by force. He was also abused in obscene language. The case actually came up against the judgement and order of the lower court which had held that sanction as required to prosecute a public servant for his duties in the capacity of a public servant, in accordance with the requirement of Section 197 was a necessity. The petitioners had come to the High Court against this among others. The Hon'ble High Court discussed this case in the light of the facts of this case and the ratio of decisions of other cases decided earlier in para 6, 7 and 8 of the judgement. Extracts from the aforesaid judgements are as given in the following lines:

Sec. 294 I.P.C. is intended to prevent obscene acts being performed in any public place to the annoyance of others. No precise or arithmetical definition of the word 'Obscene' which covers all possible cases, can be given. It will have to be judged on the facts of each case whether in the context of its surroundings, the questioned act is obscene or not. In *Chandrakant* Vs. *State of Maharashtra*[10], it was held that the concept of obscenity would differ from country to country, depending on the standards of morals of contemporary society. What is considered as a piece of literature in France may be obscene in England and what is considered in both countries as not harmful to public order and morals may be obscene in our country. In *Kinmlay Corporation* Vs. *Regents of University of New York*[11], dealing with "Lady Chatterley's Lover", the Supreme Court of United States of America upheld propagation as not offending freedom of expression. But Art. 19 (2)[12] of our Constitution makes all the more difference. None has attempted so far a definition of obscenity because the meaning can be laid bare without attempting a definition by describing what must be looked for.

(Para 6)

The classic definition of 'obscenity' delivered by Cockburn, C.J. in *R.*Vs. *Hicklin*[13], which stood until the passing of certain legislature in England was, 'The Test of Obscenity' is this:

"Whether the tendency of the matter charged as obscenity is to deprave and corrupt those whose minds are open to such immoral influences and in whose hands a publication of this sort may fall."

Though the observations were made in the context of a publication, the underlying idea is that obscenity is an act which has an irritating and/or immoral influence. The word 'obscene' in its ordinary sense denotes same thing which is indecent or disgusting as per Fullagar, J.[14] in R V. Close. The words "indecent" and "obscene" convey the idea of offending against propriety, indecency being at the lower and obscenity at the upper end of the scale.

(Para 7)

Life as lined by most of us is not of a hermit. It is not realistic to depict that what is not conducive to comparative common standard prevailing in the society of the day. Life itself is an inter-mixture of good and evil and of light and shadow. Obscenity is to be judged on the basis of the act itself.[15] In that the motive of the accused is irrelevant. . What is the effect of the act is the determining factor. Though annoyance is important ingredient of offence under Section 294 I.P.C., it being associated with mental condition has often to be inferred from proved facts. If there is sufficient indication of the fact that annoyance was caused because it is not specifically stated or spoken by witnesses in evidence that would not be sufficient to infer non-commission of offence under Section 294 I.P.C.

(Para 8)

It may be necessary to refer to some of the decisions of this Court and the facts involved therein, so far as they relate to Sec. 294 I.P.C. In *Abak Charan Biswal* Vs. *State*[16] abusive language hurled at complainant while in police lock up by the officer-in-charge of the Police Station was held not to be an act in discharge of official duty. In *Keshab Jena* Vs. *Pradip Kishore Das*[17], it was observed that no sanction was necessary where the police officer assaulted inside the Police Station area during investigation or where he abused a person.

6.02. Whether the Knowledge of Obscenity is an Ingredient of Offence?

The prosecution need not prove that one who sells or keeps for sale any obscene object knows that it is obscene. The prosecution need not prove something which law does not make obligatory. If knowledge were made a part of the guilty act which the prosecution may be burdened to prove it, that will place an almost impenetrable defence in the hands of offenders. Absence of this knowledge may be taken as mitigation but this does not take the case out of the Section.[18]

6.03 Value of Film Censor Board Certificate

A Film Censor Board is a high-powered board with specialised composition and has Statutory mandate to issue a certificate under Section 6 of the Cinematograph Act. The Certificate represents the judgement of a body of persons who are statutory functionaries for the specific purpose of adjudging the suitability of film for public exhibition. However, this does not prevent a Court from judging the ingredients of Section 292 and Sec. 293 should such a matter is presented before it for adjudication.[19]

6.04 Sale of Obscene Articles

Where the accused was found selling a packet of playing cards portraying lucidly obscene pictures on the reverse of the playing cards, and on raid a couple more of such playing cards recovered from his shop held that in dealing with offence under Section 292 I.P.C., it has to be kept in mind that the corrupting influence of these pictures is more likely to be upon the younger generation who has got to be protected from being an easy prey to these libidinous appeals upon which this illicit trade is based. The accused, therefore, cannot be dealt with leniently.[20]

6.05 Whether Sec. 292 Offends Art. 19 of the Constitution?

Sec. 292 I.P.C. does not offend Art 19 (2) of the constitution. In deciding a question whether a novel and the portions which are the subject matter of the charge must be judged by the Court in the light of the ingredients of Sec. 292 of the I.P.C. and the provisions of the Constitution. A balance should be maintained between freedom of speech and expression and public decency and morality, but when the latter is substantially transgressed, the former should give way. Obscenity without a preponderating social purpose or profit cannot have the constitutional projection of freedom of speech and expression and obscenity is treating with sex in a manner appealing to the carnal side of human nature, or is possessed with that tendency. Such a treating with sex is offensive to modesty and decency but the extent of such appeal in a particular book, etc., are matters for consideration in each of the individual cases.

The aforesaid observations were made in dealing with the book titled "Lady Chatterley's Lover" which was declared as obscene.[21]

So there are contradictory views as regards obscenity by the Supreme Court of U.S.A. and the Supreme Court of India on the same book, titled "Lady Chatterley's Lover".

In 1986, a Central Act titled, "The Indecent Representation of Women (Prohibition) Act, 1986 (referred to the Act in this book) was enacted presumably after the demand made by the woman's group in a few big cities of the country. The salient feature of this Act is that the expression "indecent representation of women" has been defined vide Sec. 2(c). Sec. 3 prohibits advertisement of indecent representation of women. Section 4 relates to prohibition of publication or sending by post of books, pamphlets, etc., containing indecent representation, the offences punishable under this Act have been made cognizable and bailable. Section 6 is titled as penalty which goes up to 5 years imprisonment and a fine up to a maximum of Rs. one lakh.

Three classes of forces have come to welcome and appreciate the Act.[22] The first consists of certain urban women group, through whose efforts the Act has come. The second group comprise of conservatives and the old-timers from the middle class houses who think that through this Act, Indian culture shall be imposed on all the advertising agencies and a respect for woman has developed among the members of the community. The third force behind the Act is the Government which thinks that it has gained popularity by catering to the public demand but the Government, in the garb of this Act, has seized the opportunity to acquire more powers for itself by enacting this toothless Act. The old law, in this respect, the Section 292–294 of I.P.C., if enforced in right earnest, is sufficient to deal with the situation. Any amount of legislation is not going to make any dent in the prevailing condition unless there is functioning sharp teeth behind the same. An ineffective law may be a piece of decoration for the Statute book and a ready explanation for the State before the public or the parliamentary forum that a law has been enacted for the benefit of the people as per demand and the law will take care of, but actually it serves no purpose. There are many journals which freely portray the different portions of woman's body in nude and semi-nude postures. One very popular weekly journal being published from Bombay would invariably portray a young woman's body in its inside pages. Of course, previously it used to print that on the last page. Advertisement of manufactured products through TV is a frequent occurrence with women. Even motor cycles advertise to show that if one possesses a motor cycle of the particular brand, young women or girls would seek lifts. Even cigarette manufacturers advertise that if one smokes a particular brand, young ladies will come near that smoker. Unfortunately, young women are also available to serve as models for such advertisements. As a matter of fact, modelling is becoming a popular career for young girls.

Modern films is another source which portray all sorts of violence against women. For instance some films starts with a rape or a gang-rape scene. At times, the young wife or the fiance of the hero (usually a Police Inspector) or the adolescent sister is shown as being kidnapped, tortured and raped in an attempt to force that honest police inspector to come to terms with the smugglers or undesirables or the mafia king and/or to hand over the relevant papers to him. Such a portrayal is not only obscene but undesirable too as the same, in addition to corrupting the young mind, teaches to the undesirables, that this is the most effective weapon to take retaliatory action against the person enforcing law with all sincerity and honesty. We find in films many nasty songs rendered in a vulgar fashion than the controversial 'Choli' song of Khalnayak. More curious thing is that the same passes the scrutiny of the Censor. The film song which once used to be a piece of art with simple orchestra such as sarangi, flute, harmonium, violin, tabla, and/or mridangam, has now been replaced by worthless songs with meaningless wordings, an orchestra comprising of hundred persons or so but having no touch of Indian music which is the developed art. There is no match to our Indian system of music (both Hindustani and Karnatak) but inspite of it, our music directors and producers of films do not attach any importance to the same. It is disgusting to note that new words have been coined for the film songs such as 'ILU, ILU' or 'one, four, three' (meaning thereby, I love you). The expressions 'I love you' and a few slangs of abuses would invariably find occurring in the modern Hindi films. Frequent embracing and kissing in films has now become the order of the day. In films we find hero and heroine tightly embracing each other and rolling on the green grass innumerable times. There is no logic in portrayal of such love scenes. In the films of yesteryears love scenes could be demonstrated even without touching the body of each other and the public could appreciate even through the movement of eyes. Some films cross all limits of vulgarity as per Indian thoughts that it becomes disgusting for any Indian having a place of pride of its own culture. Such films are designed only to be a Box Office success, even by polluting the minds of the adolescents and youngmen. It is surprising that they pass the test of the Censor Board and are granted certificate under Section 6 of the Cinematographic Act.

No amount of legislation or enactment can serve any purpose unless the same is strictly enforced. The I.P.C 1860, is so perfect and complete that by making a little amendment in the punishment clause only and through strict enforcement with a purpose of honesty can set things right. More laws mean more resources for bribe money, if not honestly implemented. Our present machinery has become rotten and the need of the hour is to provide a freedom to the people from the ruffians in various fields by strictly applying the law to situation, if situation so requires. Enactment without strict enforcement is an exercise in futility.

REFRENCES

1. The Random House Dictionary of the English Literature (College Edition), Allied Publishers Pvt. Ltd., Bombay, Delhi, Calcutta, Madras, Banglore, pp. 817, Col. 2.

2. Edited by Dermot Walsh S Adrian Poole, "A Dictionary of Criminology, Second Indian Reprint (1983), Universal Book Stall," New Delhi, pp. 149.
3. *Chandrakant Kalyandas Kakodkar* Vs. *The State of Maharashtra & Others*, 1970 Cr L J 1273=AIR 1979 SC 1390.
4. Ins. by Act 36 of 1969, vide S. 2.
5. Sec. 292 was renumbered as sub-section (2) of that Section Vide Sec. 2 of Act 36 of 1969.
6. Subs. by Act 36 of 1968, vide Sec. 2.
7. *Ibid.*
8. *Ibid*
9. 1992 Cr L J 3041 (HC).
10. AIR 1974 SC 1290=1974 Cr L J 1044 (SC).
11. (1959)3 Law Ed. 2d., 1512.
12. Art 19(2) of the Constitution—*Protection of certain Rights regarding freedom of speech* etc.;

(1) All citizens shall have the right:
   (a) to freedom of speech and expression;
   (b) to assemble peaceably and without arms;
   (c) to form associations or unions;
   (d) to move freely throughout the territory of India;
   (e) to reside and settle in any part of India;
   (f) to acquire, hold and dispose of property; and
   (g) to practice any profession, or to carry on any occupation, trade or business.

(2) Nothing in sub-clause (a) of clause (1) shall affect the operation of any existing law in so far as it relates to, or prevent the State from making any law relating to libel, slander, defamation, contempt of Court or any matter which offends against decency or morality or which undermines the security of, or tends to overthrow, the State.

13. (1868) LR 3 QB 360.
14. (1948) VLR 45.
15. B K Adarsh V. U O I, AIR 1990 AP 100.
16. 1988 Cr L J 1038=(1987) CLT 659.
17. 1989 (2) OCR 34.
18. *Ranjit D Udeshi* Vs. *State of Maharashtra*, AIR 1965 SC 881=1965 (2) Cr L J 8.
19. *Rajkapor* Vs. *State*, AIR 1980 SC 258=1980 Cr L J 202=(1980) 1 SCC 43.
20. *Uttam Singh* Vs. *Delhi Administration*, AIR 1974 SC 1230=(1974) Cr L J 923=(1974) 3 SCR 722.
21. *Ranjit D Udeshi* Vs. *State of Maharashtra*, AIR 1965 SC 881= 1965 (2) Cr L J 8.
22. Madhu Kishwar & Ruth Ruth, "The Sexes" The Illustrated Weekly of India, August 7, 1988, pp. 38 (39).

THE INDECENT REPRESENTATION OF WOMEN (PROHIBITION) ACT, 1986
(Act. No. 60 of 1986)*

(23rd December 1986)

An Act to prohibit indecent representation of women through advertisements or in publications, writings, paintings, figures or in any other manner and for matters connected therewith or incidental thereto.

Be it enacted by Parliament in the thirty-seventh year of the Republic of India as follows:

1. *Short title, extent and commencement*

(1) This Act may be called the Indecent Representation of Women (Protection) Act, 1986.

(2) It extends to the whole of India, except the State of Jammu and Kashmir.

(3) It shall come into force on such date as the Central Government may, by notification in the Official Gazette appoint.

2. *Definition:*

In this Act, unless the context otherwise requires,

(a) "advertisement" includes any notice, circular, label, wrapper or other document and also includes any visible represen tation made by means of any light, sound, smoke or gas;

(b) "distribution" includes distribution by way of samples whether free or otherwise;

(c) "indecent representation of women" means the depiction in any manner of the figure of a woman, her form or body or any part thereof in such a way as to have its effect of being indecent, or derogatory to, or denigrating woman or is likely to deprave, corrupt or injure the public morality or morals;

(d) "label" means any written, marked, stamped, printed or graphic matter affixed to, or appearing upon, any package;

(e) "package" includes box, cotton, tin or other container;

(f) "prescribed" means prescribed by rules made under this Act.

3. *Prohibition of advertisements containing indecent representation of women:*

No person shall publish or cause to be published, or arrange or take part in publication or exhibition of, any advertisement which contains indecent representation of women in any form.

4. *Prohibition of publication or sending by post of books, pamphlets, etc. containing indecent representation of women:*

No person shall produce or cause to be produced, sell, let to hire, distribute, circulate or send by post any book, pamphlet, paper, slide, film, writing, drawing, painting, photograph, representation of figure which contains indecent representation of women in any form.

Provided that nothing in this section shall apply to:

(a) any book, pamphlet, paper, slide, film, writing, drawing, painting, photograph, representation of figure,

(i) the publication of which is proved to be justified as being for the public good on the ground that such book, pamphlet, paper, slide, film, writing, drawing, painting, photograph, representation of figure is in the interest of science, literature, art, or learning or other objects of general concern; or

(ii) which is kept or used bonafide for religious purposes.

(b) any representation sculptured, engraved, painted or otherwise represented on, or in

(i) any ancient monument within the meaning of the Ancient Monument and Archaeological Sites and Remains Act, 1958, or

(ii) any temple, or on any car used for the conveyance of idols, or kept or used for any religious purpose;

(c) any film in respect of which the provisions of part II of the Cinematographic Act, 1952 will be applicable.

5. *Power to enter and search:*

Subject to such rules as may be prescribed, any Gazetted Officer authorised by the State Government may, within the local limits of the area for which he is so authorised:

(a) enter and search at all reasonable times, with such assistance, if any, as he considers necessary, any place in which he has reason to believe that an offence under this Act has been or is being committed;

(b) seize any advertisement, or any book, pamphlet, paper, slide, film, writing, drawing, painting, photograph, representation or figure which he has reason to believe contravenes any of the provisions of this Act;

(c) examine any record, register, document or any other material object found in any place mentioned in clause (a) and seize the same if he has reason to believe that it may furnish evidence of the commission of an offence punishable under this Act.

Provided that no entry under this sub-section shall be made into a private dwelling house without a warrant.

Provided further that the power of seizure under the sub-section may be exercised in respect of any document, article or thing which contains any such advertisement, including the contents, if any, of such document, article or thing if the advertisement cannot be separated by reason of its being embossed or otherwise from such document, article or thing without affecting the integrity, utility of saleable value thereof.

(2) The provisions of the Code of Criminal Procedure, 1973, shall so far as may apply to any search or seizure under this Act as they apply to search or seizure made under Section 94 of the said Code.

(3) Where any person seizes anything under clause (b) or clause (c) of sub-section (1), he shall, as soon as may be, inform the nearest Magistrate and take his orders as to the custody thereof.

6. *Penalty:*

Any person who contravenes the provision of Section 3 or Section 4 shall be punishable on first conviction with imprisonment of either description for a term which may extend to two years, and with fine which may extend to two thousand rupees, and in the event of a second or subsequent conviction with imprisonment for a term of not less than six months but which may extend to five years and also with a fine not less than ten thousand rupees but which may extend to one lakh rupees.

7. *Offences by companies:*

(1) Where an offence under this Act has been committed by a company, every person, who, at the time of the offence was committed, was in charge of, and was responsible to, the company for the conduct of the business of the company, as well as the company, shall be deemed to be guilty of the offence and shall be liable to be proceeded against and punished accordingly.

Provided that nothing contained in this sub-section shall render any such person liable to any punishment, if he proves that the offence was committed without his knowledge or that he has exercised all due dilligence to prevent the commission of such offence.

(2) Notwithstanding anything contained in sub-section (1), where any offence under this Act has been committed by a company and it is proved that the offence has been committed with the consent or connivance of, or is attributable to any neglect on the part of any director, manager, secretary or other officer of the company, such director, manager, secretary, or other officer shall be proceeded against and punished accordingly.

Explanation: For the purpose of this section:

(a) "company" means any body corporate and includes firm or other association of individuals; and

(b) "director" in relation to a firm, means a partner in the firm.

8. *Offences to be cognizable and bailable:*

(1) Notwithstanding anything contained in the Code of Criminal Procedure, 1973, an offence punishable under this Act shall be bailable.

(2) An offence punishable under this Act shall be cognizable.

9. *Protection of action taken in good faith:*

No suit, prosecution or other legal proceeding shall be against the Central Government or any officer of the Central Government or any State Government for anything which is in good faith done or intended to be done under this Act.

10. *Power to make rules:*

(1) The Central Government may, by notification in the Official Gazette, make rules to carry out the provisions of this Act.

(2) In particular and without prejudice to the generality of the foregoing power, such rules may provide for all or any of the following matters, namely:

(a) any manner in which the seizure of advertisement or other articles shall be made, and the manner in which the seizure list shall be prepared and delivered to the person from whose custody any advertisement or other articles has been seized;

(b) any other matter which is rendered to be, or may be prescribed.

(3) Every rule made under this Act shall be laid, as soon as may be after it is made before each House of Parliament, while it is in session for a total period of thirty days, which may be comprised in one session or in two more successive sessions, and if, before the expiry of the session immediately following the sessions or the successive sessions aforesaid, both Houses agree in making any modifications in the rule or both Houses agree that the rule should not be made, the rule shall, thereafter, have effect only in such modified form or be of no effect, as the case may be, so however, that any such modification or annulment shall be without prejudice to the validity of anything previously done under that rule.

Chapter 7

Dowry and Dowry Related Crimes

7.01 What is Dowry?

Dowry has been defined in Section 2 of the Dowry Prohibition Act, 1961 (28 of 1981) in the following words:

"Dowry" means any property or valuable security given or agreed to be given either directly or indirectly;

(a) by one party to a marriage to the other party to the marriage; or

(b) by the parents of either party to a marriage or by any other person to either party to the marriage or to any other person,

at or before any time after the marriage in connection with the marriage of the said parties but does not include dower or mehr in the case of persons to whom the Muslim Personal Law (Sariat) applies.

Explanation I: Omitted by Act 63 of 1984.

Explanation II: The expression "valuable security" has the same meaning as in Section 30 of the Indian Penal Code 45 of 1869.

Sec. 30 Valuable Security:

The words "valuable security" denote a document which is, or purports to be, a document whereby any legal right is created, extended, transferred, restricted, extinguished or released or whereby any person acknowledges that he lies under legal liability, or has not a certain legal right.

Illustration

'A' writes his name on the back of a bill of exchange. As the effect of this endorsement is to transfer the right of the bill to any person who may become the lawful holder of it, the endorsement is a valuable security.

Previously, according to Hindu customs, women had no right to property; either of the parents or of the husband's family. Therefore, parents used to give to their daughters in marriage all the essential items required for starting a new establishment. The articles usually comprised of essential furnitures, utensils, clothes, jewellery and cash as per the status of the two families and the desire of girls parents. Such gifts began to be called as dowry. There never used to be any demand from the bridegroom side. In course of time, many luxurious items came in the market and began to be used and those items were included in the gifts, either voluntarily or through compulsion. The groom party started giving a list of items expected to be given as dowry and the bride's party either agreed or made amendments and requested for some relief. Marriage started being settled on the basis of items agreed to by the bride's party. As time passed on, the list became so costly that it became very difficult and disproportionate to the capacity of the bride's party. What a bridegroom or his parents could not manage themselves started asking the other side to provide. For instance, the author knows the case of a marriage wherein a petty clerk in a district court asked his would be father-in-law to give him a suit length worth Rs. 7000 plus stitching charges and a pair of shoes worth Rs. 2000. In one case the would be son-in-law asked his would be father-in-law to entertain the barat party in a Five-Star Hotel with scotch. The greed of the parents becomes unlimited. To quote for instance, a couple of illustrative cases are mentioned below:

(1) The parents of a Ph. D. girl, Dr. A.S., settled the marriage of their daughter, with a boy wherein the terms of dowry had been settled. Among other things, the boy's parents put a condition that the bride in question should not be a serving girl. However, since Dr. A.S., happened to be a highly

qualified girl and she had earlier applied for some posts at various places, she got an interview call from the UPSC. Her father was not in favour of sending the girl for the interview as her would-be home wanted a domestic girl and not a serving girl. But the mother intervened and therefore, the girl appeared in the UPSC before the Selection Committee.

Four days after this interview, was the date fixed for celebration of the engagement ceremony. The bride's parents made all the necessary arrangements and remained waiting for the other side to come as fixed earlier but they did not turn up. This incident was frustrating for the bride's party. Subsequent to that, the groom's guardian informed the girl's father that since the boy had gone outside the home on that day, they did not turn up. The girl's father was called to discuss certain matters concerning the marriage. Following the command of groom's parents, the poor bride's father went. Here he was given another list which was an amended one. In it, the bride father's liability increased. He, however, promised to inform after he would arrange for the new list. When he discussed the matter with his wife, she made a blatant refusal holding that the greed of this man had no limit and she denied giving her daughter in marriage to such a family.

The result of the UPSC was favourable to the girl and she got the appointment under the Ministry of Home Affairs which she joined and is happily serving the department.

(2) Mr. P settled the marriage of his M.Sc. (Phy.) daughter with a Navy Lieutenant boy, son of Mr. R. The terms of marriage was a substantial amount of dowry including cash, ornaments, clothes, both sides expenditure, utensils, furniture plus the price of a new Maruti car. This costed nearly four lakhs. One day just before the marriage Mr. P went to meet Mr. R to finalise itemwise programme. Mr. R told Mr. P to see the room which his daughter and son-in-law was to occupy in the house. Inside the room, Mr. R told Mr. P that the room lacked only an electric fan and curtain and Mr. P should provide these. Here Mr. P had no way but to agree to that. This can aptly be said to be a shameless demand as

after having taken such a huge sum, the greedy R did not hesitate to make a demand for a few hundreds more. The family did not have the car culture and the father-in-law did not purchase the car for his son and daughter-in-law but instead he pocketed the money.

7.02 Torturing Brides

As times have passed, the greed for dowry has taken a violent form. A newly married girl is harassed, tortured, abused, battered and vexed to the extent that the married girls are killed by pouring kerosene oil and the death is declared as accident or suicide. It is pertinent to note that only the brides have accidents in kitchen and not any other inmate of the house. A large number of such cases are hall marks of the capital city. In 1978, it could be realised that many of such deaths were shown to appear as accidents. The usual plea taken in such cases is that the victim caught fire in her clothes in the kitchen while cooking. As a matter of fact the mother-in-law or the sister-in-law never becomes a victim of such accidents. Since such incidents take place within the four walls of the house where none other than the inmates are present, no eye witness is available to prove the ghastly crime and the cases end in acquittal. There is not even 2 percent convictions.[1] According to police figures 1639 woman fell victim to dowry deaths in India. This is only a tip in the iceberg as there are several times more cases which either go undetected or unreported. The State Minister of Home is reported to have admitted on the floors of the Parliament on 16.12.91 that figures for the reported cases of dowry deaths in capital alone were 99, 108, 110, and 111 during the years 1988, 1989, 1990, and 1991 respectively.[2] Our newspapers are full of such news, instances of a few are mentioned below:

(1) Lata and Geeta, the two sisters were married to two sons of a foreman sometime in Feb-Mar 1987. Geeta and her husband were working as orderlies in a nearby nursing home. According to Geeta's complaint, their in-laws had been asking for more dowries since the day of the marriage although their brother is reported to have provided dowries beyond his means.

On April 26, 1988, a heated argument took place between the sisters and in-laws. On April 27, the two sisters went to the local hospital for a check up as Geeta was pregnant. On return they retired to their bed-rooms. Lata then came out of her room shrieking, "He has fed me with poison" and reportedly gasped vomiting. She was removed to hospital. She was unfit to give a statement and, thereafter, she died after four days of hospitalisation. An inquest was ordered by the S.D.M. The in-laws at first denied but under sustained questioning, they confessed to the crime. Arrest of Lata's husband, Geeta's husband, father-in-law and mother-in-law and sister-in-law was made in this connection.[3]

(2) Manju was married to Om Prakash in 1988 and in 1990, she went to live with her in-laws in Tota Ka Nagla village in Bulandshahr district. On July 21, 1993, her brother-in-law came to her mother, Basanti Devi in Delhi and told that Manju was seriously ill. Basanti Devi went to see her daughter but could not locate her. She was told that she died on 19.7.93 and cremated on the same day. Basanti Devi was told by her grand-daughter (the daughter of Manju) that her mother died of burn injuries. The unfortunate part of the episode is that when Basanti Devi went to register her complaint at the Kakod P.S., officials refused to register a case and asked her to go.[4]

(3) The East-District Police on March 24, 1991 seized a half burnt body of a woman from the cremation ground in Seelampur where she was reportedly cremated under suspicious circumstances by her in-laws.

The woman Vanita, 28 was married to Rajesh in 1987 and reportedly had strained relations with her in-laws. She is survived by her two year daughter. A few days back she reportedly had strained relations with her in-laws who reportedly threatened her with dire consequences.[5]

(4) The Additional and Sessions Judge Kangra (HP) convicted Shaunki Ram (Sulochna's husband), Manga Devi (Mother-in-law), Prito Devi (sister-in-law) and Mehr Chand (brother-in-law) and sentenced them to life imprisonment and fined for murdering 23 year old Sulochna Devi at Majharna village in Palampur sub-division on December 25, 1987 alleg-

edly for having brought less dowry as well as the husband wanted to remarry.[6]

(5) Jaswinder Kaur (21) was poisoned to death by her in-laws in village Maksudpur (Kapurthala district) after three years of her marriage allegedly for bringing less dowry although the father asserted that he has given sufficient dowry including such luxury items like TV and fridge besides gold ornaments and other items.[7]

(6) As many as 48 cases of bride-burning have been reported in Bihar for six months period commencing from September 1987. One Mrs. Savita Devi was murdered by her in-laws for bringing insufficient dowry.

According to D.I.G. (Atrocities against Harijans and women) the figures do not reveal the true pictures as many women might have been killed in Bihar villages which have not come to the notice of administration. Suppression of women is a fact of life in most parts of Bihar for not bringing adequate dowry. He, as well blamed the parents for this malady who remain a passive spectators of the harassment being meted out to their daughters. They wake up only when it is too late. To prove his point he cited the case of one Ragini Upadhaya whose parents did not even lodge F.I.R. till four days after her husband had burnt her to death. He cited another case of Mrs. Ruby Devi wherein her own family members supported the killer husband. Justice in the two cases could be meted out only through the efforts of women's organisation in the city.[8]

Kerala's long tradition of women being educated and then going on to earn their livelihood as nurses, teachers, secretaries apart from other professions seems to have fallen victim to the State's increasingly materialistic and consumerist society.

On November 4, 1989, four Palghat sisters committed suicide through hanging and left a suicide note whose undermentioned words highlight the Dowry problem in the State.[9]

Text of the suicide note:

"Our parents are yet to pay fully the dowry for our sister who was married sometime ago. Having sold our land and gold required for this marriage, we are not sure whether they will be able to provide anything for our marriage. Hence the decision to end our lives."

It was a well thought-out decision of the sisters that originated in deep desperation and despair. What disillusioned these young girls was the plight of their married sister Bhagyamani, married off with a cash dowry of Rs. 5000 and jewellery worth Rs. 30,000. Bhagyamani's husband, a jobless youth, wanted more and more and finally a share in 1.5 acres of land of the family.

The girls reasoned that their death could be a blessed release for their persecuted parents who might weep for a moment but finally will be relieved of the unbearable burden. This was the reaction in consequence of the marriage proposal of Santha, a VII Class student the eldest of the four whose marriage proposal aborted because of the non-availability of the dowry which led them to take this fatal decision.

Even the Syrian Christian community in Central Kerala, educated and affluent has several dowry deaths to its credit. For instance Valsamma, the daughter of a Bank officer was married to Mathew, a clerk in the local Funds Account Department with a dowry of Rs. one lakh and jewellery worth Rs. one lakh. Having exhausted the total amount of dowry, the husband started demanding a share in her father's property. He was joined by her mother who demanded consumer items like fridge. The harassment upset the newly married girl who ended her life by jumping into the well.

Another victim was Jessy Cherion, a graduate, hailing from a rich family in Ala. She was married to Sally Cheriyan with appropriate dowry, but she was allegedly subjected to physical and mental torture in the family pursuit for more dowry. They even removed her six year old son from her, driving her to end her life in desperation.

The demand for dowry in Kerala as in other states, varies according to the status of the bridegroom. Thus a boy in Civil Service, engineers, doctors, Bank Officers and others in the status of an officer collect lakhs even when the girl is employed and contributes to the family income as the boy himself. The greed for status symbol like TV, fridge, car, air-conditioner in every part of the country has contributed to the growing harassment of young brides.

Incidentally most girls in Kerala are educated and a substantial number of them are employed and have the opportunity to mix with men but still they believe in arranged marriages where dowry is a pre-condition. None of them have the courage to raise a voice against the giving of dowry and making it a pre-condition for settlement of marriage.

7.03 Amending Criminal Law

To meet the disquieting situation, Chapter XXA and a new section 498-A has been inserted into the I.P.C. (1860) by Criminal Law Amendment Act (No 46 of 1983) and according to it:[10]

"whoever, being the husband or the relatives of the husband of the woman, subjects such woman to cruelty shall be punished with imprisonment for a term which may extend to three years and shall also be liable to fine."

"Cruelty" for the purpose of this Section means:

(a) any willful conduct which is of such a nature as is likely to drive the woman to commit suicide or to cause grave injury or danger to life, limb or health (whether mental or physical) of the woman; or

(b) harassment of the woman where such harassment is with a view to cocrce her or any person related to her to meet any unlawful demand for any property or valuable security or is on account of failure by her or any person related to her to meet such demand."

The offence under Section 498-A is cognizable if information relating to the commission of the offence is given to an officer in charge of a police station by the person aggrieved by the offence or by any person related to her by blood, marriage or adoption or if there is no such relative, by any public servant. The offence is also non-bailable and triable by a First Class Magistrate.

A new Section (Sec. 304-B) has been inserted vide Section 10 of Act no. 43 of 1986, with effect from 19.11.1986 and runs as follows:

304-B. Dowry Death:

(1) Where the death of a woman is caused by any burns or bodily injury or occurs otherwise than under normal circumstances within seven years of marriage and it is shown that soon before her death, she was subjected to cruelty or harassment by her husband or any relative of her husband for, or in connection with any demand for dowry, such death shall be called "dowry death", and such husband or relative shall be deemed to have caused her death.

Explanation: For the purpose of this sub-section, "dowry" shall have the same meaning as in Section 2 of the Dowry Prohibition Act, 1961 (28 of 1961).

(2) Whoever commits dowry deaths shall be punished with imprisonment for a term which shall not be less than seven years but which may extend to imprisonment for life.'

The offence is cognizable, non-bailable and triable by a Court of Sessions.

7.04 Presumption as to Proof in Such Cases

'Sec. 113-A of Evidence Act—Presumption as to abetment of suicide by a married woman:

When the question is whether the commission of suicide by a woman has been abetted by her husband or any relative of her husband and it is shown that she had committed suicide within a period of seven years from the date of her marriage and that her husband or such relative of her husband has subjected her to cruelty, the court may presume, having regard to all the other circumstances of the case, that such suicide had been abetted by her husband or by such relative of her husband.

Explanation: For the purpose of this Section, "cruelty" shall have the same meaning as in Section 498-A of the Indian Penal Code, 1860.'

For the application of this Section, three elements viz; (a) that the woman was married, (b) that she had committed suicide within seven years of marriage and (c) that her husband or such relatives of her husband had subjected her to cruelty are required to be proved.

The expression "cruelty" will carry the same meaning as defined in Section 498-A of the I.P.C.

Sec. 113-B of Evidence Act—Presumption as to dowry death[11]

When the question is whether a person has committed the dowry death of a woman and it is shown, that soon before her death such woman has been subjected by such person to cruelty or harassment for, or in connection with any demand for dowry, the court shall presume that such person has caused the dowry death.

Explanation: For the purpose of this Section, "dowry death" shall have the same meaning as in Sec. 304-B of the Indian Penal Code (45 of 1860).'

7.05 Decided Cases

(1) *Dying declaration*:

Dying declaration is a statement, written or verbal, made by a person under the expectation of death, as to the cause of death or the circumstance leading to the death. Such a declaration becomes relevant under Section 32(1) of the Evidence Act, 1872, consequent upon the death of the victim.

In murder cases, dying declaration is given a great weight in assessing the guilt of the accused. The principle on which dying declarations are admitted in evidence is indicated in legal maxim:

"nemo moriturus mentiri"- a man will not meet his maker with a lie on his mouth.

The situation in which a man is on death bed is so solemn when he is dying, the grave position in which he is placed, is the reason in law to accept the veracity of his statement. It is for this reason, the requirement of oath and cross-examination are dispensed with. Besides, should the dying declaration be dispensed with and excluded, it will result in miscarriage of justice because the victim being the only eye-witness in a serious crime, the exclusion of the statement would leave the court with a scrap evidence. The Supreme Court in several judgements have set the principles governing acceptability of dying declaration which could be summed up as under.[12]

(i) There is neither a rule of law nor of prudence that dying declaration cannot be acted upon without corroboration—*Mannu Raja* Vs. *State of M.P.*, (1970) 2 SCR 764.

(ii) If the court is satisfied that the dying declaration is true and voluntary, it can base conviction on it without corroboration—*State of U.P.* Vs. *Ramsagar Yadav*, AIR 1985 SC 416: *Ramavati Devi* Vs. *State of Bihar*, AIR 1983 SC 164.

(iii) This court has to scrutinise the dying declaration carefully and must ensure that the declaration is not the result of tutoring, prompting or imagination. The deceased had the oppurtunity to observe and identify the assailants and was in a fit state to make the declaration—*Ramchandra Reddy* Vs. *Public Prosecutor*, AIR 1976 SC 1994.

(iv) Where dying declaration is suspicious, it should not be acted upon without corroborative evidence—*Rashid Beg* Vs. *State of M.P.*, 1974 (4) SCC 264.

(v) Where the deceased was unconscious and could never make any dying declaration, the evidence with regard to it is to be rejected—*Kake Singh* Vs. *State of M.P.*, AIR 1982 SC 1021.

(vi) A dying declaration which suffers from infirmity cannot form the basis of conviction—*Ram Manorath* Vs. *State of U.P.*, 1981 SCC (cri) 581.

(vii) Merely because a dying declaration does not contain the details as to the occurrence, it is not to be rejected—*State of Maharashtra* Vs. *Krishnamurthi Laxmipati Naidu*, AIR 1981 SC 617.

(viii) Equally, merely because it is a brief statement, it is not be discarded. On the contrary, the shortness of the statement itself guarantees truth—*Surajdeo Ojha* Vs. *State of Bihar*, AIR 1979 SC 1505.

(ix) Normally the court, in order to satisfy whether the deceased was in a fit mental condition to make the dying declaration look up to the medical man for his opinion. But when the eye-witness has said that the deceased was in a fit and conscious state to make this dying declaration, the medical opinion cannot prevail—*Nanahan Ram and Another*, Vs. *State*, AIR 1989 SC 912.

(x) Where the prosecution version differs from as given in the dying declaration, the said declaration cannot be acted upon—*State of U.P.* Vs. *Madan Mohan*, AIR 1989 SC 1519.

(2) *Plurality of dying declaration:*

In the instant case, the victim made four dying declarations.

The first one was recorded by Constable Abhal Mamainya and at that time the victim, Kanta was conscious. As per this dying declaration, while the deceased was sleeping in the Osari, and father-in-law, mother-in-law and others were sleeping in the pali, at about midnight, the accused poured kerosene oil and ignited her. Because the deceased shouted, people from round about gathered and fire was extinguished. Thereafter, her father-in-law, maternal aunt-in-law and sister-in-law and two or three other persons took her in a cart.

The second dying declaration was recorded by the Taluka Magistrate Bhalchandra Prabhashanker Trivedi at 6 am after ascertaining from the doctor whether she was in a fit condition of health. This recording was done while only the doctor was allowed in the room. It was in question and answer form. According to this, while she was sleeping in the osari, her mother-in-law poured kerosene.

The deceased's father came at 7.30 am. After the recording of declaration the Magistrate had ended. The oral declaration made to her father Jadav revealed that her mother-in-law had poured kerosene oil. Jadav impressed the trial court as a truthful witness.

The fourth dying declaration was recorded by the Sub-Inspector Tavade. This recording had been rightly discarded by the court. The court believed the other dying declarations placing reliance on the judgement in *Mohan Lal* Vs. *State of Maharashtra*;[13] wherein the Supreme Court had held, that where there are more than one in statement in the nature of dying declaration, one first point of time must be preferred. The Supreme Court while maintaining the sentence awarded by the High Court expressed deep concern for women in the following words:

> "Everytime a case relating to dowry death comes up, it causes ripples in the pool of conscious of this Court. Nothing could be more barbarous, nothing could be more henious than this sort of crime. The root cause of killing young bride or daughter-in-law is avarice and greed. All tender feelings which along make the humanity noble, disappear from the heart. Kindness, which is the hallmark of human culture is buried. Sympathy to the fairer sex, the minimum sympathy

is not even shown. The seedling which is uprooted from the original soil and is to be planted in another soil to grow and bear fruits, is crushed."

(3) Whether Sec. 304-B has retrospective application ?

A substantive provision creating a new offence has no retrospective effect. Where the death of the victim took place on 13.6.1986 and the new Section came into force with effect from 19.11.1986, the accused is protected under Article 20 (1) of the Constitution, as held by the Supreme Court in case of *Soni Devraj Bhai* Vs. *State of Gujrat.*[14]

(4) Whether presumption u/S 113 B is rebuttable ?

If a case under the provisions of the Dowry Act or the penal provision related to it, is established, then the courts are to be stringent in dealing with the culprits. However, the cardinal principle of criminal law that until guilt is established, the person accused of it should not be punished only because a lesson is to be given to the person involved in the crime or the court is morally satisfied about the commission of the crime. The courts, while taking stringent view and despite the obligation of making the Legislative enactment a success, have also to keep in mind that the charge should be made out.[15]

Where the suicide by wife was within seven years of the marriage through intake of insecticides, and during investigation, it was not disclosed that the husband or any of the relatives was oppressive, or in any manner cruel towards the deceased. The fact of maltreatment came up only during the trial. It was held that the prosecution has failed to prove that the husband was guilty of cruelty towards his wife. The court declined to apply presumption under section 113-B of the Ev. Act.[16] But where the wife died by hanging within one year of marriage and only two witnesses, father and brother of the deceased were examined to prove the maltreatment and harassment meted out to the deceased because of demand of dowry, held that the prosecution case was established and only two witnesses, being relatives to the deceased did not come in the way of conviction of the accused.[17]

In the case of *Mohanlal & Another* Vs. *The State of Punjab,*[18] the admitted position was that the wife had committed suicide by burning herself. Her husband and the mother-in-law were cited as accused who had allegedly abetted her to commit suicide. There was no allegation about the accused being present at the time of the occurrence. The only evidence was that on other occasions they used to maltreat the deceased and used to tell her that she has not brought sufficient dowry. This fact was not taken as sufficeint to connect the accused with the crime. On the other hand in case of *Smt. Shyama Devi* Vs. *State of West Bengal* (DB)[19] in Cr Appeal No. 183 decided on Feb. '20 , 1987 by the Calcutta High Court, the evidence of the relatives of the deceased without being corroborated from any person outside the family or residing in the vicinity of the house of the in-laws, was taken to be sufficient evidence regarding the demand of dowry and torture or harassment to the lady.

In the case of *Wazir Chand and Another* Vs. *State of Haryana,*[20] burn injuries sustained by housewife caused her death. The prosecution case was that the victim committed suicide by setting herself on fire. The evidence regarding the smell of kerosene from the clothes of the deceased, improbability of sustaining burn injuries accidently from stove, deliberate delay in taking the deceased to the hospital or to a nursing home, deliberately avoiding her to be taken to Civil Hospital and instead taking her to a nursing home where sufficient medical aid in respect of burn injuries was not available and suppressing cries of the victim by putting on loudly a radio or a T.V. set being insufficient, were not found reliable and the conviction under Section 306 was not sustained. However, the conviction under Section 498A was sustained because of the material on record relating to repeated dowry demand made and harassment meted out to was deceased housewife by accused husband and father-in-law.

In the case of *P.B. Bikashpathi and Others* Vs. *The state of A.P.,*[21] drinking and coming late of the husband coupled with beating and demanding dowry was taken to amount to cruelty, as defined in Sec. 498A I.P.C. in view of the legal effects of Section 113B of the Evidence.

7.06 Conclusion

Unfortunately young girls in India are taught to be docile, respectful who should serve the parents of the husband and worship the husband as 'Pati Parmeshwar'. They are hardly taught to retaliate against injustice being perpetrated against them. They must be taught to save themselves before it is too late after pouring kerosene oil. At least, they can firmly catch the person lighting matches on her body. The author knows a case, where a highly affluent boy started beating his wife, who had also come with a good amount of dowry and this continued for sometime. One day the wife also beat her husband in retaliation and that day was the end of her ordeal.

The parents, if possible, give necessary training in Judo and Karate to the girls which may serve as a protective weapon at all times.

REFERENCES

1. Rukmani Anandani, "Documenting Violence against Women" *Hindustan Times* (Delhi Edition), dated 18.2.89.
2. News Item, "3186 Cases of crimes against women, in 91," *Hindustan Times*, Delhi Edition, dated 17.12.91.
3. By a Staff Reporter, "In-Laws held for poisoning woman" *Times of india*, dated 5.5. 1988.
4. H.T. Correspondent, "Mystery surrounds death" *Hindustan Times* (Delhi Edition), 7.8.93.
5. "Police seize Half-burnt body of women" *H T* (Delhi Edn.), dated 26.3.91.
6. From Correspondent,"Life term for four in dowry death" *Tribune*, dated 3.1.1989.
7. Express News Service, "Dowry Death Alleged", *Indian Express* (Chandigarh Edition), dated 26.10.1986.
8. Times of India News Service, "Bride- burning cases in Bihar go unreported". *Times of India*, dated 7.4.1988.
9. Leena Menon, "News Watch—Who killed the Palghat Sisters" *Indian Express*, dated Dec. 4, 1989.
10. Vide Section 7 of the Criminal Law (Amendment) Act No. 46 of 1983.
11. Ins. in the Dowry Prohibition (Amendment) Act, 1986.
12. *Paniben* Vs. *State of Gujrat*, I (1992) CCR 1100(SC).
13. AIR 1982 SC 839.
14. I (1992) CCR 59(SC).
15. *Gurditta Singh* Vs. *State of Rajasthan*, I(1992) CCR 471 (DB).
16. *Ashok Kumar* Vs. *State of Punjab*, 1987 Cr L J 1412.
17. *Dalip Singh and Others* Vs. *State of Punjab*, (1988) (1) Crime 211.
18. 1984 Chandigarh Law Reporter, 647.
19. Cited in Para 16 of the Judgement by the Rajasthan High Court in *Gurditta Singh* Vs. *State of Rajasthan*, I (1992) CCr 471 (DB).
20. 1989 SCC (Cri) 105.
21. 1989 Cr L J 1181.

Chapter 8

Criminal Assaults

8.01 Introduction

By criminal assault, we mean sexual assault in the form of rape. This expression has been defined vide Section 375 of the Indian Penal Code, 1860, in the following words:

375 Rape: A man is said to commit "rape" who, except in the case hereinafter excepted, has sexual intercourse with a woman under circumstances falling under any of the six following descriptions:

Firstly: Against her will.

Secondly: Without her consent.

Thirdly: With her consent, when her consent has been obtained by putting her or any person in whom she is interested in fear of death or of hurt.

Fourthly: With her consent, when, the man knows that he is not her husband, and that her consent is given because she believes that he is another man to whom she is or believes herself to be lawfully married.

Fifthly: With her consent, when, at the time of giving such consent, by reason of unsoundness of mind or intoxication or the administration by him personally or through another of any stupefying or unwholesome substance, she is unable to understand the nature and consequences of that to which she gives consent.

Sixthly: With or without her consent, when she is under sixteen years of age.

Explanation: Penetration is sufficient to constitute the sexual intercourse necessary to the offence of rape.

Exception: Sexual intercourse by a man with his own wife, the wife not being under fifteen years of age, is not rape.

Local amendment:

(Introduced prior to Act 43 of 1983 by Act 30 of 1950)

Manipur: In its application to the Union Territory of Manipur, in Section 375:

(a) in clause Fifthly, for the word "Sixteen" substitute the word "Fourteen", and

(b) in the Exception, for the word "fifteen" substitute the word "thirteen".

Out of the total rape cases reported in the country during the year 1991, 24.9 percent cases (2596) were reported from Madhya Pradesh, followed by Uttar Pradesh with 13.6 percent (1417) cases, Maharashtra with 8.905 percent (906) cases, Bihar with 8.63 percent (878) cases, Rajasthan with 7.892 percent (803) cases and Andhra Pradesh with 6.526 per cent (665) cases and these six states taken together account for nearly 70 percent of the cases.

Among the seven Union Territories, a total of 236 cases have been reported out of which Delhi accounts for 90.7 percent of the cases (214) while Lakshdweep has the unique distinction of no case of rape.

The agewise distribution is as under:

Below 10 years	1099
Between 10 to 18 years	2630
Between 18 to 30 years	5377
30 years and above	1319

Victims of rape were highest in the age-group 18–30 years which accounted for 51.7 percent. However, it is a matter of grave concern that in recent years 'Paedophilia', that is child rape (Children below 10 years) have increased manifold, that is from 394 in 1990 to 1099 in 1991. This was due to sharp rise of 1284.6 percent in Uttar Pradesh and 186.4 percent in Madhya Pradesh. In the Union Territory of Delhi 32 cases of child rape were reported during the year 1991 as against none during the three years period from 1988 to 1990.[1]

8.02 Punishment for Rape

Commission of rape on the person of a woman is the worst form of crime which imparts on the victim a life-long stigma inspite of the fact that the act is committed forcibly without her consent. Section 376 of the I.P.C. prescribes punishment which till 1983 used to be imprisonment for life or with imprisonment of either description which may extend to 10 years and shall also be liable to fine, unless the woman raped is his own wife and is not under 12 years of age in which case he shall be punished with imprisonment of either description for a term which may extend to two years, or with fine, or with both.

This was the position which existed previously but an important incident occurred in Maharashtra which envied widespread resentment. In that case a 15 year rustic married woman approached the Police Station to lodge a complaint in some case but the accused constable at the Police Station instead of looking into her grievance raped her and a colleague of the same constable made attempts at rape against her. The Sessions Judge acquitted the accused person, the High Court awarded five years imprisonment and on an appeal before the Supreme Court, the Apex Court restored the judgement of the Trial Court.[2] As a result of the widespread resentment, an amendment in the rape laws were made. Section 375 was changed by making substitutions in Clause 'thirdly' and 'fifthly' and inserting Clause 'sixthly' Section 376 was changed and four new Sections viz; 376A, 376B, 376C and 376D were inserted. The amended Section 376 and the new Sections so introduced run as under:

"376 Punishment for Rape[3]

(1) Whoever, except in the cases provided for by sub-section (2), commits rape shall be punished with imprisonment of either description for a term which shall not be less than seven years but which may be for life or for a term which may extend to ten years and shall also be liable to fine unless the woman raped is his own wife and is not under twelve years of age, in which case, he shall be punished with imprisonment of either descrip-

tion for a term which may extend to two years or with fine or with both.

Provided that the court may, for adequate and special reasons to be mentioned in the judgement, impose a sentence of imprisonment for a term of less than seven years.

(2) Whoever:

(a) being a police officer commits rape:

(i) within the limits of the police station to which he is appointed; or

(ii) in the premises of any Station House whether or not situated in the police station to which he is appointed; or

(iii) on a woman in his custody or in the custody of a police officer subordinate to him; or

(b) being a public servant, takes advantage of his official position and commits rape on a woman in his custody as such public servant or in the custody of a public servant subordinate to him; or

(c) being on the management or on the staff of a jail, remand home or other place of custody established by or under any law for the time being in force or of a women's or children's institution takes advantage of his official position and commits rape on any inmate of such jail, remand home, place or institution; or

(d) being on the management or on the staff of a hospital, takes advantage of his official position and commits rape on woman in that hospital; or

(e) commits rape on woman knowing her to be pregnant; or

(f) commits rape on a woman when she is under twelve years of age; or

(g) commits gang rape,

shall be punished with rigorous imprisonment for a term which shall not be less than ten years but which may be for life and shall also be liable to fine.

Provided that the court may, for adequate and special reasons to be mentioned in the judgement, impose a sentence of imprisonment of either description for a term of less than ten years.

Explanation 1: Where a woman is raped by one or more in a group of persons acting in futherance of their common intention, each of the person shall be deemed to have committed gang rape within the meaning of this sub-section.

Explanation 2: "Women's or children's institution" means an institution, whether called an orphanage or a home for neglected women or children or a widow's home or by any other name, which is established and maintained for the reception and care of women or children.

Explanation 3: "Hospital" means the precincts of the hospital and includes the precincts of any institution for the reception and treatment of persons during convalescence or of person requiring medical attention or rehabilitation.

376-A Intercourse by a man with his wife during separation:

Whoever has sexual intercourse with his own wife, who is living separately from him under a decree of separation or under any custom or usage without her consent, shall be punished with imprisonment of wither description for a term which may extend to two years and shall also be liable to fine.

376-B Intercourse by public servant with woman in his custody:

Whoever, being a public servant, takes advantage of his official position and induces or seduces, any woman, who is in his custody as such public servant, or in the custody of a public servant subordinate to him, to have sexual intercourse with him, such sexual intercourse, not amounting to the offence of rape, shall be punished with imprisonment of either description for a term which may extend to five years and shall also be liable to fine.

376-C Intercourse by Superintendent of jail, remand home, etc.:

Whoever, being the superintendent or manager of jail, remand home or other place of custody established by or under any law for the time being in force or of the women's or children's institution takes advantage of his official position and induces or seduces any female inmate of such jail, remand home, place or institution to have sexual intercourse with him, such sexual intercourse not amounting to the offence of rape, shall be punished with imprisonment of either description for a term which may extend to five years and shall also be liable to fine.

Explanation 1: "Superintendent" in relation to a jail, remand home or other place of custody or a women's or children's institution includes a person holding any other office in such jail, remand home, place or institution by virtue of which he can exercise any authority or control over the inmates.

Explanation 2: The expression "women's or children's institution" shall have the same meaning as in Explanation 2 to sub-section (2) of Section 376.

376-D Intercourse by any member of the management or staff of a hospital with any women in that hospital:

Whoever, being on the management of a hospital or being on the staff of a hospital takes advantage of his position and has sexual intercourse with any woman in that hospital such sexual intercourse not amounting to the offence of rape shall be punished with imprisonment of either description for a term which may extend to five years and shall be liable to fine.

Explanation: The expression "hospital" shall have the same meaning as in explanation 3 to sub-section (2) of Section 375.

A disquieting feature of the pattern of crime that is emerging now is that the members of the police force, by and large, are the main indulgent. Whoever turns to the pages of newspaper, he comes across such news. As a matter of fact, policemen are supposed to provide protection to the weak, infirm and the women. There are instances that even legislatures have been indulged in such criminal acts. The incidence of gang-rape, incestuous sex-activities and paedophelia are on increase. Instances are that even a child of four months have not been spared.

8.03 Criminal Assaults Committed by Policemen

There are a large number of cases of rapes being committed by policemen are on record. However, a few cases are cited by way of example:

(1) On the night of February 19/20, 1988, a number of policemen including homeguards and chowkidars invaded a small tribal village, Pararia, falling within Deoghar district of Bihar situated only 30 miles away from the district headquarters and committed rape on village women. Initially no police

case was instituted which invited widespread resentment and some political party and a woman organisation took up the matter in all seriousness. Thus a case was instituted, charge-sheet was filed and the accused persons were put on trial. The investigation being half-hearted, the outcome of the trial was the acquittal of the accused person. According to Ms. Anjana Prakash, the Assistant Public Prosecutor in the case the quality of investigation was dubious.[4]

(2) Dabi Pada is a small hamlet comprising of tribal population who are extremely poor. On the night of the 16th November 1986, a force of policemen stormed into the village and started breaking and wantonly destroying any and everything. The residents grabbed their children and ran for their lives in the nearby hills and forests where they continued for several days as shelterless.

On November 18, 1986, the policemen returned and dragged five tribals to Danpur Police Station, illegally detained them for five days during which they were brutally assaulted. On November 19, 1986, Smt. Takudi and her daughter Saman were dragged into the Police Station. Here they were beaten, sexually molested and red chilli powders were smeared on lathis and such lathis were thrashed into their private parts. They stopped only when Takudi (60 yrs) became unconscious. The victims were taken to Banswara hospital for treatment for a couple of days and then allowed to return home. On November 30, the two were again dragged to Danpur Police Station and illegally detained till the 3rd December, beaten and humiliated. Saman was again subjected to rape.[5]

(3) A police informer accompanied by another policeman went to the victim, a 27 year old woman and asked her to accompany them to the nearby police picket of the Kalkaji P.S. She reportedly resisted and the police party allegedly forced her to come alongwith them. Some four or five residents of the Jhuggi cluster went with her to the police picket. Constable 'NK', one of the accompanying policemen alongwith other staff of the police picket, allegedly bashed up the residents and they ran away. The constable then allegedly raped the woman and threatened her up with dire consequences if she reported the matter to anyone. Mean-

while other residents of the area rushed to the local leaders and apprised them of the incident. The victim was found on the roadside in a state of shock and she narrated the incident.

When the residents went to the Chitranjan Park P.S., the staff refused to register a case and they were shooed away. Some policemen are also alleged to have offered to the victim a substantial amount to get the matter hushed up. Kalkaji P.S. registered a case after intervention by the local political leaders.[6]

(4) A CRPF jawan and four others allegedly raped a 25 year old woman in front of her friend in Budha Jayanti Park on April 2, 1991. The victim had gone to the park with Satnam to meet a park employee where the Jawan took them to a wooded area where he was joined by four others. Two of them held Satnam and the rest raped her.[7]

(5) The People's Union for Democratic Rights (PUDR) conducted case studies on custodial rapes of five cases from R.K. Puram, Chandani Chowk, Seemapuri, Alaknanda and Baljit Nagar and came to the conclusion that the women were raped in active connivance with and by policemen.[8]

Alongwith these five cases, the PUDR obtained the list of custodial rape cases compiled by Delhi Police since January 1988. These 14 cases include three instances which involved the participation in the crime of civilians alongwith the police. According to the conclusion drawn by the PUDR, the victims of custodial rapes are mostly members of the city's 1.6 million labour force.

The cognizance of the case is built up, on the presumption that a case of rape is dependent on the point of denial of consent. Unless the victim exhibits a mauled body of her own as evidence of physical coercion or of the offences, as evidence of her resistance, preferably both, she is deemed to be a consenting party although evidence of rape may be from trivial circumstantial evidence to Medical report.

In the R.K. Puram case, the investigating officer allegedly put legal statutes which suggested "their building a case of consent". In this case, the woman was allegedly raped in the P.S. and let off. On her complaint on the following day, three policemen were suspended and later arrested. The ingredients of the case were criminal intimidation and committing offence in furtherance of the common intention of committing rape but initially a case under Section 376B was instituted which later on was converted to an offence under Section 376 I.P.C. The offence in addition to custodial rape was also gang rape.

In the Seemapuri case which occurred on Jan. 10, 1990, a victim, a widow migrant from Himachal Pradesh was raped by a civilian and a couple of policemen. The cops were summarily dismissed, arrested and a criminal case launched against them. Incidentally she was allegedly branded as a prostitute and she refused to identify the two constables and practically there was no charge against the constables. According to PUDR, branding her a prostitute was a weapon to silence her.

The lodging of complaints also takes some time as the woman has to muster courage and support before exposing herself as a person whose chastity has been violated. However, this delay sometimes is viewed as doubt.

Since the investigation of cases are undertaken by the fellow policemen, witnesses are afraid of coming forward to depose against a policeman.

Although an Amendment has been made in Cr. P.C. that in trial of a rape case, the statement of the victim is recorded in camera, yet how many people know this fact. The poor victim woman generally knows that the trial will be conducted in open court and all the people hearing her statement will know the story of her being sexually assaulted. On this account many incidence of criminal assault case are not even reported.

8.04 Incestuous Rape

Incest is a sexual intercourse/or marriage between two persons who are so closely related that marriage or sexual act between them are forbidden or prohibited through custom or rituals. The great difficulty in such cases is the availability of evidence as the victim and the criminal, at times, are closely related and in most cases, the victim is a dependent member of the criminal in the same house.

According to a report lodged with Hauz Khaz Police, the prosecutrix alongwith her younger brother and accused father were present in the house on April 30, 1987. The girl and her brother were watching TV when his father (45 yrs), a three-wheeler driver came into the room, took his daughter into his cot and committed criminal assault on her which was seen by a cousin of the victim and the mother, who also arrived at that time. A case was instituted but during trial, the prosecutrix and the mother turned hostile and cousin could not be available for the evidence as he was not found at the address given before the police. And what could have been a minimum of seven year jail term for criminally assaulting his minor daughter ended in acquittal.[9]

"Fathers are known to have laid down their lives to defend the honour and lives of their daughter...Here is a classic example of depraved mind and lusty father who did not pause for a while before satisfying his carnal desire with his own flesh and blood."[10]

The above-mentioned remarks were given by the Metropolitan Magistrate Mr Pratap Chadha of Sahadara in case against Prem Chand for raping his own daughter, whose mother had left the home on account of his extramarital relationship with one Snehlata. On November 2, 1990 Prem Chand allegedly raped his daughter with the help of his mistress Sneh Lata who held her hands during the act. This became a frequent act till she became pregnant and had abortion and finally she went to her mother and narrated her tale and the matter was reported in the Seelampur P.S. on August 20. Unfortunately on Aug. 23., an A.S.I. of Police threatened the girl if she opened her mouth.

A 53 year old man was arrested for allegedly raping his recently widowed daughter-in-law in Tilak Vihar on 8.2.1990 while the daughter-in-law was sleeping in one of the rooms of the house when the father-in-law committed this act. She cried out when the accused was nabbed by the neighbours.[11]

Millions of present day adults are victims of incest. A recent study in the U.S. has brought on to the surface that 12 to 15 million female children are subjected to incestuous abuse every year. Response to incest are radically varied and it ranges from trauma to acceptance, denial to open admission, depression, guilt, shame or indifference. In this, the social beasts not only exploit the weak but display utter depravity of character. One 'BK' of Tilak Nagar in Delhi was so shamed on account of the cousin's lust that she burnt herself in bath room of her house after recording the story of her plight in the walls of her bathroom.[12]

8.05 Retaliatary Action by the Victims

'Ge' was attempting to force his daughter 'Sa' for the past three years to enter into an incestuous relation with him. One afternoon, while he was trying to force his evil design on the hapless girl where he lowered the daughter with a rod and the rod came down on 'Sa's' shoulders who, cried with pain and fear, mustered courage to snatch the rod from her father's hand and inflicted a deadly blow on his head which ended the sordid tale that was supposed to follow.

A woman, mother of three, went to the toilet during midnight was met by her brother-in-law roaming around. The fellow tried to sexually assault her. She accompanied her to a room where she castrated him with a blade which she was carrying.[13]

Where rape was committed on a blind girl who was a helpless person on account of her physical infirmity caused by the blindness and in a sexual assault on her there was no injury on her person except an abrasion on her cheeks, the court held that the probability factors are so overwhelming that it would amount to adding insult to the injury to insist on corroboration. Conviction therefore, could be maintained.[14]

Where the victim girl was first waylaid by her agnatic uncle, Gagan Behari Samal and liquor was forced into her mouth and, thereafter, she was tied to a chair and raped by the said uncle and another person, Prafulla, the Supreme Court of India, recorded the following:

> "Her uncontroverted testimony has been accepted by all the courts and the courts concurrently found that she was raped without her consent. It has been tried to be contended on behalf of the appellants, that the amended Section 114A of the Evidence Act was inserted into the Act after the date of commission of the instant case. Therefore, assumption as envisaged under Section 114(A) is not applicable in the instant case. This submission is of no avail as the victim girl

protested and struggled while she was subjected to sexual assaults by the accused persons. This clearly shows an absence of consent on the part of the victim girl apart from the legal presumption under Section 114(A) of the Evidence Act. The defence story is not substantiated by cogent evidence."

In result, the appeal is dismissed and order of conviction passed by the High Court is maintained.[15]

8.06 Men in High Position

The National Commission of women has found Orissa's Panchayat Raj Minister, Hon'ble Sri D. Raut, guilty of outraging the modesty of Kutra Block Chairperson, who is a lady and urged the State Government to conduct a regular trail of the accused Minister in a Criminal Court. The Commission also found the Superintendent of Police, the District Magistrate and the then sub-collector, Kutra Sundergarh, guilty of dereliction of duty in failing to protect a lady against whom offence of outraging the modesty of a woman has been committed and the act in question amounts to offence u/s 354 I.P.C.

According to the Commission, the District Magistrate played an "indifferent and timid role" and instead of trying to help the lady indulged in shielding the guilty. He was helped in this by the Superintendent of Police and the sub-collector who probably acted as an agent of the Hon'ble Minister and was rewarded with a promotion within a month of the incident. The only officer, whose conduct was above board, and indeed "irreproachable" was the Block Development Officer, who was harassed and penalised.

The necessity of enquiry arose out of a complaint filed before the National Commission for woman towards the close of October 1992 by the Chairperson of Kutra Block Panchayat, Sundergarh, Orissa. According to her, she was subjected to pressure by the Superintendent, the S.D.O. and the local police to withdraw her complaint and was forced to sign a paper and compelled to withdraw her F. I. R.[16]

Kulwant Kaur, a nurse from village Datta of Dharamkot, Beant Kaur from Moga, both in the age group of 20 years,

Sukhpal Kaur, barely 15 years from Talwara Village near Jagraon, all hailing from rural Punjab, struggling for a squalid existence and in search of job, are reported to have become victims of lustful politician, who under the promise of providing jobs to them have sexually exploited them.

Kulwant Kaur, a victim of the BSP M.L.A. B.S. Bhatti is reported to have died. Her aged parents now suffer from ignoble existence.

According to the police, the scandal came to light when Surnam Singh, an ex-serviceman resident of village Datta P.S. Dharamkot, Distt. Ferozpur in an affidavit had alleged that his daughter Kulwant Kaur had been raped by the M.L.A. at M.L.A. Hostel, Chandigarh. A regular case of kidnapping for purposes of illicit sex was recorded. The investigation revealed that the helpless girl, who later on disappeared under mysterious circumstances, had reported to have been gang-raped by B.S.P. M.L.A. Sri B.S. B. and three of his associates in the presence of her father on three consecutive nights, i.e. June 2, 3 and 4. She was assured that she would be provided with a job. During investigation several more cases of sexual exploitation by the M.L.A. came to light.[17]

8.07 Paediphilia

The last decade has seen some cases of child rape which is now taking an alarming proportion and depravity had gone to the extent where only very strict measures can cure the malady. Below are some of the instances:

(1) The facts of the case is that Siddik Singh, Pritam Singh aged about 26 years and Gurmal Singh Lal Singh aged about 25 years went to a brothel, house no. 989 at Budhwar Peth, Pune in the red-light area and had their association with women lodged therein and at the time of leaving Siddik Singh lifted four months child which was raped and thrown in well after killing. The Bombay High Court held that immediately after taking away the infant girl by accused No. 1, she was raped and the body was thrown into a well. The time factor and the circumstances of the case leave no doubt that the offence of kidnapping in the present case, would therefore, be squarely covered by the ingredients of

Section 363 and 366 of the I.P.C. The court further held that the depravity which is associated on an innocent infant and in such circumstances that the child lost its life would certainly justify the imposition of maximum punishment prescribed. It is difficult to conceive of any worse form of rape than what has happened in this case.[18]

(2) Naval Dubey, a young medical man, who was having the knowledge of anatomy of human being and the tender sexual organ of a minor (8 years) girl admitted that he, without forcibly and completely penetrating his male organ into the female sex organ of the 8 year minor girl had slightly penetrated within the labia majora or vulva or pudenda without rupturing the hymen and thereby satisfied his lust after emission of semen. The Supreme Court held that the offence of rape as defined in Sec. 375 was complete and the accused was liable to receive punishment as prescribed under Section 376 I.P.C.[19]

The Trial Court in this case acquitted the accused persons holding that the prosecution launched against the respondent was on account of enmity between the two families and the prosecution had not adduced any acceptable evidence for holding the respondent guilty of the offence under Section 376 I.P.C. The State preferred an appeal before the High Court. The Appellant also filed a Revision before the High Court challenging the legality of the Trial Court's judgement and further one Jay Rao of New York (U.S.A.) on the basis of an article relating to this incident that appeared in a German Magazine titled 'DER SPIEGEL' and after visiting Jabalpur sent a petition of grievance addressed to the Chief Justice of India with a copy of the Chief Justice of M.P. The High Court of Jabalpur disposed off the three petitions holding Nawal Dubey guilty of the offence only under Section 354 I.P.C. and sentenced him to pay a fine of Rs. 3000, in default to suffer simple imprisonment for six months and also directed a sum of Rs. 2000 out of the fine amount, if collected, to be paid to the victim as compensation.

The state did not prefer any appeal against the judgement before the Apex Court. However, the father of the victim girl has appealed before the Supreme Court and the Apex Court finding him guilty under Section 376 I.P.C. ordered the respondent to undergo R.I. for 7 years and to pay a fine of Rs. 25,000 in default, therefore of, to suffer R.I. for a further period of 1 year 6 months. The fine of Rs. 25,000, if realised, should be paid to the victim girl.

Before parting with the judgement, the S.C. pointed out with deep concern that though all sexual assaults on female child do not come to light there is an alarming and shocking increase of sexual offences committed on children. The reason assigned by the Supreme Court is that the children are ignorant of the act of rape and are not able to offer resistance and become easy prey to the desire of lusty brutes who display the unscrupulous deceitful insidious art of luring female children and young girls. Therefore, such offenders, who are menace to the civilised society should be mercilessly and inexorably punished in the severest terms. According to the Supreme Court, the judges who beared the sword of justice should not hesitate to use that sword with utmost severity and to the full and to the end if the gravity of the offences so demands.

The principal question which remains to be answered is that the father of the infant victim girl fought the case to the Supreme Court and had the satisfaction of the getting the wrong-doer punished. However, according to the facts of the case, the accused doctor had sexually abused several other girls and such specific instances never came before any court. Justice in respect of all such cases remained denied for want of any action from any quarter.

(3) On 13.7.1991, the accused Kartar Singh called Anuradha (8 years) and Divya (6 years) to his railway quarter and made the two girls sit on his right and left thighs respectively. He inserted his penis in the mouth of Anuradha and discharged semen in her mouth and on this account she vomited. The petitioner, Kartar Singh, then thrust his penis in the mouth of Divya and discharged urine in her mouth. Anuradha further told the police that the petitioner had outraged their modesty by putting his fingers into and attempting to penetrating his penis into their private parts. Anuradha also said that the appellant had also bitten on her left cheek.[20]

Held by the High Court, that so far as the charge under Section 377 I.P.C. is concerned, it consists of a carnal intercourse committed against the order of nature or in an unnatural manner by one with another person. The act of the petitioner of inserting his penis into the mouth of these two tender girls, prima facie is brutish, beastly, barbarous, depraved and lustful. Learned Counsel for the petitioner contends that the petitioner is alleged to have discharged semen in the mouth of Anuradha and after this he would not have been capable of committing any type of intercourse with the other girl, Divya alias Gullu. Thus no offence can be said to have been made out. It is difficult to agree with this contention also. The second act attributed to the petitioner is also of the same nature as the one allegedly committed by him with Anuradha. He is alleged to have discharged urine in her mouth, which, if true is equally carnal. The statement of Anuradha, prima facie, seems to inculpate the petitioner with an offence under Section 376 I.P.C. read with Section 511 I.P.C. because he made an attempt to penetrate his penis into the private part of the girls after fingering them.

The above three are representative cases cited in this volume. More cases of sexual depravity of this type are not being cited for paucity of space but the moot question is whether the law is adequate to tackle the problem associated with the incidence of child rape.

Legal experts and social activists believe that the only way to stem the root is by bringing into effect a strong and deterrent legislation. The present law is inadequate to meet the situation, so far as it relates to the rape cases. There is another case which is quoted by way of example.

8.08 Shortcoming of Amended Act

The present day law does not seem to protect the interests of rape victims. The legal procedures only make it easier for the accused to go either scot-free or escape with a minor punishment. In case *Premchand* Vs. *State of Haryana,*[21] Suman Rani was abducted and raped by one Ravi Shanker. While on his way from Bhawani Khera (from where she was abducted) to Jammu via Bhiwani, the two were checked at Patram Gate by police. They were taken to the police post, and kept in different rooms.

The two policemen then raped Suman Rani, one by one. There after Suman Rani and Ravi Shanker were taken to the Railway Station where they were left. On the said accusation, Ravi Shanker took his trial under Section 366 I.P.C. and the two constables, who gang-raped the victim under Section 376 I.P.C. In the joint trial, the Trial Court awarded seven years R.I. to Ravi Shanker and ten years R.I. to the two constables. In their appeal before the High Court, the conviction against Ravi Shanker was set aside and those against the two constables were maintained.

In appeal before the Supreme Court, the Apex Court while observing that an offence of this nature has to be dealt with condign punishment but taking into account the peculiar facts and circumstances of the case coupled with the conduct of the victim girl, do not call for minimum sentence as prescribed under Section 376(2) proviso to the Section. The proviso to the Section can be involved in the present case and a sub-minimum sentence will meet the ends of justice. The Supreme Court on the strength of this proviso reduced the sentence to 5 years, which was virtually the period undergone in sentence as under-trial prisoner.

The aforesaid judgement of the Supreme Court invited wide-spread criticism from Social Organisations and members of the legal community on the following grounds:[22]

(1) The important issue in this case was of consent on which the proof of the offence rested. The Supreme Court did not disprove the proof. Since the punishment is prescribed for the offence of rape without making any distinction whether the woman is virtuous or is a woman of easy virtue.
(2) The fact that the woman was found in the companay of a boy and the opinion of the medicolegal expert about her being 'used to sexual intercourse' was used as a weapon against the girl to reduce the gravity of the offence thereby reducing the sentence. Law does not provide any relaxation of offence committed against a women of questionable character or even prostitute who too, has rights on her person, and the law is bound to protect her rights by passing sentence appropriately in accordance with the law.
(3) The judgement of the Supreme Court has set a precedent that even public servants of the category as mentioned in

the Act can rape a girl, who is used to sexual intercourse, and taken into custody by the custodians of law and order and get away with concessioned sentence.

(4) This judgement, in effect has affected the seriousness of the Criminal Law (Amendment) No. 43 of 1983".

It is a matter of serious concern that the following portion of the sub-section (1) of Section 376, be omitted by another amendment.

"Provided that the Court may, for adequate and special reasons to be mentioned in the judgement, impose a sentence of imprisonment for a term of less than seven years."

8.09 Right of Private Defence in Sexual Assualt Cases

Section 96 to Section 106 of Chapter IV of the Indian Penal Code (1860), deals with the "Right of Private Defence". The following Sections of this Chapter are relevant in this context.

96. *Things done in private defence:*

Nothing is an offence which is done in the exercise of the right of private defence.

97. *Right of private defence of the body and of property:*

Every person has a right, subject to the restrictions contained in Section 99, to defend.

First: His own body, and the body of any other person, against any offence affecting the human body;

Secondly: The property, whether movable or nonmovable, of himself or of any other person, against any act which is an offence falling under the definition of theft, robbery, mischief, or criminal tresspass, or which is an attempt to commit theft, robbery, mischief or criminal tresspass.

99. *Act against which there is no right of private defence:*

There is no right of private defence against an act which does not reasonably cause the apprehension of death or of grievous hurt, if done, or attempted to be done, by a public servant acting in good faith under colour of his office, though that act may not be strictly justifiable by law.

There is no right of private defence against an act which does not reasonably cause the apprehension of death or of grievous hurt, if done, or attempted to be done, by the direction of a public servant acting in good faith under colour of his office, though that direction may not be strictly justifiable by law.

There is no right of private defence in case in which there is time to have recourse to the protection of the public authorities.

Extent to which the right may be exercised:

The right of private defence in no case extends to the inflicting of more harm than it is necessary to inflict for the purpose of defence.

Explanation I: A person is not deprived of the right of private defence against an act done, or attempted to be done, by the direction of a public servant as such unless he knows or has reason to believe, that the person doing the act is such public servant.

Explanation II: A person is not deprived of the right of private defence against an act done or attempted to be done, by the direction of a public servant, unless he knows, or has reason to believe, that the person doing the act is acting by such direction, or unless such person states the authority under which he acts, or if he has authority in writing, unless he produces such authority, if demanded.

100. *When the right of private defence of the body extends to causing death:*

The right of private defence of body extends, under the restrictions mentioned in the last proceeding section, to the voluntary causing of death or any other harm to the assailant, if the offence which occasions the exercise of the right be of any of the descriptions hereinafter enumerated namely:-

First: Such an assault as may reasonably cause the apprehension that death will otherwise be the consequence of such assault.

Secondly: Such an assault as may reasonably cause the apprehension that grievous hurt will otherwise be the consequence of such assault.

Thirdly: An assault with the intention of committing rape.

Fourthly: An assault with the intention of gratifying unnatural lust.

Fifthly: An assault with the intention of kidnapping or abduction.

Sixthly: An assault with the intention of wrongfully confining a person under circumstances which may reasonably cause him to apprehend that he will be unable to have recourse to the public authorities for his release.

The use of the right of private defence against criminal assault on the honour of a woman is not taken seriously and the police also keeps telling people that one should not take law in his own hand. Section 100 I.P.C. has been provided for self-defence as the law-makers were aware of the fact that police protection will not be available at all time. Clause Thirdly of Section 100 I.P.C. is an appropriate law that smashes misconceptions that murders are always intentional. What is required is the creation of an awareness among the people, particularly among women, that they have a right to save their honour even by killing a person who is trying to rape them.[23] Below are some of the cases where this rights are reported to have been exercised.

(1) Trinath hit his brother Kirtan Gaud who was trying to rape his own daughter in front of his wife and a couple of strangers. The head injuries caused on him by the hitting with an iron rod resulted in his death. Trinath was arrested on the charge of murdering his own brother. The matter came up for hearing before the Division Bench of Bombay High Court wherein the Judges, Hon'ble Mr. Justice M. Saldanha and Mr. Justice S.P. Kurudkar passed an order of acquittal to Trinath holding that right to self-defence under Clause Thirdly to Sec.100 was extended to a Third party. According to the court's judgement, this right extended to a person who tried to save a woman from being raped.

(2) One Dularibai, the wife of a Bhillai Steel Plant employee, killed her husband's friend in her own house, who, during one summer afternoon in 1985 dropped in her house in the absence of her husband with the dubious intentions. She brought him down, strangled him with an electric wire in a reflex action after which she ran out of her house. A case of murder was registered against her. During trial she stuck to

her statement. She was acquitted by the court and praised by the Judge for using her right of private defence legally available under the provisions of Section 100 I.P.C. The court further remarked "I wish more women exercised this right".

(3) There is another widely publicised case which came up in the year 1987. A policeman entered the room of a young girl staying in a room in Golden Temple at Amritsar with the intention of committing rape on her. The girl showed a great presence of mind by pretending to be resigned to fate and asked the constable to put off his dress. While commencing to do this, she grabbed his revolver and shot him dead. She was charged with the offence of murder but was acquitted under Section 100 I.P.C., Clause Thirdly.

8.10 Proposed Amendment of the Rape Laws[23]

The draft Bill on sexual violence has been prepared by a group of 11 women activists representing the National Commission for Women (NCW). If passed, the Bill is likely to achieve its objective in reducing a victim's ordeal. The following improvements have been suggested:

(1) Section 375 A is sought to be inserted. It categorises "aggravated sexual assault". It includes the following:

"(i) Sexual assault by those enjoying power or authority.
(ii) Sexually assaulting minors, mentally or physically disabled persons and pregnant woman by any person;
(iii) Protracted assault of a minor or a woman."

According to the existing law, the punishment provided under the law is a minimum of seven years in rape as such and a minimum of ten years for gang rape, custodial rape of minors with provision of a lesser sentence at the discretion of the court for adequate and special reasons to be mentioned in the judgement. This provision has been used and claim for lesser sentences has been made on its strength. To aviod this, the Bill seeks to introduce the use of discretion by the court but that discretion to reduce the sentence shall not be below the minimum mandatory sentence prescribed under the Act.

The draft Bill further focusses its attention to ensure that the sexual antecedents of a victim are not cited during the course of trial. At present, resort to this is taken in order to weaken the case of a victim in order to secure acquittal or substantial reduction in sentence of the accused.

The draft Bill, in addition, suggests a series of recommendations for recording of the medical evidence wherein it would be considered compulsory for the medical man to record the statement of the victim. It further suggests for recording of the statement of a victim below the age of 12 years by a female police officer or by a social worker in the presence of a relative or a friend and ensuring that the interrogation is done either in the victim's house or at a place of her choosing.

8.11 Conclusion

As regards the sign of a good and sound administration, it has been mentioned in 'Mahabharat' that if a beautiful and young women in costly jewellery and attractive costume fearlessly and unhesitatingly goes out of her house without requiring the need of an accompanist or a guard and returns safe that is indicative of a good and sound administration.

REFERENCES

1. Chapter X, "Victims of rape, Crimes in India,1991", National Crime Records Bureau, pp. 16–87
2. *Tukaram* Vs. *State of Maharashtra*, (1979) 2 SCC 143=1979 Scc (Cri) 381=AIR 1979SC 185=1979 Cr L J 939.
3. Section 375, 376, 376A, 376B, 376C and 376D substituted vide Sec. 3 of the Act 43 of 1983 (Amendment)Act replacing the original Section 375 and 376 I.P.C. respectively.
4. H. Sengupta, "Paradia Verdict", Rape of Justice, *India Today*, May 3, 1988 pp. 78–86.
5. Sri Lata Swaminathan, "Endless night in Dahi Pada", *Express Magazine*. Jan. 25, 1987.
6. H.T. correspondent, "Cop held for rape", *Hindustan Times* (New Delhi), dated Feb. 13, 1990.
7. H.T. Correspondent, "Alleged Rape by Jawan", *Hindustan Times* (New Delhi Edn.), dated April 4, 1991.
8. H.T. correspondent, "Rape by Policemen—Most cases drag on P.U.D.R.", *Hindustan Times* (Delhi Edn.), dated May 29, 1990.
9. H.T. News Item, "Man held for raping daughter acquitted", *Hindustan Times*, dated Aug. 2, 1987.
10. H.T. News Item, "Man in Custody for Raping Daughter", *Hindustan Times* (Delhi Edition), dated Sept. 19, 1991.

11. H.T. Correspondent, "Held for raping daughter-in-law" *Hindustan Times* (Delhi Edn.), dated Feb. 16, 1990.
12. "Crossing Bloodlines-Incest: The Unspoken Trauma", *Femina,* June 1992, pp. 6–11.
13. By a Staff Reporter, "Woman Castrates Brother-in-law", *Times of India* (Delhi Edn.), dated August 10, 1993.
14. *Rabindra Narayan Das* Vs. *State of Orissa,* I (1992) CCR 403 (Orissa).
15. *Gagan Bihari Samal& Another* Vs. *State of Orissa,* II (1992) CCR 157 (159) SC-June 92 issue.
16. Satyam Mohapatra, "Rout Found guilty by Panel", *Times of India* (Delhi Edition), dated 3.7.1993.
17. From Gobind Thukral, "Victims of a Politicians' Lust", *Hindustan Times* (Delhi Edition), dated June 21, 1993.
18. *Siddik Singh Pritam Singh* Vs. *The State of Maharashtra,* II (1993)CCR 1671 (DB) Bom. H C. June 1993 issue.
19. *Madan Gopal Kakkad* Vs. *Naval Dubey & Another,* II(1992) CCR 88 (SC)= 102 (2) crimes 168.
20 *Kartar Singh* Vs. *State* (Delhi Administration), 1993 Cr I.J. 1483.
21 *Premchand & Another* Vs. *State of Haryana,* AIR 1989 SC 937.
22 J. Purewal, "What Price Virtue", *Newswatch, The Indian Express* (Chandigarh) Feb. 1989.
23 Legal and Consumer Forum, "The Effective Legal Weapon against Rape", *Deccan Chronicle* (Hyderabad), dated Sept. 11, 1993.
24. Minu Jain, "Plugging the Loopholes" 4–10 July 1993, `*SUNDAY*'- Anand Bazar Publications, pp. 42.

Chapter 9

Matrimonial Offences

9.01 Introduction

Chapter XX of the Indian Penal Code, 1860, relates to the offences dealing with matrimonial cases. The Chapter contains seven Sections (493 to 498A). These are as under:

"493. Cohabitation caused by a man deceitfully inducing a belief of lawful marriage

Every man who by deceit causes any woman who is not lawfully married to him to believe that she is lawfully married to him and to cohabit or have sexual intercourse with him in that belief, shall be punished with imprisonment of either description for a term which may extend to ten years, and shall also be liable to fine."

Notes:

This Section is analogous to Section 375, that is; rape; and a man is said to commit "rape" who, except in the case hereinafter excepted has sexual intercourse with a woman under circumstances falling under any of the following descriptions:

"*Fourthly*: With her consent, when the man knows that he is not her husband, and that her consent is given because she believes that he is another man to whom she is or believes herself to be lawfully married."

A case of this type occurred in the second half of the 16th Century.[1] One Martin Guerre, a youngman of twenty years absconded from his village in Languedoe, under fear of being charged with theft, leaving behind his young wife and an infant son. Martin Guerre listed as a soldier and became extremely intimate with a comarade of bad character named Arnauld de Tilh (or Dutille). Eight years after the disappearance of Martin Guerre, Arnauld de Tilh appeared in the place of Martin Guerre, represented himself as Martin Guerre and since he was very intimate with Martin Guerre, he could convince that he was Martin Guerre and could carry on as an imposter successfully for several years. At the end of several years there was a quarrel with Martin's uncle when the latter denounced the former. Of the 150 witnesses, 40 swore that he was Martin Guerre, 50 were definite that he was not and the rest sixty were indecisive. Arnould was condemned after the trial.

A case of sexual exploitation by one Vaisnvavacharya (39 years) of Radhaballabh temple in the tiny city of Dehgam near Ahmedabad (Gujarat) by luring women devotees into sexual relationship has been reported by stating that the Goswami was their husband in the previous birth has been reported from Gujarat.[2]

"*494. Marrying again during lifetime of husband or wife:*

Whenever, having a husband or wife living, marries in any case in which such marriage is void by reason of its taking place during the life of such husband or wife, shall be punished with imprisonment of either description for a term, which may extend to several years, and shall also be liable to fine.

Exception: This section does not extend to any person whose marriage with such husband or wife has been declared void by a court of competent jurisdiction, nor to any person who contracts a marriage during the life time of a former husband or wife, if such husband or wife, at the time of the subsequent marriage, shall have been continually absent from such person for the space of seven years, and shall not have been heard of by such person as being alive within that time provided the person contracting such subsequent marriage shall, before such marriage takes place, inform the person with whom such marriage is contracted of the real state of facts so far as the same are within his or her knowledge."

Notes:

The act of second marriage during the lifetime of one spouse, who has not been divorced, is called 'Bigamy'. Bigamy is a matrimonial offence according to marriages law of the country. The social custom of the State of Goa is based on the family laws of the Portuguese Civil Code, 1867,[3] titled as "The Usages and Customs of Gentile Hindus of Goa." This law is incorporated in the Family Laws of the State. The Code aims at safeguarding on the "grounds of justice or convenience, the customs, religion and family organization" (viz: joint family which the Hindus were until then observing). It is a Code which recognises the Caste System; it is one which permits polygamy among Hindus; as also relegates the girl child to a second position. For both, polygamy and adoption are allowed only in the absence of a male child.

Article 3 of the Usage and Customs provides for simultaneous polygamy in specific cases including absence of issues by the wife of the previous marriage until she attains the age of 25 years; absolute absence of male issues, the previous wife having completed the age of 30 years; ten years having elapsed from the last pregnancy; and separation on any legal ground when proceeding from wife and there being no male issue among others.[4] A strong controversy blew up in Rajasthan during the year 1985 regarding the then Education Minister of the State who had a previously married wife living in his native place in Bhilwara and he was living with another woman at Jaipur and they were living together as husband and wife allegedly after their marriage in 1965 in a Jaipur temple.

Bigamy is not only an offence under the I.P.C. but is an offence under most of the Marriage and Divorce Laws; such as Parsi Marriage and Divorce Act, 1936, The Indian Christian Marriage Act, 1872, The Indian Divorce Act, 1869 (Applicable to Indian Christians), The Special Marriage Act, 1954 and the Hindu Marriage Act, 1955.

For prosecution under Section 494 I.P.C. which has been placed on the Statute book for purposes of punishing a spouse who violates the sanctity of a marriage contract by fraudulently substituting it by another to the prejudice of the aggrieved spouse. In applying this Section, a court will have to adopt an approach of practicability in so far as evidence, direct, oral or circumstantial which can prove the charge will have to be good enough and this does mean only evidence of the actual solemnisation of the marriage in keeping with religious rites and ceremonies.[5]

Proof of second marriage has great importance for prosecution of the accused in such cases. In a case, it is, therefore, necessary to allege form of marriage as well as essential ceremonies required for solemnization of a valid marriage and then to lead some evidence to prove the same.[6] The admission of the petitioner is of no avail to the complainant. The mere fact that the petitioner is photographed with the woman is itself not enough to maintain the conviction of the petitioner under Section 494 of the I.P.C.[7]

The *Bhaurao Shankar Lokhande* Vs. *The State of Maharashtra*[8] held that no conviction under Section 494 I.P.C. would be possible unless it is established that the second marriage is one that would have been valid in all respects but for the existence of the first marriage.

Where there is proof of a marriage having taken place, a presumption that all legal formalities are complied with as per Section 114 and 101 of the Evidence Act[9] and the burden to prove to the contrary is on the one challenging the validity of the marriage. This view has been culled from an old decision of the Privy Council in *Mauji Lal* Vs. *Chandrabai Kumari*,[10] where it was held that where a ceremony of marriage undoubtedly took place, the strong presumption is in favour of the marriage and applies to the forms and the ceremonies necessary to constitute it a valid marriage.

The offence of bigamy hits at the very root of the social institutions of marriage and the framers of the Indian Penal Code have categorically classified it as a serious criminal offence having regard to its deletatious fall out in the subsisting marriage. This offence is often alleged but rarely held to be proved before the courts. While interpreting Section 494 I.P.C., which has been the subject matter of many decisions of the High Courts and the Supreme Court on different facts and circumstances, the court has to bear in mind that a party contracting a second marriage during the subsistence of the first one, essentially put on guard by the fact that the consequences could be serious to both the persons involved in that act and invariably, therefore, keeps the marriage, particularly the ceremony part of it, as secret as possible. The aggrieved spouse is confronted with the situation of the parties living together, openly professing to be husband and wife, possibly acknowledging the paternity of the children. When these facts are complained of before a court of law in a proceeding under Section 494 I.P.C., the aggrieved spouse is confronted with the legal requirement of proving the factum of the second marriage and in absence of being able to do so, in the majority of prosecution under Section 494 I.P.C., the wrong doer is acquitted by the Criminal Courts.[11]

"495. Same offence with concealment of former marriage from person with whom subsequent marriage is contracted:

Whoever, commits the offence defined in the last preceding section having concealed from the person with whom the subsequent marriage is contracted, the fact of the former marriage, shall be punished with imprisonment of either description for a term which may extend to ten years, and shall also be liable to fine."

Notes:

The ingredients of the facts of the cases under Section 495 required to be proved are the same as the ingredients of cases under Section 494 I.P.C. but one more fact that is, the factum of concealment of the former marriage has also to be proved. As a matter of fact, the parties now-a-days get the video-tape of the entire proceedings made in addition to the photographs taken on various occasions. These in addition to the invitation cards of the marriage and reception would constitute strong documentary proof of the marriage. For the proof of the legitimacy of the children, DNA, fingerprinting tests of the mother, father and the child/children would be the conclusive proof of the paternity of the child.

"496. Marriage ceremony fraudulently gone through without lawful marriage:

Whoever, dishonestly or with a fraudulent intention, goes through the ceremony of being married, knowing that he is not thereby lawfully married, shall be punished with imprisonment of either description for a term which may extend to seven years and shall also be liable to fine."

"497. Adultery:

Whoever has sexual intercourse with a person who is and whom he knows or has reason to believe to be the wife of another man, without the consent of connivance of that man, such sexual intercourse not amounting to the offence of rape, is guilty of the offence of adultery, and shall be punished with imprisonment of either description for a term which may extend to five years, or with fine, or with both. In such case the wife shall not be punishable as an abetter".

Notes:

Adultery means a sexual intercourse with a married woman with consent and the law provides punishment up to a term of imprisonment of five years with fine. The woman however is exempted from any punishment. However, in matrimonial laws, the repercussion of an adulterous act is wider in as much as it can result in a decree of divorce. Both under the Special Marriage Act, 1954 and Hindu Marriage Act, 1955, as amended from time to time, if the husband or the wife has had a voluntary sexual intercourse with any other person than his/her own spouse, the other party gets a ground for breaking the marriage, that is; through judicial separation or divorce.. The difference between judicial separation and divorce is that in the former case, the parties are to wait for one year after which any one of the two, can move the court for a decree of divorce stating specifically that during the period under question, there was no intercourse between them. In the case of divorce petition, if the same has been granted the parties can immediately remarry provided the period of appeal has expired or the appeal has been dismissed.

Under the Indian Divorce Act, 1869, governing the Indian Christians, a wife can dissolve the marriage on the ground of adultery while in the case of judicial separation, the chances of reunion are kept alive. On the other hand, in case of divorce, the separation is complete. The husband can seek divorce on the ground that his wife has been guilty of unchastity. Section 34 of the Indian Divorce Act, 1869 gives a right to the husband to seek compensation from the adulterer.

Under the Parsi Marriage and Divorce Act, 1936, governing the marriage and divorce laws of the Parsi Zorastrian, a decree of divorce can be obtained by the wife on the ground that the husband has, since the marriage committed adultery or rape or an unnatural offence. The husband can also give up his wife, if the latter has committed an act of infidelity. Since a Muslim marrying under the Muslim personal law, can divorce his wife at any time without assigning any reason and without the intervention by a court, The Muslim Law givers or the commentators have not given any reason or specified any ground for this. However, after the enactment of the Muslim Marriage Dissolution Act, a provision has been made by which the wife also gets the right to repudiate her marriage if her husband associated himself with women of evil repute or lives an infamous life.[12]

It may be kept in mind that an allegation of a lewd life is a grave charge. Besides being a social stigma, it is fraught with far reaching legal consequences. The allegations must, therefore, be proved beyond an iota of doubt. Courts are never happy to break marriages and they make all efforts to see them reunited.

Judges are also not unaware of the fact that the illicit sexual relationship amounting to adultery is performed in strict secrecy and, therefore, direct evidence is very difficult, rather impossible to obtain. Various relations between the persons belonging to opposite sexes, not married to each other, can be gathered from circumstantial evidences.[13]

9.02 Shortcomings of the Section 497 I.P.C.[14]

The offence of adultery, as defined in Section 497 suffers from the undermentioned defects:

(a) The Section is applicable in those cases where the female partner is the wife of another man. Thus if a man maintains a sexual relationship with an unmarried woman, or concubine, or a keep or a prostitute, even in the same premises, it is not an offence of adultery. Under the provision of prevention of Immoral Trafic Act, 1956, as amended in 1978 and 1986, a woman is punished by law if she allows several persons to have access to her for sexual intercourse in lieu of consideration. But no such ban has been put on the husband against his extra-marital relations. He has the liberty to choose a sex partner from amongst unmarried girls, widows or mistresses or he can visit prostitutes. The situation with respect to Muslim women are one of observing conjugal faithfulness but the husband can afford to be unfaithful to the wife in sex matters. The Muslim husbands, are enjoying the facility of non-registration of marriages and the benefit of oral 'Talaq' with obligations only to maintain the divorced wife for a period extending to three month only after the oral Talaq.

(b) The husband can, even with the connivance of or the consent of the woman's husband, enjoy sexual pleasure. Thus in each case of prostitution, it can be shown that the woman had a husband and the so-called husband connived or consented to the sexual act, in that event no prosecution can be launched against the person who indulge in this type of sexual activities. This is supported by the fact that somebody else's wife with whom a husband is making love is not punishable under the provision of Section 497 I.P.C., the woman not being an abetter. In an act, which amount to a criminal activity with the active connivance of another person involved in the act is neither an abettor nor an accomplice, is against the principal of law.

(c) Under the provision of Section 198 Cr. P.C. (1973), it is the husband who is the aggrieved person in an act of sexual intercourse with his wife. This right is available to the husband of the wife adulterated, whereas, the woman whose husband has been adulterated has no such right to proceed against the woman who had adulterated her husband. This does not make any sense of the right given to a wife vide Section 198 (1) (c) Cr. P.C. to lodge a complaint against her husband for a bigamous marriage act of her husband.

(d) There are a couple of more problems for such wives. Firstly they have no right under any law of the court so far to a matrimonial home although there is also no law that she must get out of the husband's home even though the husband is the wrongdoer. This, however is the accepted practice. Secondly under Section 125 Cr. P.C., the wife leading a life of adultery is not entitled to maintenance whereas the wife of the man practising adultery can refuse to live with her husband and yet claim maintenance from him.

The law as it exists today seems to undermine the family by marriage only by giving right to maintenance to illegitimate child but not to illegitimate wife.

Section 497 of the I.P.C. is discriminatory in nature as the husband enjoys the right to sue the man who had an adulterous sexual act with his wife but the wife has no such right under the law to sue the woman who enticed her husband or with whom her husband had indulged in sexual act.

498. Enticing or taking away or detaining with criminal intent a married woman

Whoever takes or entices away any woman who is and whom he knows to be the wife of any other man, or from any person having the care of her on behalf of that man, with intent that she may have illicit intercourse with any person, or conceals or detains with that intent any such woman, shall be punished with imprisonment of either description for a term which may extend to two years, or with fine or with both.

498. Husband or relative of husband of a woman,[15] subjects such woman to cruelty shall be punished with imprisonment for a term which may extend to three years and shall also be liable to fine.

Explanation: For the purpose of this section, "cruelty" means-

(a) any wilful conduct which is of such a nature as is likely to drive the woman to commit suicide or to cause grave injury or danger to life, limb or health (whether mental or physical) of the woman; or

(b) harassment of the woman where such harassment is with a view to coercing her or any person related to her to meet any unlawful demand for any property or valuable security or is on account of failure by her or any person related to her to meet such demand.

9.03 Child Marriage

The marriage of Mamta, a three month old nursing baby with a toddler aged one years in early 1990 in a village under the Bundi District of Rajasthan epitomised the farcical extent to which the age old custom of child marriage can go.[16] This is not an isolated case but one among many being solemnised in Rajasthan inspite of the existence of Child Marriage Restraint Act. The law enforcing agencies are helpless spectators to such marriages making a mockery of the provisions of the Act. The custom is prevalent among all Hindus and it is the social sanctions that enable it to continue in sharp violation of biological, ethical and legal considerations.

Child marriage has little religious sanction and at one time it had the logic of protecting the honour and chastity of girls from the Muslim rulers. However, now the practice thrives on monetary and superstitious grounds. For most parents girls are a liability which could be discharged by giving her in marriage and earlier the girls are married off, the better it is. Besides this, a bride is more often seen as addition of a hand in the family to take care of domestic chores like cooking, cleaning of the house and grazing cattles or as farm labourer. In some cases, she brings in bride money. Little consideration is given to the fact that there are chances of such girls becoming widows before knowing the importance of marriage in life. Besides the useless social custom, Rajasthan has the distinction of such social custom as female infanticide and sati. Their prevalence shows that laws, however lofty they may be, are not a check upon the age-old obsolete illegal customs. There should be sustained and vigorous efforts to wean people away from retrograde practices. This is a task which the society as a whole should take up.

REFRENCES

1. Guy's Forensic Medicine, 15, Cited in Lyon's Medical Jurisprudence for India, Vth. Edition (1914), Thacker Spink & Co. Calcutta and Simla, pp. 52.
2. Uday Madhurkar, "A Godman's Gaffe" *India Today*, Feb. 15, 1988.
3. Kumkum Chadha, "The Law that breaks the Constitution," *The Hindustan Times* (mag. Section), dated Aug. 8, 1993 (sunday).
4. Kumkum Chadha, " Goa's Obsolete Laws, Polygamy for Hindus, No Nikah for Muslim", *Hindustan Times*, Dated Aug. 1, 1993.
5. *Indu Bhagya Natekar* Vs. *Bhagya Pandurang Natekar, & Others*, II (1992) CCR 1954.
6. *Ashok Kumar Chopra* Vs. *Krishna Kumari*, I (1992) CCR 574 (P.&H).
7. *Guru Charan Singh* Vs. *The State of Punjab*, I (1992) CCR 228.
8. AIR 1965 Sc 1564.
9. *Linga Malik* Vs. *Ajudha Malkani*, AIR 1974 SC 107.
10. (1911) ILR 38 Cal. 700(PC).
11. *Indu Bhagya Natekar* Vs. *Bhagya Pandurang Natekar & Others*, II (1992) CCR 1954.

12. D.K. Bhatia, "Adultery and Marriage, Laws", *Hindustan Times* (Delhi Edition), March 18, 1987.
13. *A.S. Puri* Vs. *K.L.Ahuja*, 1970 Cr. L J 1441, AIR 1970 Del. 214.
14. Krishan Mahajan, "The Husband's woman," *The Hindustan Times* (Del. Ed.) dated Jan. 19, 1988.
15. Ins. by Cr. Law (Amendment) Act, 1983 (Act 46 of 1983), Sec. 2. (This Section has received discussion in this Volume in Chapter on Dowry related offences.)
16. Child Marriage, Editorial Column of *Hindustan Times*, dated 2.5.1990.

Chapter 10

Divorce and Maintenance

10.01 Introduction

The expression divorce means:[1]

(a) Judicial declaration dissolving a marriage in whole or in part;
(b) any formal separation of man and woman according to custom as among uncivilised tribe;
(c) to break the contract of marriage between oneself and one's spouse.

Besides the penal provisions for faulty solemnisation of marriages, matrimonial faults may entitle one of the spouses to seek divorce through an order of the Court.

The provisions in relation to divorce are as under:

(1) *The Indian Divorce Act, 169:*

The provisions of this Act are applicable to Indian Christians. Under the Act, both husband and wife may present a petition for dissolution of marriage.

S.10. When husband may petition for dissolution:

Any husband may present a petition to the District Court or to the High Court, praying that his marriage may be dissolved on the ground that his wife has, since the solemnization thereof, been guilty of adultery.

When wife may petition for dissolution:

Any wife may present a petition to the District Court or to the High Court, praying that her marriage may be dissolved on the ground that, since the solemnization thereof, her husband has exchanged his profession of Christianity for the profession of some other religion and gone through a form of marriage with another woman;

or has been guilty of incestuous adultery,

or of bigmay with adultery,

or of marriage with another woman with adultery,

or of rape, sodomy or bestiality,

or of adultery coupled with such cruelty as without adultery would have entitled her to a divorce 'a mensa et tora'

or of adultery coupled with desertion, without reasonable excuse, for two years or upwards.

CONTENTS OF PETITION

Every such petition shall state, as distinctly as the nature of the case permits, the facts on which the claim to have such marriage dissolved is founded.

(2) *The Parsi Marriage and Divorce Act, 1936:*

This Act was enacted in 1936 and later amended in the year 1988, It lists the following faults, which constitute valid grounds for seeking divorce.

32. *Grounds for divorce*

Any married person may sue for divorce on any one of the following grounds, namely:

(a) that the marriage has not been consummated within one year after its solemnization owing to the willful refusal of the defendant to consummate it;

(b) that the defendant at the time of the marriage was of unsound mind and has been habitually so up to the date of the suit.

Provided that divorce shall not be granted on this ground, unless the plaintiff: (1) was ignorant of the fact at the time of the marriage, and (2) has filed the suit within three years from the date of the marriage;

[2][(bb) that the defendant has been incurably of unsound mind for a period of two years or upwards immediately preceeding the filing of the suit or has been suffering continuously or intermittently from mental disorder of such kind and to such an extent that the plantiff cannot reasonably be expected to live with the defendant.

Explanation: In this clause:

(a) the expression "mental disorder" means illness, arrested or incomplete development of mind, psychopathic disorder or any other disorder or disability of mind and includes schizophrenia,

(b) the expression "psychopathic disorder" means a persistent disorder or disability of mind (whether or not including subnormality of intelligence)—which results in abnormally aggressive or seriously irresponsible conduct on the part of the defendant, and whether or not it requires or is susceptible to medical treatment;]

(c) that the defendant was at the time of marriage pregnant by some person other than the plaintiff.

Provided that divorce shall not be granted on this ground unless: (1) the plaintiff was at the time of the marriage ignorant of the fact alleged, (2) the suit has been filed within two years of the date of marriage, and (3) marital intercourse has not taken place after the plaintiff came to know of the fact.

(d) that the defendant has since the marriage committed adultery or fornication or bigamy or rape or an unnatural offence.

Provided that divorce shall not be granted on this ground, if the suit has been filed more than two years after the plaintiff came to know of the fact.

[3][(dd) that the defendant has since the solemnization of the marriage, treated the plaintiff with cruelty or has behaved in such a way as to render it in the judgement of the Court improper to compel the plaintiff to live with the defendant.

Provided that in every suit for divorce on this ground it shall be in the discretion of the court whether it should grant a decree for divorce or for judicial separation only.]

(c) that the defendant has since the marriage voluntarily caused grievous hurt to the plaintiff or has infected the plaintiff with venereal disease or where the defendant is the husband, has compelled the wife to submit herself to prostitution.

Provided that divorce shall not be granted on this ground, if the suit has been filed more than two years (i) after the infliction of the grievous hurt, or (ii) after the plaintiff came to know of the infection, or (iii) after the last act of compulsory prostitution;

(f) that the defendant is undergoing a sentence of imprisonment for seven years or more for an offence as defined in the Indian Penal Code.

Provided that divorce shall not be granted on this ground, unless the defendant has prior to filing of the suit undergone at least one years's imprisonment out of the said period;

(g) that the defendant has deserted the plaintiff for at least[4] [two years].

(h) that [5][* * *] an order has been passed against the defendant by a Magistrate awarding separate maintenance to the plaintiff. And the parties have not had marital intercourse for [6](one year) or more since such decree or order ;

(i)[7][* * *] ;

(j) that the defendant has ceased to be a Parsi[8] [by conversion to another religion.]

Provided that divorce shall not be granted on this ground if the suit has been filed more than two years after the plaintiff came to know of the fact.

(3) DISSOLUTION OF MUSLIM MARRIAGE

Under the Mohamden Law, there are three distinct modes in which a Muslim marriage can be dissolved and the relationship between the husband and the wife terminated to result in an irrevocable divorce. These are:

(i) Where the husband unilaterally gives a divorce in accordance with any of the forms approved by the Mohamedan Law, namely *'Talak ahsan'*. This consists of a single pronouncement of divorce during *'tuhr'* (period between menstruation) followed by abstinence from sexual intercourse for the period of *iddat*; or 'talak ahsan' which consists of three pronouncements made during the successive Tuhrs, no intercourse taking place between tuhrs; and lastly *'talak-ul-biddat'* or *'talak-i-badai'* which consists of three pronouncements made during a single tuhr either in one sentence or in three sentences signifying a clear intention to divorce the wife, for instance, the husband uttering 'TALAQ' ('I divorce thee irrevocably' or 'I divorce thee, I divorce thee.) The third form referred to above is, however, not recognised by the Shia Law.

A divorce or talaq may be given orally or in writing and it becomes irrevocable, if the period of iddat is observed though it is not necessary that the woman divorced should come to know of the fact that she has been divorced by her husband.

(ii) By an agreement between the husband and the wife whereby a wife obtains divorce by relinquishing either her entire or part of the dower. This mode of divorce is called *'Khula'* or *'Mubarat'*. This form of divorce is initiated by the wife and comes into existence if the husband gives consent to the agreement and releases her from the marriage tie. Where, however, both parties agree and desire a separation resulting in a divorce, it is called 'Mubarat'. The gist of these modes is that it comes into existence with the consent of both the parties particularly the husband, because without his consent this mode of divorce would be incapable of being enforced. A divorce may also come into existence by virtue of an agreement either before or after the marriage by which it is provided that the wife should be at liberty to divorce herself in specified contingencies which are of a reasonable nature and which again are agreed to by the husband. In such a case, the wife can repudiate herself in the exercise of the power and the divorce would be deemed to have been pronounced by the husband. This mode of divorce is called *'tawfiz'*.

(iii) By obtaining a decree from a Civil Court for dissolution of marriage under Section 2 of the Dissolution of Muslim Marriage Act, 1939 which also amounts to a divorce under the law obtained by the wife. For the purposes of maintenance, this mode of divorce is governed by Clause (c) of sub-section (3) of Section 127 of the Cr P.C., (1973) whereas the divorce given under modes (1) and (2) would be covered by clause (b) of sub-Section (3) of the Section 127.[9]

The Muslim Personal Law (Shariat) Act, 1937 was the outcome of the Ulema seeking Government intervention to oust the customary laws in force, especially in the then undivided Punjab and the N.W.F.P and to bring all Muslims under a common Shariat umbrella.[10] Under the Customary Law in operation in these provinces, the Muslim landlords were taking advantage of the then prevailing Hindu Law to bequeath their entire property of their male heirs denying the daughters their share under the Islamic Law.

The Dissolution of Muslim Marriage Act, enacted in 1939 was sponsored by the 'Ulemas'. Although Koran permits dissolution of marriage by the woman in case of necessity, under the Hanafi Law obtaining divorce in India. A Muslim woman seeking divorce would lose her faith. This was leading to conversion of women bent on getting out of unwanted alliance. To bring about an end to it, the Ulema proposed enactment or a law empowering Muslim Judges to dissolve Muslim marriages in specified circumstances.[10]

Under the Dissolution of Muslim Marriage Act, 1939, the wife is entitled to dissolve the marriage on the following grounds (Section 2 of the Act):

(i) that the whereabouts of the husband have not been known for a period of four years;
(ii) that the husband has neglected or has failed to provide for her maintenance for a period of two years;
(iii) that the husband has been sentenced to imprisonment for a period of seven years or upwards;
(iv) that the husband has failed to perform, without reasonable cause, his marital obligations for a period of three years ;
(v) that the husband was impotent at the time of marriage and continues to be so;
(vi) that the husband has been insane for a period of two years or is suffering from leprosy or a virulent veneral disease;
(vii) that she, having been given in marriage by her father or other guardian before she attained the age of fifteen years, repudiated the marriage before attaining the age of eighteen years: provided that marriage has not been consummated;

(viii) that the husband treats her with cruelty, that is to say
- (a) habitually assaults her or makes her life miserable by cruelty of conduct even if such conduct does not amount to physical ill treatment, or
- (b) associates with women of evil repute or leads an infamous life, or
- (c) attempts to force her to lead an immoral life, or
- (d) disposes of her property or prevents her religious profession or practice, or
- (e) obstructs her in observance of her religious profession or practice, or
- (f) if he has more wives than one, does not treat her equitably in accordance with the injunction of the Qoran.

(ix) On any other ground which is recognised as valid for the dissolution of marriages under Muslim Law.

Provided that:

(a) no decree shall be passed on ground of (iii) until the sentence has become final;

(b) a decree passed on ground (i) shall not take effect for a period of six months from the date of such decree and if the husband appears either in person or through an authorised agent within that period and satisfies the court that he is prepared to perform the conjugal duties the court shall set aside the said decree; and

(c) before passing a decree on ground (v) the court shall, on an application by the husband make an order requiring the husband to satisfy the court within a period of one year from the date of such order that he has ceased to be an impotent, and if the husband so satisfies the court within such period, no decree shall be passed on the said ground.

The pronouncement of three Talaq in one sitting by the Muslim husbands is playing havoc with the lives of thousands of women in the country due to the purported irrevocability.[11]

Firoz Bakht Ahmad[12] records a case where Bilquess was divorced by her husband Dilshad by uttering the word 'Talaq' in one sitting. After tempers cooled down, they wanted to reunite as the husband realised the mistake. He brought the case to three '*muftis*' , Sheikh Ataur Rahman Madani, Sheikh Obeidur

Rehman and Sheikh Jamil Ahmad Madani of the Jamaite-Ahle Hadis, a religious body of the Muslims who declared that three pronouncements in one sitting are not to be considered as one under the Islamic Law which says that three such pronouncements at an interval of one month each can only be considered as 'Talaq' as mentioned in the Holy Quran's Sura, 'At Talaq' (Chapter 28: Verse 64, 4).

Many Jurists hold that a divorce takes effect if it is pronounced three times even at one sitting. However, noted Islamic theologicians Imam Ahmad-ibn-e-Hanbul and Iman-ibn-e-Teymia are reported to have rejected this opinion and regards the words spoken in one sitting as one pronouncement and separation, therefore, does not come off at the end of three such declaration, but only when they are separated each by an interval of one month. The law in prescribing three pronouncements in three sittings at intervals of one months is to leave open room for reconciliation. This intention is defeated by recognising the three pronouncements delivered at a single sitting of having the effect of final separation.

The truth is that a Muslim woman is at a disadvantage The situation is worse in India. Even Pakistan has enacted the "Muslim Family Law" in 1961 wherein progressive demands of Pakistani women have been given effect to. One of the important provisions of the Act is that divorce must be carried out under judicial process and control and that it should not be purely private unilateral action.

(4) *Special Marriage Act, 1954:*

This Act is an attempt to make provision for a secular form of marriage and is applicable to all irrespective of caste and religion. Those who marry under the provisions of this law are out of the barriers of their personal laws. Section 27 of the Act embodies the conditions of marriage or faults for seeking marriage.

Section 27 runs as under:

27. Divorce:

(1) Subject to the provisions of this Act and to the rules made thereunder, a petition for divorce may be presented to the

district court by the husband or the wife on the ground that the respondent

(a) has, after the solemnization of the marriage, had voluntary sexual intercourse with any person other than his or her spouse; or

(b) has deserted the petitioner for a continuous period of not less than two years immediately preceding the presentation of the petition; or;

(c) is undergoing a sentence of imprisonment for seven years or more for an offence as defined in the Indian Penal Code (45 of 1860); or

[13][* * * *]

(d) has since the solemnization of the marriage treated the petitioner with cruelty; or

(e) has been incurably of unsound mind, or has been suffering continuously or intermittently from mental disorder of such a kind and to such an extent that the petitioner cannot reasonably be expected to live with the respondent.

Explanation: In this clause:

(a) the expression "mental disorder" means mental illness, arrested or incomplete development of mind, psychopathic disorder or any other disorder or disability of mind and includes schizophrenia;

(b) the expression "psychopathic disorder" means a persistent disorder or disability of mind (whether or not including sub-normality of intelligence) which results in abnormally aggressive or seriously irresponsible conduct on the part of the respondent, and whether or not it requires or is susceptible to medical treatment; or

(f) has been suffering from venereal disease in a communicable form; or

(g) has [13][* * * *] been suffering from leprosy, the disease not having been contracted from the petitioner; or

(h) has not been heard of as being alive for a period of seven years or more by those persons who would naturally have heard of the respondent if the respondent had been alive.

Explanation: In this Sub-section the expression "desertion" means desertion of the petitioner by the other party to the marriage without reasonable cause and without the consent or against the wish of such party, and includes the wilful neglect of the petitioner by the other party to the marriage and its grammatical variations and carnate expressions shall be construed accordingly;

(I-A) A wife may also present a petition for divorce to the district court on the ground,

(i) that her husband has, since the solemnization of the marriage, been guilty of rape, sodomy or bestiality;
(ii) that in a suit under Section 18 of the Hindu Adoptions and Maintenance Act, 1956 (78 of 1956), or in a proceeding under Section 125 of the Code of Criminal Procedure, 1973 (2 of 1974) or under the corresponding Section 488 of the Code of Criminal Procedure, 1898) (5 of 1898), a decree or order, as the case may be, has been passed against the husband awarding maintenance to the wife notwithstanding that she was living apart and that since the passing of such decree or order, cohabitation between the parties has not been resumed for one year or upwards.

(2) Subject to the provisions of this Act and to the rules made thereunder, either party to a marriage, whether solemnized before or after the commencement of the Special Marriage (Amendment) Act, 1970 (29 of 1970). May present a petition for divorce to the district court on the ground:

(i) that there has been no resumption of cohabitation as between the parties to the marriage for a period of one year or upwards after the passing of a decree for judicial separation in a proceeding to which they were parties; or
(ii) that there has been no restitution of conjugal rights as between the parties to the marriage for a period of one year or upwards after the passing of a decree for restitution of conjugal rights in a proceeding to which they were parties.

(5) *The Hindu Marriage Act, 1955:*

The Hindu Marriage Act, 1955 was enacted in order to regulate the system of marriage through legal provisions. The Act, although does not include the word 'Divorce' in the title, includes a Section on 'Divorce' as well. Amendment to the Act was carried out in several times, (vide Act no. 73 of 1956, 58 of 1960, 44 of 1964, 68 of 1975 and 2 of 1978). Either party to a marriage can move the Court for dissolution of the marrige. However, the Act provides for extra ground to the wife in addition to the other grounds available to both the parties. Sec. 13 runs as under:

13. DIVORCE

(1) Any marriage solemnized, whether before or after the commencement of this Act, may, on a petition presented by either the husband or the wife, be dissolved by a decree of divorce on the ground that the other party—

(i) has, after the solemnization of the marriage, had voluntary sexual intercourse with any person other than his or her spouse; or

(ia) has, after the solemnization of the marriage, treated the petitioner with cruelty; or

(ib) has deserted the petitioner for a continuous period of not lees than two years immediately preceding the presentation of the petition;

(ii) has ceased to be Hindu by conversion to another religion;

(iii) has been incurably of unsound mind, or has been suffering continuously or intermittently from mental disorder of such a kind and to such an extent that the petitioner cannot reasonably be expected to live with the respondent.

Explanation: In this clause:

(a) the expression "mental disorder" means mental illness, arrested or incomplete development of mind, psychopathic disorder or any other disorder or disability of mind and includes schizophrenia;

(b) the expression "psychopathic disorder" means a persistent disorder or disability of mind (whether or not including sub-normality of intelligence) which results in abnormally aggressive or seriously irresponsible conduct on the part of the other party, and whether or not, it requires or is susceptible to medical treatment; or]

(iv) has, been suffering from a virulent and incurable form of leprosy; or

(v) has, been suffering from venereal disease in a communicable form; or

(vi) has renounced the world by entering any religious order; or

(vii) has not been heard of as being alive for a period of seven years or more by those persons who would naturally have heard of it, had that party been alive.

Explanation: In this sub-section, the expression "desertion" means the desertion of the petitioner by the other party to send or against the wish of such party. And includes the wilful neglect of the petitioner by the other party to the marriage. And its grammatical variations and cognate expression shall be construed accordingly.

(I-A) Either party to a marriage, whether solemnized before or after the commencement of this Act, may also present a petition for the dissolution of the marriage by a decree of divorce on the ground:

(i) that there has been no resumption of cohabitation as between the parties to the marriage for a period of one year or upwards after the passing of a decree for judicial separation in a proceeding to which they were parties; or

(ii) that there has been no restitution of conjugal rights as between the parties to the marriage for a period of one year or upwards after the passing of a decree for restitution of conjugal rights in a proceeding to which they were parties.

(2) A wife may also present a petition for the dissolution of her marriage by a decree of divorce on the ground:

(i) in the case of any marriage solemnized before the commencement of this Act. That the husband had married again before such commencement or that any other wife of the husband married before such commencement was alive at the time of the solemnization of the marriage of the petitioner.

Provided that in either case the other wife is alive at the time of the presentation of the petition; or

(ii) that the husband has, since the solemnization of the marriage, been guilty of rape, sodomy or bestiality; or

(iii) that in a suit under Section 18 of the Hindu Adoptions and Maintenance Act, 1956 (78 of 1956), or in a proceeding under Section 125 of the Code of Criminal Procedure, 1973 (2 of 1974), [or under the corresponding Section 488 of the Code of Criminal Procedure, 1898 (5 of 1898)], decree or order, as the case may be, has been passed against the husband awarding maintenance to the wife notwithstanding that she was living apart and that since the passing of such decree or order, cohabitation between the parties has not been resumed for one year or upwards; or

(iv) that her marriage (whether consummated or not) was solemnized before she attained the age of fifteen years and she has repudiated the marriage after attaining that age but before attaining the age of eighteen years.

Explanation: This clause applies whether the marriage was solemnized before or after the commencement of the Marriage Laws (Amendment) Act, 1976 (68 of 1976).

State Amendment:

Uttar Pradesh: In its application to Hindus domiciled in U.P. and also when either party to the marriage was at the time of marriage a Hindu domiciled in U.P., in Section 13:

(i) in sub-section (1) after clause (i) insert and deem always to have been inserted the following:

"(i-a) has persistently or repeatedly treated the petitioner with such cruelty as to cause a reasonable apprehension in the mind of the petitioner that it will be harmful or injurious for the petitioner to live with the other party; or". And

(ii) for clause (viii) (since repealed) substituted and deem always to have been so substituted the following:

"(viii) has not resumed cohabitation after the passing of a decree for judicial separation against that party, and

(a)a period of two years has ellapsed since the passing of such decree, or

(b)the case is one of exceptional hardship to the petitioner or of exceptional depravity on the part of other party."

10.02 Divorce Among Tribals

Divorce among the tribals are very simple although the same is seldom practised. The common cause of divorce are barrenness or incompatibility. Divorce generally among the Khasis takes place under mutual agreement. When a couple agrees to divorce, they exchange five cowries. The wife gives five cowries to the husband who returns them with his five. The ten cowries is thereafter, returned to the husband who, if he throws them on the ground, then the divorce is complete. Word goes round the members of the community that the divorce has been effected. The Karbis obtain a divorce by presenting a gourd to the girl's parents. Among the Kacharis, a betal leaf is torn into two to complete separation.[14]

The incidence of divorce among the Banjaras is almost nil. The bride has no rights in respect of divorce. In the event of torture of the wife by the husband, the wife's father brings back the woman and she gets a share in her father's property and this is done after a full legal procedure.[15]

There is yet very simple procedure among certain Tribes in Rajasthan where separation is effected after a ceremony in which the husband tears the 'Chunari' of the wife.

The simple procedure of divorce among the tribals is fast deteriorating and is being replaced by the culture of the enlightened society and the process of marriage and divorce is now getting diluted.

10.03 Maintenance

Chapter IX of the [Criminal Procedure Code, 1973] provides for 'order for maintenance of wives, children and parents.' In addition, Section 126, Sec. 127 and Section 128 outline procedure, alteration of allowance and enforcement of order of maintenance respectively. The four Sections run as under:

CRIMINAL PROCEDURE CODE, 1973

Chapter IX

ORDER FOR MAINTENACE OF WIVES, CHILDREN AND PARENTS

125. Order for maintenance of wives, children and parents:

(1) If any person having sufficient means neglects or refuses to maintain

(a) his wife, unable to maintain herself, or
(b) his legitimate or illegitimate minor child, whether married or not, unable to maintain itself, or
(c) his legitimate or illegitimate child (not being a married daughter) who has attained majority, where such child is, by reason of any physical or mental abnormality or injury unable to maintain itself, or
(d) his father or mother, unable to maintain himself or herself,

a Magistrate of the first class may, upon proof of such neglect or refusal, order such person to make a monthly allowance for the maintenace of his wife or such child, father or mother, at such monthly rate not exceeding five hundred rupees in the whole,* as such Magistrate thinks fit, and to pay the same to such person as the Magistrate may from time to time direct.

Provided that the Magistrate may order the father of a minor female child referred to in clause (b) to make such allowance, until she attains her majority, if the Magistrate is satisfied that the husband of such minor female child if married is not possessed of sufficient means.

Explanation: For the purposes of this Chapter,

(a) "minor" means a person who, under the provisions of the Indian Majority Act, 1875 (9 of 1875) is deemed not to have attained his majority;
(b) "wife" includes a woman who has been divorced by, or has obtained a divorce from, her husband and has not remarried.

(20 Such allowance shall be payable from the date of the order, or, if so ordered, from the date of the application for maintenance.

* Raised to Rupees Fifteen hundred in Proposed Criminal Bill No. XXXV of 1994.

(3) If any person so ordered fails without sufficient cause to comply with the order, any such Magistrate may, for every breach of the order, issue a warrant for levying the amount due in the manner provided for levying fines, and may sentence such person, for the whole or any part of each month's allowance remaining unpaid after the execution of the warrant, to imprisonment for a term which may extend to one month or until payment if sooner made.

Provided that no warrant shall be issued for a recovery of any amount due under this section unless application be made to the court to levy such amount within a period of one year from the date on which it became due.

Provided further that if such person offers to maintain his wife on condition of her living with him, and she refuses to live with him, such Magistrate may consider any grounds of refusal stated by her, and may make an order under this section notwithstanding such offer, if he is satisfied that there is just ground for so doing.

Explanation: If a husband has contracted marriage with another woman or keeps a mistress, it shall be considered to be just ground for his wife's refusal to live with him.

(4) No wife shall be entitled to receive an allowance from her husband under this section if she is living in adultery, or if, without any sufficient reason, she refuses to live with her husband, or if they are living separately by mutual consent.

(5) On proof that any wife in whose favour an order has been made under this section is living in adultery, or that without sufficient reason she refuses to live with her husband, or that they are living separately by mutual consent, the Magistrate shall cancel the order.

Corresponding Law: S. 488(1) to (5) of Act V of 1898.

126. Procedure:

(1) Proceedings under Section 125 may be taken against any person in any district-

(a) where he is, or
(b) where he or his wife resides, or
(c) where he last resided with his wife, or as the case may be, with the mother of the illegitimate child.

(2) All evidence in such proceedings shall be taken in the presence of the person against whom an order for payment of maintenance is proposed to be made or, when his personal attendance is dispensed with, in the presence of his pleader, and shall be recorded in the manner prescribed for summons cases.

Provided that if the Magistrate is satisfied that the person against whom an order for payment of maintenance is proposed to be made is wilfully avoiding service, or wilfully neglecting to attend the court, the Magistrate may proceed to hear and determine the case ex parte and any order so made may be set aside for good cause shown on an application made within three months from the date thereof subject to such terms including terms as to payment of costs to the opposite party as the Magistrate may think just and proper.

(3) The court in dealing with applications under Section 125 shall have power to make such order as to costs as may be just.

Corresponding Law: S. 488 (f) to (8) of Act V of 1898.

127. Alteration in allowance:

(1) On proof of a change in the circumstances of any person, receiving, under Section 125 a monthly allowance, or ordered under the same section to pay a monthly allowance to his wife, child, father or mother, as the case may be, the Magistrate may make such alteration in the allowance as he thinks fit.

Provided that if he increases the allowance, the monthly rate of five hundred rupees in the whole shall not be exceeded.

(2) Where it appears to the Magistrate that, in consequence of any decision of a competent Civil Court, any order made under Section 125 should be cancelled or varied, he shall cancel the order or, as the case may be, vary the same accordingly.

(3) Where any order has been made under Section 125 in favour of a woman who has been divorced by, or has obtained a divorce from her husband, the Magistrate shall, if he is satisfied that:

(a) the woman has, after the date of such divorce, re-married, cancel such order as from the date of her remarriage;

(b) the woman has been divorced by her husband and that she has received, whether before or after the date of the said order, the whole of the sum which, under any customary or personal law applicable to the parties, was payable on such divorce, cancel such order,

(i) in the case where such sum was paid before such order, from the date on which such order was made;

(ii) in any other case, from the date of expiry of the period, if any, for which maintencance has been actually paid by the husband to the woman;

(c) the woman has obtained a divorce from her husband and that she had voluntarily surrendered her rights to maintenance after her divorce, cancel the order from the date thereof.

(4) At the time of making any decree for the recovery of any maintenance or dowry by any person to whom a monthly allowance has been ordered to be paid under Section 125, the Civil Court shall take into account the sum which has been paid to, or recovered by, such person as monthly allowance in pursuance of the said order.

Corresponding Law: S. 489 of Act V of 1898.

128. Enforcement of order of maintenance:

A copy of the order of maintenance shall be given without payment to the person in whose favour it is made, or to his guardian, if any, or to the person to whom the allowance is to be paid; and such order may be enforced by any magistrate in any place where the person against whom it is made may be, on such Magistrate being satisfied as to the identity of the parties and the non-payment of the allowance due.

Corresponding Law: S. 490 of Act V of 1898.

Notes:

VALIDITY AND PROOF OF MARRIAGE

Where the respondent wife allegedy left the house of the husband as he got annoyed due to ther incapability to beget a child and started ill-treating her and inflicted assaults. She had no income, therefore, the Magistrate granted an interim maintenance of Rs. 200 per month. The husband claimed that there was no question of any claim as no marriage has been solemnised, on the other hand, the wife filed a copy of the voter's list where she was described as the wife of the petitioner. She also produced Ration Card, wherein the name of the respondent was entered as the wife of the petitioner. The only fear of the petitioner was that in case if the proof of the marriage is not made out, he will not be in a position to recover the interim maintenance paid by the petitioner. The High Court directed, the Trial Court to pass an appropriate order protecting the rights of the petitioner to recover maintenance amount paid to the respondent by way of interim maintenance in case he succeeds in his plea.[16]

In a claim for maintenance by Kulshan Bibi from the petitioner Zaiuddin Khoda Buksh, the wife's claim of a valid marraige was denied by the petitioner asserting that the opposite party was the former maidservant of his father and further attacked on her character and reputation. The wife examined six witnesses including herself. The evidence of one Smt. Rehana Khatoon (PW 6) a tenant at 78 Baithak Khana Road for 5 years, was considered as reliable. She said that she saw the petitioner and the respondent living as husband and wife during her stay as tenant on the Baithak Khana Road. Discussing the question of proof of marriage, the court made the following observation:[17]

> "A proceeding under Section 125 Cr P.C. is not a punitive in nature but serves as a measure against a social oppression suffered by the categories of persons mentioned in Cl. (a) to (c) of Section 125(1). It has been held by the Supreme Court in *Bhagwan Dutt* Vs. *Kamla Devi*[18] that the Section is not intended to provide for a full and final determination of the status and personal rights of the parties. The jurisdiction conferred by the Section on the Magistrate is more in the nature of a preventive, rather than remedial jurisdiction. It is certainly not punitive. In case *Jiban Dey Sarkar* Vs. *Gopalji Dey Sarkar*,[19] it was held that the proof of marriage must depend on facts and circumstances of each case and no hard and fast rule can be laid down. In my opinion, the evidence on record which brings out sufficient facts and circumstances to support the claim of the opposite party that she is the wife of the petitioner cannot be negatived. The proceeding for maintenance under the provisions of the Code of Crimi-

nal procedure, being not a punitive proceeding, does not require that proof of act or omission beyond reasonable doubt."

Maintenance to Illegitimate Child and Proof of Paternity

The object of Sec. 125 Cr. P.C. is to provide a summary remedy to save dependents from destitution and vagrancy and this is meant to serve a social purpose, apart from and independent of the obligations of the parties under their personal law. The right of the child, legitimate or illegitimate under the Code is an individual right in his or her own rights independent of the mother. When a woman claims maintenance on behalf of a minor child born out of wedlock against his alleged putative father, the onus is on her to show that the child could only have been born through the alleged father under the circumstances of an exclusive relationship.[20] In such a case, the woman being a highly interested person, the court has a duty to see that her statement gets some independent corroboration, direct or circumstantial that the claimant could have conceived the child when she and the alleged father had access to each other.

While deciding the case of entitlement of a child, only paternity and not legitimacy has to be seen. When maintenance is claimed for an illegitimate child from an alleged father, it is not enough that the defendent would have been the father, but the court has to find out that in all reasonability no one else could have been the father.[21]

In the absence of a legal marriage, presumption under Section 112 of the Evidence Act is not available. Even then the proof of access by the putative father and non-access by others are matters which the court can take into account in evaluating the evidence. The result of DNA test by itself could be taken as conclusive in deciding paternity. I have no hesitation in confirming that Kunhiraman is the putative father of Manoj.[22]

Obligation of Husband to Maintain his Wife

Where the respondent had a son who is also earning and it is the obligation of the son to maintain his father and mother, the husband would not be absolved of the liability to maintain his wife under certain circumstances. The liability of the husband to maintain his wife under the provisions of Section 125(1) of the Cr. P.C., 1973 is not subject to the right of the mother to get maintenance from the son.[23]

LIABILITY OF THE WIFE TO REMAIN WITH HUSBAND WHILE RECEIVING MAINTENANCE

The finding about the second marriage is thus clearly upheld and this furnishes a justification to the petitioner to live spearately and claim maintenance allowance and make the husband liable to pay the same.[24]

There was no obligation cast on appellant 1 to live with the respondent no. 1 because he had created a situation by marrying another woman while the first marriage is still subsisting. The petitioner cannot be refused maintenance on that ground.

MAINTENANCE TO SECOND WIFE

The second marriage, while the first marriage is still subsisting is void by itself. The provisons of Section 125 Cr. P.C. does not provide for granting maintenance to a second wife of a person when the first marriage of that person is subsisting and his first wife is living.[25]

MAINTENANCE TO STEP MOTHER

Section 125 is a benevalent legislation which provides for discharge of obligations to maintain person who deserve to be maintained. Broad meaning, therefore, is to be given to the term, 'mother'. Accordingly I am inclined to hold that stepmother is included in the term mother under Section 125 Cr. P.C.[26]

MAINTENANCE—REFUSAL AND NEGLECT TO MAINTAIN

Where the husband does not care for his wife, and does not take care to maintain his daugher, it is a case of neglect or refusal to maintain his wife and daughter.

The Ld. Judge, Family Court surprisingly did not take into consideration this aspect of the matter merely on the ground that allegations of cruelty as contained in the application are not proved and arrived at a conclusion that is no proof of neglect or refusal to maintain the appellant by the respondent and dismissed the application filed under Sec. 125 Cr. P.C. as far as the appellant is concerned. This appraoch of the Ld. Judge does not appear to be correct. A Hindu wife belonging to the poor family having no source of personal income does not desert her husband commanding a status in the society particularly while she is pregnant. There must, therefore, be some reason for her to leave the house of her husband. From the facts on record, we are satisfied that it is case of refusal or neglect by the respondent to maintain his wife and the Ld. Family Court Judge was wrong in rejecting the application for maintenance filed by the appellate.[27]

Father's Liability to Maintain Daughter

The facts of *Balkar Singh* Vs. *Harvinder Kaur*[28] case is that the respondent was the daughter of the petitioner born out of the wedlock of the petioner with Amarjit Kaur. The marriage was dissolved by an order of the Court. Maintenance of Rs. 300 per month was granted to each of the two, wife and the daughter. Subsequently, Amarjit Kaur remarried and the maintenance allowed to her and the daughter was stopped. Amarjit Kaur while desiring to keep the daughter with her, had promised not to demand maintenance for her daughter as well. The High Court held that the father had the obligation to pay for the maintenance to the daughter as the daughter had not surrendered her rights and she could not be debarred from claiming maintenance as the mother cannot barter her claim for maintenance for some other consideration.

Maintenance to a Muslim Wife

In Islam, marriage is not a sacrament but a contract. The husband's responsibility is supposed to be confined to payment of 'Dower' and maintenance till the period of Iddat but a history was created by the Supreme Court judgement in Shah Bano case, who was divorced by her husband, a prosperous lawyer of Indore in a traditional Muslim manner after 43 years of marriage. She did the most unusual thing to go to the court. The matter finally went to the Supreme Court of adjudication where a five judge Bench headed by the Chief Justice of India ruled as under[29]

> "The liability imposed by Section 125 of Cr P.C., 1973 to maintain close relatives, who are indigent is founded upon

the individual's obligation to the society to prevent vagrancy and destitution. This is the moral edict of the law and the morality cannot be clubbed with religion."

Defenders of women's rights were quick to applaud the Supreme Court's decision, but their joy was short-lived as in a dramatic turn about, Shah Bano called a press conference and announced her desire that the Supreme Court could withdraw the order.

However, in its judgement, the Supreme Court had taken care to study Quoran as well. It appears from the judgement where certain verses from Quoran had been quoted and held that there was no conflict between Section 125 and Muslim Personal Law on the question of Muslim husband's obligations to provide maintenance for his divorced wife.[30] A section of Muslim community strongly opposed this judgement holding that the judgement in question was an attack on their religion. This led the Parliament to enact "Muslim Women Protection of Rights on Divorce Act, 1986". Section 3 (reproduced below) makes provision for giving of the Mahr or other properties of Muslim woman at the time of divorce.

3. *Mehr or other properties of Muslim woman to be given to her at the time of divorce:*

(1) Notwithstanding anything contained in any other law for the time being in force, a divorced woman shall be entitled to

(a) a reasonable and fair provision and maintenance to be made and paid to her within the Iddat period by her former husband;

(b) where she herself maintains the children born to her before or after her divorce, a reasonable and fair provision and maintenance to be made and paid by her former husband for a period of two years from the respective dates of birth of such children;

(c) an amount equal to the sum of mehr or dower agreed to be paid to her at the time of her marriage or at any other time thereafter according to Muslim law; and

(d) all the properties given to her before or at the time of marriage or after her marriage by her relatives or friends or the husband or any other relatives of the husband or his friends.

(2) Where a reasonable and fair provison and maintenance or the amount of Mehr or dower due has been made or paid or the properties referred to in caluse (d) of sub-section (1) have not been delivered to a divorced woman on her divorce, she or any one duly authorised by her, may, on her behalf, make an application to a Magistrate for an order for payment of such provision and maintenance, Mehr or dower or the delivery of properties as the case may be.

(3) Where an application has been made under sub-section (2) by a divorced woman, the Magistrate may, if he is satisfied that

(a) her husband having sufficient means, has failed or neglected to make or pay her within the iddat period, a reasonable and fair provision and maintenance for her and the children; or

(b) an amount equal to the sum of mehr or dower has not been paid or that the properties referred to in clause (d) of sub-section (1) have not been delievered to her,

make an order, within one month of the date of the filing of the application, directing her former husband to pay such reasonable and fair provision and maintenace to the divorced woman as he may determine as fit and proper having regard to the needs of the divorced woman, the standard of life enjoyed by her during her marriage and the means of her former husband or, as the case may be, for the payment of such mehr or dower or the delivery of such properties referred to in clause (d) of sub-section (1) to the divorced woman.

Provided that if the Magistrate finds it impracticable to dispose of the application within the said period, he may, for reasons to be recorded by him dispose of the application after the said period.

(4) If any person against whom an order has been made under sub-section (3), fails without sufficient cause to comply with the order, the Magistrate may issue a warrant for levying the amount of maintenance or mehr or dower due in the man-

ner provided for levying fines under the Code of Criminal Procedure, 1973 (2 of 1974),[31] and may sentence such person, for the whole or part of any amount remaining unpaid after the execution of the warrant, to imprisonment for a term which may extend to one year or until payment, if sooner, made, subject to such person being heard in defence and the said sentence being imposed according to the provisions of the said Code."

Section 4 of the Act, provides for order for payment of maintenance. The Section runs as under:

"4. *Order for payment of maintenance:*

(1) Notwithstanding anything contained in the foregoing provisions of the Act or in any other law for the time being in force, where a Magistrate is satisfied that a divorced woman had not remarried and is not able to maintain herself after the iddat period, he may make an order directing such of her relatives as would be entitled to inherit her property on her death according to Muslim Law to pay such reasonable and fair maintenance to her as he may determine fit and proper, having regard to the needs of the divorced woman, the standard of life enjoyed by her during her marriage and the means of such relatives and such maintenance shall be payable by such relatives in the proportions in which they would inherit her property and at such period as he may specify in his order.

Provided that where such divorced woman has children, the Magistrate shall order only such children to pay maintenance to her, and in the event of any such children being unable to pay such maintenance, the Magistrate shall order the parents of such divorced woman to pay maintenance to her.

Provided further that if any of the parents is unable to pay his or her share of the maintenance ordered by the Magistrate on the ground of his or her not having the means to pay the same, the Magistrate may, on proof of such inability being furnished to him, order that the share of such relatives in the maintenance ordered by him be paid by such of the other relatives as may appear to the Magistrate to have the means of paying the same in such proportion as the Magistrate may think fit to order.

(2) Where a divorced woman is uanble to maintain herself and she has no relatives as mentioned in sub-section (1) or such

relatives or any one of them have not enough means to pay the maintenance ordered by the Magistrate or the other relatives have not the means to pay the shares of those relatives whose shares have been ordered by the Magistrate to be paid by such other relatives under the provision to sub-section (1), the Magistrate may, by order, direct the State Waqf Board established under Section 9 of the Wakf Act 1954 (29 of 1954), or under any other law for the time being in force in a State, functioning in the area in which the woman resides, to pay such maintenance as determined by him under sub-section (1) or, as the case may be, to pay the shares of such relatives who are unable to pay, at such periods as he may specify in his order."

Notes:

In case titled *Arab Ahemadha Abdulla and Others* Vs. *Arab Bail Mohmuda Bail Mohmuna Saiyadbhai and Others,*[32] the Gujrat High Court held that a divorced Muslim woman is entitled to maintenance and the maintenance is not limited to Iddat period only. However a contrary view has been taken by a Full Bench of the A.P. High Court in case titled *Usman Khan Bahmani* Vs. *Fatimunissa Begam and Others,*[33] after analysing the provisions contained in Section 3(1)(a) of the Act and the history of the legislation. The Full Bench held that the Sec. 3(1)(a) envisaged the making of reasonable and fair provision and payment of maintenace to the divorced wife commensurate with the period of Iddat. A contrary view would defeat the purpose for which the legislation was made. The provisions contained in Section 4 casting liability on the relatives or the Waqf Board, as the case may be, for payment of maintenance to the divorced woman, if the divorced woman is not remarried or is unable to maintain herself after the Iddat period, fortifies the view that the liability to pay the maintenance does not extend beyond the period of Iddat. They also took into account the provisions contained in Seciton 5 which provided that if the husband and wife exercised their option in the manner provided, they would be governed by Sections 125 to 128 and the provisions contained in Section 7 reinforced the view taken.

The view that Section 125 of the Code of Criminal Procedure, 1973 would have no application to the case of a divorced Muslim woman who is governed by the provisions of the Act of 1986 has been dispelled .[34]

SECTION 125 Cr.P.C. AND SECTION 4 OF MUSLIM WOMEN (PROTECTION OF RIGHTS ON DIVORCE) ACT, 1986 COMPARED

SECTION 125	SECTION 4
LIABILITY TO MAINTAIN IS ON	
Husband	Relatives of the woman, failing which, Waqf Board
MAXIMUM LIMIT	
Rs. 500	No maximum limit has been fixed
ADULTERY - AS GROUND FOR REFUSAL	
Adultery makes a woman lose her rights to receive maintenance	Adulterous life does not affect the payment of maintenance
GUIDELINES FOR FIXATION OF AMOUNT	
No guidelines, except that the amount shall be limited to Rs. 500 irrespective of the means of the husband	Magistrate can fix the amount of maintenance having regard to need of the woman, the standard of life enjoyed by her during the marriage and the means of the relatives
JURISDICTION	
Proceeding can be taken up in any district where the person is or where he or his wife resides, or where he last resided with his wife	Proceeding under the Act can be taken up in the area where the divorced woman resides, that is to say, that if the wife after divorce moves her residence away from the place of residence of the husband, then the Magistrate of the new place of residence will have the jurisdiction
APPLICABILITY	
Section 125 Cr P.C. applies to every person and gives options to the Muslims as well, if they choose to do so and agreed to by the parties	Sec. 4 is applicable to the Muslims only.

REFERENCES

1. The Random House Dictionary of the English Language (College Edition) Allied Publishers Pvt. Ltd. Bombay, Calcutta, Madras, Banglore.
2. Ins. by Amendment Act No. 5 of 1988, Sec. 8(i).
3. Ins. by Amendment Act No. 5 of 1988, Sec. 8(ii).
4. Subs. by Amendment Act No. 5 of 1988, Sec. 8(iii).
5. Omitted by Amendment Act No. 5 of 1988, Sec. 8(iv) (1).
6. Subs. by Amendment Act No. 5 of 1988, Sec. 8(iv) (2).
7. Omitted by Amendment Act. No. 5 of 1988, Sec. 8(v).
9. *Zohra Khaton* Vs. *Ibrahim*, (1981) 2 SCC 509=1981 SCC (Cri) 517.
10. G.S. Bhargava, "Towards a Common Civil Code," *Hindustan Times*, dated 21.2.1993.
11. News Item, "Muslim Women too have rights", *Hindustan Times*, dated 10.7.1993.
12. "Talaq, Talaq, Talaq, The three words that Separate" *Hindustan Times* (Delhi Edition), dated Sunday July 18, 1993.
13. Omitted by Act no. 68 of 1976.
14. Ranjit S. Mooshahary, "Of Marriages and Morals" *Times of India*, Sunday Review, dated 1987.
15. Bhim Singh Jadhav, "The divorce among Banjaras is nil" *Dharmayug*, dated 16th to 31th of October 1991, P16.
16. *Amar Singh @ Umrao Singh* Vs. *Prem*, I(1992) CCR 608 (Punj. & Har): [*Balbir Singh* Vs. *Smt. Maya & Othes*, 1990(1) Recent Criminal Reporter, 28 relied on.]
17. *Ziauddin Khoda Baksh* Vs. *Kulshum Bibi*, II(1992) CCR 210 6.
18. 1975 SCC (Cri) 563.
19. 88 Cal. WN 1010.
20. *Ahalya Bariha* Vs. *Chhelia Padhan*, II(1992) CCR 1670 [*B. Mahadeva Rao* Vs. *Yashoda Bai*, AIR 1962) Mad. 141 and *Durai Raju* Vs. *Neela*, 1976 Cr. LJ 1507 rel. on.]
21. *Ahalya Bariha* Vs. *Chhelia Padhan*, II(1992)CCR 1670 [*Most. Jagir Kaur & Another* Vs. *Jaswant Singh*, AIR 1963 SC 1521 followed.]
22. *Kunhi Raman* Vs. *Manoj*, I(1992) CCR 286 (Kerala).
23. *Arumagham* Vs. *Thulasi Nachammal*, II (1992) CCR 1780.
24. *Badam Bai* Vs. *Kanhaiyalal*, III (1992) CCR 2702.
25. *Savitri Devi & Others* Vs. *Harish Chandwa*, III (1992) CCR 228 (ALL).
26. *Kripasandhu Pradhan* Vs. *Kaina Pradhan*, II(1992) CCR 1526 (Orissa).
27. *Jaspal Kaur* Vs. *Manjeet Singh*, II (1992) CCR 1145 (Raj).
28. II(1992) CCR 1274).
29. Tavleen Singh, "Shah Bano Case—Fundamental Issue", *India Today*, December 15, 1985, pp. 154–55.
30. *Mohammad Ahmad Khan* Vs. *Shah Bano Begum*, (1985)2 SCC 566 1985 SCC (Cri) 245.
31. Refer to Sections 421 to 424 of Cr. PC (1973).
32. AIR 1988 Guj 141.
33. AIR 1990 AP 225.
34. *M.D. Yunus* Vs. *Bibi Phankani* @ Tasrun Nisa, (1987)2 Crimes 241; *Abid Ali* Vs. *Msst. Raisa Begam*, (1988)1 Raj LR 104: *Abdul Gafoor* Vs. *A.V. Pathumma Beevi*, 1989 Cr. LJ 1224 (Kerala): *Rizwana Begum* Vs. *Motiullah*, 1989 Cr LJ (NCC) 155.

Chapter 11

Exploitation of Women

11.01 Introduction

Exploitation of women is an age-old phenomenon. The concept that a man is superior to a woman is given to the boys and girls from the very beginning of the life. The very depiction of Goddess Lakshmi (wife of Vishnu) continuing to press the feet of her husband, while he is lying on serpent bed spread in 'Kshir-Sagar' (Ocean of milk) is a step towards that. The superiority of man over a woman takes its root on seeing such pictures. Bhisma in Mahabharat states that a woman should possess the virtues like fidelity, forgiveness, absence of guile, piety and truthfulness in order to please Lakshmi, the goddess of wealth. Parvati, the wife of Shiva, says that for a woman there is no god, except her husband and a woman should be kind even to an unkind and irate husband. Purana says that by serving her husband in thought, words and deeds, a woman secures the same spiritual and heavenly worlds that her husband does with great efforts.[1] Tulsidas, in Ramayan, through a verse has bracketted a woman with 'Shudra', moron, drum and animal and all of them deserve beating. Hinduism has attributed certain derogatory remarks like fickle-minded, sensual, seducer of man, tricky, folly, greedy, impurity, inconsistent, cruel and root of all evils.

Power of man over woman is not just physical but also psychological. When society demands that a woman commit sati upon her husband's death, it emphasises the belief that she is no longer fit to protect herself against the world. She must make way for some male inheritor to her husband's property.[2]

Incidentally, a woman is endowed with the fatal combination—intelligence, beauty and gullibility of a kind specific to intelligent and beautiful woman. This constitutes a special vulnerability to exploitation.[3] She is exploited in home, offices, employment and everywhere and in almost all communities.

11.02 Woman as Saleable Commodity

The Mondappatta Tribals in pockets of Ganjam district in Orissa are reported to have been selling their wives to stave off their hunger. Mortgaging and selling wives has sanction of the tribal community. The going rate varies between Rs. 60 and Rs. 300, depending upon the looks and health of the girl.

Mondappattas are basically nomadic people but some of them have taken to settled life and they reside mostly on the outskirts of the villages around Aska, Bhanjnagar, Chitki and Rambha. The population of the tribe is nearly one thousand. Being socially boycotted, they are the poorest among the poor. It is a matter of surprise that they are not reported to be covered by any poverty amelioration scheme.[4]

11.03 Child Marriage as Mode of Exploitation

Not only the child marriage is banned in India, but the age of marriage for boys and girls has been raised to 21 and 18 years respectively. A valid marriage is one which performed between consenting adults and a child before attaining adulthood is not expected to judge its implications. Child marriage is bad for health of children and adolescents. In addition, the country cannot afford luxury of child marriage on account of its overgrown large population. But inspite of it, child marriages are being performed on a regular basis in Rajasthan and yearly melas are held. Unfortunately, the administration turns a blind eye to that. A study conducted by Family Planning Foundation of India (FPFI) some five years ago have estimated that there were more than one crore girls who were married when they were not even 11 years. A survey of the urban population has revealed that the majority of women were married when they were below 18 years of age.[5]

The FPFI has not come out with anything new when it gives

the prescription: large-scale processes of development with emphasis on education, especially for women. The National Institute of Nutrition at Hyderabad has given evidence of the direct linkage between socio-economic factors and the family size. It has come up with a theory that the number of children is depended upon the literacy level of the mother—the number coming down in a steady curve from six for illiterate woman to two for those who are in possession of a University degree. It also discoverd that poverty and illiteracy were directly correlated to child marriage. The correlation between literacy, health facilities and population growth rates are borne out by Kerala's example. It is above average in the first two factors and has the lowest population growth rate in the country.

The plight of young girls, especially in eastern Uttar Pradesh for those belonging to weaker sections remain pathetic in the rural areas. They continue to be treated as unequal to their brothers, denied education beyond primary school level, often given away in marriage before they have learnt the meaning of sex and exploited in sundry other ways. They remain outside the pale of welfare schemes launched specifically for their benefits.[6]

These facts have been highlighted by a survey sponsored by the National Media Centre, New Delhi on behalf of the United Nations Children Fund and conducted by Prof. S.N. Singh of Benaras Hindu University. The survey revealed that the lower caste girls are married between the age of five and eleven years. The consent of the girl is never taken. Among the Scheduled Caste, the Chaudhary decides the question as to who will marry whom. There is no dowry system among the poorer section of the society but the better off among them are gradually imitating the upper caste people and are adopting the evil system of dowry.[6]

For a girl, marriage is the most important problem and on account of the difficulty of the guardians in locating a suitable bridegroom for an educated bride, and the inability of the poor parents to pay the price of such grooms, the girl's parents clear off this burden through early marriage when bridegroom price does not soar high. According to a report almost all the daughters of Dumma village in Deogarh district become brides before the age of ten years. Elders of the village hold their poverty responsible for the rampant child marriage. The cost of marriage inclusive of dowry is directly proportional to the age of the girl. The chain effect leads to early motherhood. For instance one Kishori Devi married at the age of 11 years became mother of four children in the next 11 years. The absence of any health support system of the pregnant woman and frequent spells of pregnancy often lead to fatality to the already malnourished and anaemic mothers. Infant mortality and pregnancy deaths are quite high in this village.[7]

11.04 Illiteracy—A Major Cause of Indirect Exploitation

"Educate a woman and you educate a family: Educate a man and you educate one person" emerged as the underlying theme of a National Seminar on "Reforms for Women: Future Options."[8]

Speaking on the occasion, the Indian Prime Minister urged women to educate themselves to be able to stand up for an equal place in the society and once education is taken care of, women will be equipped to make use of the legislation as a weapon for their rightful place in the society. However, the Hon'ble Prime Minister did not consider the fact that the initiative for educating the children in almost all the houses are taken by the male members and in a majority of cases, girl's education gets the lowest priority.

The picture of education in this country as revealed by 1991 Census is 52 per cent of the total population. The ratio of women literates, who constitute nearly 50 per cent of the population is much lower as compared to the male counterpart. Out of a population of nearly 84 crores, only 13 crores of women were counted as literates which is nearly 21 per cent of the total literate population. Even in the State of Kerala which boasts of total literacy, only 1.11 crores of women are literate out of a total population of 1.48 crores whereas the total male literates are 1.15 crores out of a total male population of 1.42 crores. In U.P. at the end of the decade 1981–1991, 3.33 crores of male literates exist as against 1.37 crores of females. Similar is the situation in M.P. where the literate male population is 1.61 crores against the population of female literates which stands at 73 lakh. In Orissa, the ratio is 83 lakh males as against 45 lakh females and in Rajasthan the position is still worse as there are only 34 lakh females in that category as against 1.01 crores male.[9]

In some of the Urban cities, the position is not very encouraging. For instance, in Chandigarh 2.52 lakh men are literate as against only 1.73 lakh females. In Delhi 35.70 lakh men are counted as literate as against 23.78 lakh females. In big cities like Patna, Allahabad, Bombay and Calcutta, the figures for literate males and females are as under:[9]

City	Literate males	Literate Females
Allahabad	12 lakh	4.49 lakh
Bombay (Greater)	42 lakh	30 lakh
Calcutta	44 lakh	31 lakh
Patna	10.76 lakh	5.38 lakh

The picture, as is available, on the question is improving but not satisfactory.

11.05 Women in Prisons

About 44,000 women are arrested every year under the provisions of the Indian Penal Code. This does not include arrests under local and special laws. India has a total of nearly ten thousand police stations and only a few are for women. Barring one Woman Inspector General of Prisons which is in Delhi, there is no woman I.G. Prisons and in most jails, women superintendents report to and are supervised by men.[10]

The criminal law of the country stipulates the following, in respect of females:

(1) No woman shall be summoned to a police station;
(2) Only in the rarest of rare cases should a woman be remanded to police custody and in such cases, the reasons for remand should be recorded by the Judicial Magistrate; and
(3) A woman suspect should be searched by a woman only.

Inspite of these provisions, women are taken into custody, summoned to the police station and detained on the most flimsy grounds. Sometimes they are kept in informal custody, which is not correctly recorded or the entries are tampered with and during such informal custodies all sorts of illegal things happen.

The system, therefore, is heavily balanced against the woman in custody whether under the police or the prison. The long history of prison reform has failed to alleviate their sufferings. In 1836, Lord Macaulay first set up a committee to go into the question of prison reforms. The resultant commission of enquiry into Jail Management and Discipline of 1864, recommended that women prisoners should be kept separate from male prisoners.

The Indian Jails Committee of 1919, again laid stress on segregation of women prisoners from men. It categorically stated that the object of imprisonment is not to isolate the offender from society, but to make efforts to reform and rehabilitate the offender so that the prisoner can be absorbed in the society on release. Unfortunately when it comes to women, even the most progressive legislation encounters lukewarm support or non-implementation.

The situation of women in custody has been a matter of great concern to the Department of Human Resource Development Ministry which set up a Commission on Women Prisoners under the Chaimanship of Hon'ble Justice Mr. Krisha Iyer. The scope of the committee extended to:

(1) study the handling of women detenus,
(2) review conditions of the treatment of women in custody,
(3) examine the efficacy of services for the rehabilitation of women and to suggest measures to ensure fair and proper care of women offenders.

According to the Committee's report, women in custody are a tragic testimony to judicial futility. Women languish in asylum because there is no one to take care of them or take them back when they are cured. Wards are filthy and over-crowded with not even the bare provision of beds and pillows.

The need for separate prison accommodation for women inmates has been emphasised repeatedly yet there is indifference in implementation. There are nearly 4000 women prisoners in India and against this, there are only six institutions for women prisoners with a sanctioned capacity for 975 prisoners. The rest are kept in wings where male prisoners are kept. In addition to this, the institutions meant for women prisoners are old buildings which have outlived their utility.

The Committee has made a long list of recommendations which is based on informations obtained through visits by its members. The important points from the recommendations are as under:

(1) A major project, "Destination deliverance of womenhood from indignity" has to be initiated to induct more women into the system to bring about better gender sensitive training for the staff, to have new buildings in the form of cottages or hostels, give more freedom and introduce useful crafts so that on release they become self-reliant persons.
(2) Custodial facilities should be set up separately for convicted and under-trial women. As it is, the existing malpractices in various forms of custody tend to be prejudicial to women, it is a necessity and their small number should not be taken as a limiting factor for providing suitable separate custodial conditions for women.
(3) Since no policy is effective unless it has an enforcing mechanism, the committee has recommended the constitution of a Statutory Autonomous Body to be designated as "The National Authority on Custodial Justice to Women". This Authority should have representatives of the criminal justice system, voluntary agencies, media, medicine, etc., to be presided by a distinguished personality to be selected for the job solely on merit and commitment. The key function of this body will be to assist in maintaining a high standard of professional competence. In addition, the body will also be responsible for the compilation of an annual report which will be in the nature of a critical assessment of the quantitative and qualitative parameters of the status of women and girls in custody.
(4) The Committee has also laid stress on the setting up of mobile judicial camps as an immediate modality for rendering speedy justice to women in custody.

It remains to be seen how far the Committee's recommendations will succeed in getting implemented.

11.06 Distress Sale of Girls

A racket involving the sale of girls from other States particularly from Bihar and West Bengal was unearthed as a flourishing business in Kashmir valley mostly in the far flung areas. The success of the racket is attributed to high bride price which many men are unable to cough up and in consequence they remain unmarried.[11]

The girls are lured by agents of a well organised network from their homes on various pretexts like bait of a job, etc. and in some cases they are whisked away forcibly. The girls mostly belong to poor families. The going on price for the girls are Rs. 3000 to Rs. 4000 and the customers are mostly elderly persons.

Sometime back, a girl was spotted in a plane by an Air-hostess with an elderly Arab and on the initiative taken by the same Air-hostess, the girl named Ameena was rescued and the Arab was arrested for which a case was instituted in Delhi. The residents of Barkas, at Hyderabad had little interest in the 11 year old Ameena marrying a 60 year old Arab as according to them it was nothing unusual. Barkas, a place nearly 10 kms. from Char-Minar in Hyderabad is the first port to call the Arabs visiting Hyderabad for two reasons, firstly over 90 per cent of its residents are of Arab origin and secondly it is an ideal place for bride picking for the visitors. According to Masood Ansari, Managing Editor of an Urdu daily, poverty is behind the back of the poor minor girls getting married to elderly Sheikhs of Arab. The parents are forced to marry off their daughters due to a substantial dowry prevalent in the market. For instance a rickshaw puller in the local commands a dowry of Rs. 15,000. On the other hand, the parents get marriage expenses and a promise for a job in Arab. Some of the marriages do not last long as the Arabs desert their wives. The marriage episode at times assume a disproportionate dimensions and Arab marries more than one girl. In 1985, a Saudi national had got married to five girls in one night for which he was arrested.[12]

The marriages of young Muslim girls from the coastal region of Malabar district to visiting Arabs present a peculiar admixture of exploitation, veiled social sanction, mutual convenience as well as blatant violation of laws prescribing the minimum age for the marriage. The so called Arab marriages are more of a social menace than a crime. The menace comes to light when the local bride discovers to her dismay that she had been deserted along with her offspring by her Sheikh husband and she is forced to join the urchin population of the area. The illegal part of the act is that most the girls are between the ages of 12 and 16 years while the marriageable age under the law is 18 years. In 1989, a Sheikh camped at Nadapuram on the northern outskirts of the city. He announced a donation of Rs. 15,00,000 for the construction of a place of worship. He utilised the time in selecting and marrying a minor girl from the area. As the news spread, a group of Naxalites took out a protest march and surrounded the area where the Sheikh was staying but the Sheikh could outsmart them by fleeing to his country via Bangalore, and Bombay with the child bride.[13]

11.07 Exploitation of Prostitutes

The Suppression of Immoral Traffic Act, 1956 which was amended in 1986 by the Central Act No. 44 was meant to eliminate the age-old trade in flesh of women but the objective has not been served, rather it is proving counter-productive as the exploitation of women in the trade by pimps and the law-enforcing agencies have taken root.

The scheme has opened a floodgate of corruption and a lion's share of their earnings are grabbed by middleman, pimps and the law-enforcing agencies. In a day a good-looking young girl earns between Rs. 200 and Rs. 300 out of which Rs. 30 goes as rent for the small room where she handles her customers and Rs. 125 goes to the pool of pimps whose responsibility is to pay off to the police. That leaves the girl with daily income of Rs. 45 to Rs. 145. In a professional life of 10 to 15 years, a girl is sold or bartered at least 10 times and during this period they become hardened criminals and become experienced enough to run a brothel.[14] The demand of social world, Women Organisations and Veshya Kalyan Sangh of Indore (Madhya Pradesh) a registered association of the prostitutes in the country is to regularise the profession and lend dignity to women.[15–17] Prostitutes in the Port Town in Narainganj (Bangladesh) protested their eviction by an Anti-Islamic Committee. They further demanded that they may be allowed to peacefully pursue their profession.[18]

A workshop has recently been organised on the topic "Women and Law" for a period of 5 days which concluded on January 8, 1994 and was attended by eminent persons from India and abroad. The workshop stressed on prostitution and

Immoral Traffic (Prevention) Act, 1986, Rape and Sexual Assault (The Indian Penal Code, 1861) and Indecent Representation of Women (Prohibition) Act, 1986. The Workshop recommended and urged upon the Government to effectively implement a legal regulation of prostitution from disempowerment to empowerment.[19]

Prostitution cannot be abolished by simple legislation unless conditions required for its abolition are created. The following are some of the suggestions.

(1) A survey for the existing prostitutes may be conducted and they should be registered as regular prostitutes.
(2) Those among them who are willing to leave the profession may be rehabilitated in accordance with their aptitude. Vocational training and employment should be provided.
(3) The children of prostitutes who are minors should be provided teaching facilities, attempts should be made to get them married to eligible boys. All efforts should be made to see that they do not take up prostitution, pimp or middleman as their profession.
(4) The state may care to see that no new girls are recruited to the profession.
(5) Inter-state smuggling of girls and women should be checked and prevented.

All the provisions under the I.P.C. and the Immoral Traffic (Prevention) Act should be strictly enforced.

11.08 Witch-Craft, A Mode of Exploitation

Countless are the women who have to die because somebody usually a *'Ojha'* or a *'Baiga'* has branded them as witches. Such killings are rampant in tribal areas. Lack of education among them do not take out their deep faith in sorcery and they seek the solution of their life's problems through sorcery. Usually the victims of the killings of women are those who are single widows. In many cases, this kind of treatment is meted out to a woman because someone, usually a close relative, has an eye on her landed property. Since such cases enjoy certain social sanctity, it is not very often that the police swings into action against the guilty.[20]

Sukandighi, a village in Malda district in West Bengal had seen in recent times six persons, four of them women, declared witches and lynched by their own cousins with the help of other villagers because the cousins believed that three or four deaths in their family had occurred due to the evil influence of those lynched. In addition, an old family feud had also fuelled the tribal superstitions centering on witch-craft.[21] According to Sri Amarjit Singh, I.A.S.,[22] who had a three year of posting in Chaibasa [Headquarters of the district of Singhbhum (Bihar)], branding a woman as witch and getting them killed arises from the fact of their being a liability, for instance an unmarried daughter is a liability for the brother and a widow for the family.

11.09 Exploitation of Widows

According to 1951 Census, India had 123 widows per 1000 male. In 1961 Census, it came out that 10.8 per cent of total population consisted of widows as opposed to 3.70 per cent widowers. In 1971, the ratio between widower and widow was 8 and 23.[23]

The conditions of these women deserve a consideration from two angles, viz., social and economic. Among the Hindus and tribals in this country, a woman is entitled to marry with full rights only once in her life. The moment a Hindu woman becomes a widow, certain disabilities, like non-access to active participation in auspicious rituals, non-use of any decorations, like coloured clothes, glass bangles, wearing of flowers and use of any jewelery except a pair of metallic bangles get associated with widowhood. In some cases the head is shaven. Plain white cloth becomes the prescribed dress and this dress is banned for 'Sadhwas' that is, whose husbands are alive. There is now widow re-marriage among the high caste population. In those castes also where widow remarriage is allowed, the subsequent unions are solemnised through a simple ceremony and such unions suffer from certain disabilities in regard to performance of particular roles in the rituals of marriage and worship of deities. No such disability is attached to men. Although Widow Remarriage Bill was passed in the year 1856, it still requires acceptance by the Hindu society without any reservation.

It is not only the Hindu society, which makes a widow distinguishable, but respectable families of other religious groups also follow regional practices of showing discrimination against a women in widowhood. The whole idea is that a widow of any age should be unattractive. Among the Muslims, if a son dies during the lifetime of his father, then his widow does not get any share in the property of her father-in-law.[24]

Though the conditions of widows in our society caused such serious concern to the social reformers and the Widow Remarriage Act was passed, the attitude of the society towards this unfortunate group, who are an object of pity than of hate, has not made any perceptible change and the conditions of widows continue to be a blot in our society. The large group of widows, who come from different parts of the country awaiting their death in Varanasi under the belief that they will attain salvation on account of their death in Varanasi, as this city is believed to be stationed on the *Trishul* of Lord Shiva, are in a state of destitution and abject poverty. Hon'ble Mr. Justice D.K. Bawa, of Calcutta High Court has lifted the mystic veil of the holy place of Kashi when he spoke of the Bengali widows living in penury and abject poverty at the place and speaks of the human tragedy which is being enacted every day. He suggested that the hopeless Kashi widows, living in absolute misery could sue their children for legal redress, if the latter were capable of, but not helping their mothers with the barest maintenance money. He exhorted the Legal Aid Society of West Bengal to visit Kashi to study their conditions and take up their cases.[25]

The Hon'ble Judge further says that one meets these widows everywhere in Kashi wrapped in the widows white cotton saris and sitting out for the whole day on the ghats or doorways of temples and streets with begging bowls for the pilgrims to hand over some coin, or a handful of rice or sundry other articles. It may be pertinent to note that such widows are seen not only in Kashi but at several places of religious importance such as Hardwar, Mathura, Brindaban, Nawdwip Dham and Nadia district. The widows while going to these places, bank upon charity and charitable institutions which have closed their shops.

11.10 Exploitation in Employment

Art. 39(1) of the Constitution of India, guarantees equal pay for equal work for both men and women. In the light of this provision, there should not be any discrimination in payment of wages on the ground of sex. However the discrimination does exist in the payment of salaries between the male and the female workers in many establishments. The matter regarding the discrimination came up before the Hon'ble Supreme Court in India. There existed a disparity in the wage structure of Lady Stenographers (who were called 'confidential lady stenographers' and they were attached to the Senior Executives of the firm) from the male stenographers working in the same establishment. There was no difference between work of the two. However, the lady stenographers on account of their being paid less, approached the Apex Court. The Supreme Court held that there was no ground for the lady stenographers to suffer for their loyalty, integrity, sincerity and punctuality and receive less pay for possessing those qualities when they are doing the same kind of work as their male counterpart.[26]

The Rajya Sabha Committee on petitions in its 99th Report submitted to the House in 1993 recorded the following observations.[27]

> "Women workers continue to suffer from inherent inequalities in various sectors of employment and they were often paid less than men notwithstanding the laws. They are kept in conditions almost similar to imprisonment and even subjected to sexual harassment by the contractors."

The Committee noted with concern that at several places, the women workers were denied full maternity benefits. They were forced to work till advance stages of pregnancy, and in some cases their services were terminated when they proceeded on leave.

The Committee found it most shocking that the Government had failed to take adequate steps to safeguard women workers against health hazards when they were exposed to chemicals and dust. In Mysore, the Committee found that because of poor lighting conditions at the place of work of cleaning silk yarn, women workers often got serious eye problems.

At another place the Committee was told that while the Air-hostesses in Air India were grounded at the age of 45 years, the male employees continued till the age of 58 years. The Air-hostesses were not allowed to wear glasses because the male bosses in the establishment thought that it spoils their appearances. It also felt that in private companies, women were treated as objects of sex and they were recruited exclusively for selected jobs like those of private secretaries, telephone operators or receptionists in hotels.

The Committee felt that the basic problem was that in the present social and caste system prevailing in the country, a woman is still considered as "persona-non-grata". There existed entrenched centres of resistance in society because of which women continued to suffer from 'inherent inequalities'.

11.11 Bonded Labour

Parvati Bai and Shanti Bai belonging to Damoh and Jabbalpur districts of Madhya Prdesh were hired by contractors of Stone Crusher Unit on a monthly wage of Rs. 200 but full payment were never made to them. During day time, they used to lift the crushed stone and later in the evening, the driver and the few other associates of the contractor used to beat them and commit atrocities on them. Being so oppressed, they alongwith another woman Chinta Bai left the place during evening hours one day with their children consisting of two grown-ups and two infants and some household goods and in a state of terror and panic they lost the track and entered Barakhera jungle area where the children died of starvation, want of water, dehydration, and heat stroke as in the secluded deep forest, not a drop of water or morsel of food could be available.[29]

11.12 Contract Labour

There are nearly ten thousand contract labour working in sixty textile mills. More than 25 per cent of the contract labour comprise of women workers and the extreme uncertainty in their jobs made them highly vulnerable to every conceivable form of exploitation. In many cases women have been sacked for refusal to sexual advances of their employers. The low wage and sexual exploitation are symptomatic of a system where even the expression 'contract' is a misnomer, for, there is, in fact, no contract of any sort, except between the Mill and the labour contractor. The Management, instead of paying a minimum wage of Rs. 35 per day to their regular workers, get contractors to employ workers to run a particular Section of the Mill. The contractors making full use of the saturated labour market, hire destitute job-seekers, frequently for Rs. 15 par day.[30]

The National Commission on Self-employed Women and women in informal sector hold that vague labour laws is one of the primary causes for the sorry plight of the women in the country. According to the Commission, the basic purpose of these laws gets defeated because they are confined to the Statute books and are hardly implemented. In case of women workers in unorganised sectors, these difficulties are even more.[31]

The Commission had felt the necessity of evolving some kind of self-regulating mechanism so that such working women get a role not merely as beneficiaries but also as participants in the enforcement of provisions applicable to them.

The Commission made the following recommendations:

(1) A separate wing in the Labour Department be created which should have exclusive responsibility of dealing with problems of unorgainsed labour. The strength and prestige of the wing be commensurate towards the Sector of labour which accounts for 90 per cent of the total work force. Not less than 30 per cent women functionaries be appointed in this wing.

(2) The power of inspection and consequently of filing complaints, must be given to women organisations, trade union functionaries and other Government functionaries at the village level.

(3) Provisions for adequate legal aid should be made.

11.13 Sexual Exploitation

Sexual exploitation of women, not amounting to rape, is a global phenomena. Section 376B, Section 376C and Section 376D of our Penal Code prescribes punishment of imprisonment upto five years for such sexual intercourse by a public servant with a woman in his custody, sexual intercourse by the Superintendent of Jail, Remand Home, etc., with a female inmate of such jail, remand home, place or institution and intercourse by a member on the Management or Staff of a Hospital with any woman in that hospital. But inspite of these enactments, the sexual exploitation of women continues. The story of the sexual exploitation of a 14 year old class IX girl student lodged in one of the Social Welfare Department run hostel and residential school in the district of Karimnagar by a policeman within the knowledge of everybody including the Principal came to surface through press after she gave birth to a child. Everybody kept quiet because the culprit happened to be a policeman. This is not an isolated case of its kind. In 1991, there was an uproar in the state following reports of alleged physical exploitation of a number of inmates of a Schedule Caste Girls' hostel in Narayankhed in Medak district. There were even allegations that a Member of the Legislative Assembly was virtually using the hostel as a harem.[32]

The frequent exploitation, including sexual abuse of about one hundred inmates of Patna Care Home (Home for Destitute Women) by the Staff and Management of the Home and anti-social elements from outside, in active connivance with the Management Staff and the consequent torture of those inmates who refused, was reported by an Advocate of Sasaram to the Supreme Court. In consequence of the orders of the Supreme Court, the Patna District Judge visited the District Care Home and reported on the deplorable condition existing therein. However, none of the inmates, for the reasons best known to them, confirmed the allegations of sexual abuse, although the advocate came to know of it from an inmate of the Home, a young girl who flew from the Care Home to protect her life and honour.[33, 34,35]

The Hindustan Times (Delhi Edition),[36] reports the incidence of a henious type of atrocity perpetrated on a woman, Mrs. B. Devi, a mother of four children at the hands of the police in police station where her brother had been taken into custody for interrogation in connection with the murder of one Maya Devi. The woman had gone to the police station with her sister-in-law in order to serve food to her brother. She was tortured, humiliated, molested and illegally detained at the police station for three days and kept without food presumably to extract confession from her brother. But the final disgrace was slapped on her face when she was allegedly forced to have sexual intercourse with her brother who was told that if he refused, four persons in the police station would rape her in front of him.

The aforesaid disclosure was reported to have been made by the woman to newspapers at a Conference organised by Janwadi Mahila Samiti (JMS) on February 20, 1993.

Below is the classical case of exploitation of a young woman on the promise of marriage.[37]

"Kunhiraman, a wealthy middle-aged eligible bachelor acquired access to unmarried Vilasini, his neighbour working as an agent of an Insurance Company. Vilasini became pregnant and gave birth to a male child named Manoj. Kunhiraman, was recorded father in the Birth Register which the latter got removed. Vilasini filed a maintenance suit under the provisions of Section 125 Cr P.C. for the child who was a minor. Kunhiraman denied to have fathered the child stating that Vilasini was a woman of bad character. However, Vilasini had no history or evidence of connection with anybody except Kunhiraman, and that too, on the promise by the latter to marry her. The trial court allowed a maintenance of Rs. 500 per month to the child against which Kunhiraman filed a revision petition before the High Court. The High Court got the parentage of the child tested by D.N.A. (De-oxyribo-Nucleic Acid) technique and dismissed the Revision Petition declaring the Revisionist as the biological father."

There is a rampant nun running racket going on in the State of Kerala where the Italian convents faced with the problem of sharp decline in local recruitment to the cadre of nuns to run their missionary, are turning to India and Philippines through their middlemen, usually priests, who lure these girls to convents by false promises of a rosy picture. The Asian girls, instead of being trained as nurses and pursuing their career as such, are required to take up as domestic servants to do odd jobs in houses. The duty hours of such girls start at 7 am and continue till 9.30 pm. The hard duty thus performed by them hardly provides them with a monthly salary of 550,000 Lires which is equivalent to Rs. 500 in Indian currency. The middleman earns a huge amount for bringing these hapless girls to the sorry state of their lives.[38]

In the Jain religious order, mostly poor girls are initiated at a tender age into a life of self-denial and working as 'Jain Sadhvi'. Such girls are required to move about on foot in a group and have to subsist only on alms. No water or medicine is permitted during illness and every three months there is a *'Keshlochan'*, the process by which a *'Sadhvi's'* hair is pulled after applying a little ash on the hands. The process is very painful and everytime a girl is subjected to 'keshlochan', she bleeds.[39]

The Budhist women are fighting hard to obtain a status of equality, which they think are denied to all such women in the world. An International Conference of Budhist nuns was held at Bodhgaya in 1987 from February 11 to February 17. The Conference established the formation of *'Sakyadhita'* (daughter of Sakya), a worldwide Budhist Woman Organisation to fight for their reinstatement and to work out ways and means to reintroduce the *'Bhikshuni'* tradition, which is extinct although, its services in different forms do exist. On the cards, there was a proposal to establish an educational institution in India to provide religious and general education to Budhist women from all countries and a training programme for nuns contemplating ordination to the highest level. Their plea was that if Budha had broken stack and rigid social barriers to enable women to enter the order, why it is not possible for the *'Bhikshunis'*, who were custodians of *'Dharmas'*, to merely accept an older order fully approved by Lord Budha.[40]

11.14 Insensitivity towards Women

During early Seventies, a case of systematic killing of young unmarried girls at Mawat (in Maharashtra State) came to the surface. The place was not far from the local police station. This was done by a man who was under the belief that by such killings, he would get huge wealth. The case finally came in appeal before the Supreme Court. Ten years after that gory incident another case of one Waddar Sunkappa (56) an arrack addict from Bellary, who was arrested in January 1986 for killing a woman has come to light. The man has admitted that he had the distinction of killing 44 *'Jogithis'* (nomadic women priests) in the State of Karnataka over the last decade by smashing their heads with stones, although he had no grudge with any one of them. But he did so, because he needed money to foot the bills of his drinks as *'Jogithis'* are nomads, as such it was not possible to make identification of the victims after they were killed and disfigured. This was precisely the success of the accused as local records of *'Jogithis'* continued to be missing.[41]

11.15 Religious Heads and Women

In a seven days *'Mahayagya'* for obtaining world peace, organised from March 27, to April 2, 1988, at Pura Mahadeva,[42] a place hardly 25 kms from Meerut (U.P.), the Shankarcharya of Puri Swami Niranjan Tirth (72) declared that Hindu women should not be allowed to study *'Vedas'*. He reiterated that Shastras sanctified voluntary 'sati' and debarred women from studying *'Shastras'*. According to him, a woman become sati, earned three and half crores years of happiness in heaven and salvation for the husband and father's family.

In 1993, one Mrs. Arundhati Raychowdhary stood up to recite *'Vedic hymns'* at a function in Calcutta University. On this occasion Swami Nischalanand, the Shankaracharya of Puri, who happened to be the Chief Guest, refused to permit her to do so and threatened to walk out of the function if she did not obey his dictate.

It may be pertinent to point out that the *'Vedas'* belong to our earliest traditions which was an oral one and belong to the category of *'Shruti'* (one that is heard). The rishis, who are described as the Seers of the hymns (*Mantra Drishta*), belonged to both the sexes. In this context, names of women seers are also mentioned and include Shradha Kakayani, whose name is mentioned in Rig-Veda (Mandals 10, Sukta 23), Saarpragni (Rig Veda: 10.37), Vaghambhrini (Rig Veda 10.33) and Yami, who is also mentioned as one of the seers of a hymn (10.3) in the *Rig Veda*.

Some of other women seers who are mentioned include Ghosa, Lopmudra, Sikata-Nivavari, Apalla and Aditi.

Against the backdrop, it is inconceivable that women *'Rishis'* could have passed on their creations without using their voices since the only tradition (*parampara*) or method available to them was the oral (*vachik*) one. Even the Mahabharat refers to Kunti as being an authority on reciting the '*Atharva Veda*'.[43]

Unfortunately the right wing members of the clergy in India have felt much threatened by the rise of the well educated and enlightened women among the female flock of worshippers. They, therefore, try to keep women quiet and out of sight in the name of religion and snub them rudely when they stand up to speak in public.[44]

It may not be out of place to point out that a certain religious head has opposed the move by Election Commission for Identity Cards for voters by way of Election Reform to avoid bogus voting holding that photographing women is prohibited by the religion. It means therefore, that either the bogus voting should continue or a section of women voters get debarred from casting their votes and exercise franchise. It is common day experience that photograph has become a way of life to perpetuate memorable events of life. It is another thing that the preparation of I. Cards of women could be undertaken by women officers only. There may be even another demand for taking necessary arrangement for providing booths meant for women voters by women polling officers and perhaps this may meet the necessity of getting *pardanashin* ladies out of the gaze of men.

11.16 Prohibition for Girls from Marrying a Person of Choice

According to law, the marriageable ages for boys and girls in India are 21 and 18 years respectively. The law gives another right to the eligible persons to choose their spouse provided they are outside the prohibited blood relationship.

A sociological survey was conducted at Vikram University in M.P.[45] It could be known that about 60 per cent of the female students expressed themselves in favour of inter-caste marriage as the same had several advantages like ending of dowry system, preventing girls from becoming dowry victims, effecting a social change and ending caste barriers and caste disparity.

However, inter-caste marriage and marriage without the consent of elders in a house are still a taboo in Indian rural society. The infamous Mahrana hanging of two Jatav boys and a Jat girl from an old bargad tree near a Shiva temple at the entrance of a village (Mehrana) about 160 kms from New Delhi at the behest of the members of the local Panchayat community bear testimony to the day when human beings turned into beasts.[46] The fact was that the boy and girl lived together for a few days and wished to marry each other.

There is another case also on records. In mid-December, 1986, one Satwanti ran from home and joined one Jai Singh in Faridabad (Haryana). They got married in a nearby temple and later registered their marriage in a Court in Panipat in January 1987. But the society's strong disapproval compelled Satwanti to beg Jai Singh to kill her with an axe which she brought with her and Jai Singh, being dazed, killed her as desired by her. While himself trying to commit suicide, he was caught by the police. The tragic story brings into focus how society, often in the form of family and social relationship, tries in vain to regulate human relationships. It is symptomatic of the desire prevalent in people in authority to control other people's urges, emotions and desires.[47]

REFERENCES

1. Towards Equality (1974), Report of the Committee on the 'Status of Women in India', Government of India, Ministry of Education and Social Welfare, Department of Social Welfare, New Delhi, pp. 40–41.
2. Jaya Jaitley, "Women: They don't have even basic right to live", *Times of India,* dated April 4, 1988.
3. Iqbal Massod, "Personal viewpoint, Winner takes nothing if she is a woman," *Express Magazine* (Delhi) September 16, 1984.
4. Express News Service, "Selling wives to stave off hunger", *The Indian Express*, (Delhi Edition) pp. 4, May 31, 1988.
5. Editorial Column, "Child Marriage", *Hindustan Times* (Delhi Edition), dated July 18, 1988.
6. Janak Singh, "Pathetic Plight of Girls in Rural East Uttar Pradesh", TOINS, *Times of India,* April 22, 1988.
7. Pranav Kumar Chaudhary,"A Yadav village full of Child Brides in Deoghat", *The Sunday, Times of India,* (Delhi Edition), dated January 9, 1994.
8. Hindustan Times Correspondent, "P.M. Accent on Woment's Education" *Hindustan Times* (Delhi Edition), dated 22.8.1991.
9. A. Qureshy, "Women Lag in Literacy", *Hindustan Times* (Delhi Edition), dated September 2, 1993.
10. Subhadra Butalia, "Women in Jails are in the coustody of Apathy," *Times of India* (Delhi Edition), May 11, 1988.
11. The Times of India News Service (Srinagar), "Racket in Sale of Girls in Kashmir", *Times of India* (Delhi Edition), dated April 30, 1986.

12. Asok Das, "Barkas Bride Market Thriving," *Hindustan Times* (Delhi Edition) dated September 14, 1991.
13. Rathin Das, "Cluld Marriages with Arabs regular in Malabar Hills," *Hindustan Times* (Delhi Edition), dated September 27, 1991.
14. Dilip Awasthi in Sonauli and Kapur, "The Border Trafficking—Bordallas battle Police", *India Today*, dated August 15, 1089, pp. 66–67.
15. I.B. Mahboobin, P.O. Box 11035, "Prosituties Lot" in the Column 'Letters to the Editor' *Hindustan Times*, dated December 31, 1988.
16. News Item, "Call to legalise Prostitution", *Indian Express* (Chandigarh), dated April 25, 1989.
17. Suresh Malhotra, "M.P. Prostitutes up in Arms", *Hindustan Times* (Delhi Edition), dated June 12, 1989.
18. News Item (from Dacca), "Protests by Bangla Prostitutes," *Hindustan Times*, dated October 27, 1991.
19. Hindustan Times Correspondent, "Legal Regulation of Prostitution Mooted", *Hindustan Times* (Delhi Edition), dated January 9, 1994.
20. Editorial Note, "Witch-hunting Bihar", *Hindustan Times* (Delhi Edition), dated January 13, 1993.
21. Subhamoy Chatterji, "Witch-hunting—Deprivation behind gruesome Practice", *Hindustan Times* (Delhi Edition), dated August 30, 1993.
22. A.J. Philips, "Witch Hunt of Women", *The Hindustan Times* (Delhi Edition), Sunday Magazine, October 11, 1987.
23. Towards Equality (1974), Report of the Committee on the ' Status of Women' in India, Min. of Education and Social Welfare, New Delhi, pp. 77.
24. *Ibid.*, pp. 79
25. Ashis Chakrabarty, "Widows Tragedy Scars a Holy City," *Hindustan Times* (Delhi Edition), dated December 27, 1993.
26. *M/s Mackinon Mackenizie & Co. Ltd.* Vs. *Andrey D'Costa and Another*, 1987(2) SLR 690=AIR 1987 SC 1281=1987 Lab. IC 961=(1987) 2 SCC 469=(1987)3 JT 34 1987 SCC(Lab.)100.
27. Hindustan Times Correspondent, "Women Workers, Victims of Inherent Inequalities", *Hindustan Times* (Delhi Edition), dated August 29, 1993.
28. Sec. 2(h) and Section 4 of "Equal Renumeration Act 1978".
29. R.C. Mathur, "Bonded Labour in Uttar Pradesh Political Twist to Death of Five Kids" *Hindustan Times* (Delhi Edition), dated June 6, 1992.
30. Ramesh Menon, "Contract Workers, Of Inhuman Bondage", *India Today*, Nov. 30, 1985, pp. 122–123.
31. News Item, "Vague Labour Laws, fail to protect Women, "*Hindustan Times* (Delhi Edition), dated Jan. 15, 1988.
32. Ashok Das, "A Hostel used as a Harem", *Hindustan Times* (Delhi Edition), dated September 15, 1993.
33. Legal Correspondent, "Supreme Court Notice on Abuse of Women," *Times of India* (Delhi Edition), dated November 19, 1987.
34. Legal Correspondent, "Patna Care Home for Women not safe", *Hindustan Times* (Delhi Edition), dated, January 29, 1988.
35. Legal Correspondent, "Care Home Conditions—Pathetic, Miserable", *Times of India* (Delhi Edition), dated March 29, 1988.
36. Hindustan Times Correspondent, "Women's rule Tale of Torture", *Hindustan Times* (Delhi Edition), dated February 20, 1993.

37. *Kunhiraman* Vs. *Manoj*, I (1992) CCR 286.
38. Leela Mohan (reporting from Rome), "No Holiday for Kerala Nuns", *Express Magazine*, January 11, 1987.
39. N.K. Singh (In Indore) "The Runaway Nun", *India Today*, January 31, 1987, pp. 89.
40. Farzand Ahmad, "Revolt of the Nuns", *India Today*, March 15, 1987, pp. 133.
41. Srinivasa Prosad, "The Brute of Bellary", *India Today*, May 15, 1986, pp. 122.
42. Raminder Singh (in Pura Mahadev), "Religious Rukus", *India Today*, April 30, 1988, pp. 171.
43. Mrinal Pandey, "Women and Vedas", *Hindustan Times* (Delhi Edition), dated January 28, 1994.
44. Kumkum Chadha, "Shastras disprove Shankaracharya", *Hindustan Times*, dated January 26, 1994.
45. Hindustan Times Correspondent (from Bhopal), "Intercaste wedding preferred by girls", *Hindustan Times* (Delhi Edition) dated September, 1993.
46. Gargi Parsai, " Tortured, drugged and hanged" *Hindustan Times*, dated March 30, 1991.
47. Niranjan Mukhopadhaya (investigates the bizarre murder of a bride), "Insight—An Act of Love", *The Hindustan Times*, Sunday Magazine, March 8, 1987.

Chapter 12

Postscript

In the foregoing chapters, many subjects which have a bearing on causing atrocities on women have been discussed. In this chapter, it is proposed to discuss some of the residual topics, as it is felt that without including them, proper justice to the subject shall remain incomplete. These are presented as under:

12.01 Female Criminality

The traditional female role is confined to the job of keeping one self at the service of the emotional and physical requirement of others, mainly that of the husband, children or the elders in the family of the husband. The entire social, cultural, political and legal milieu is shaped in woman's total subjugation to men, who consider women as object primarily to fulfil the sexual needs. At times, this is made a right and executed through brutal force and when faced with such dehumanising situation, women take up cudgel to fight against injustice and victimization, they are, frequently, labelled as criminals and are required to face prosecution and conviction. To quote for instance, the famous Phulan Devi,[1] born in a family of a fish-catcher in 1957 and married at the age of 13 years was first implicated in a theft case in 1979 by her cousin, who wanted to grab her landed property. Circumstances forced her to take to banditary where she became a gang leader and allegdly force revenge in Bahmai. Thereafter she surrendered to the Madhya Pradesh Police and concluded her criminal career.

Phulan Devi was in Gwalior Jail for a period covering 12 years and then she was reported to have fallen ill and under the orders of the Supreme Court she was brought to Tihar Jail for treatment in Delhi. The Supreme Court had further ordered that for all the criminal cases of Uttar Pradesh, she be tried at Delhi. Subsequently the Janata Dal Government was formed by the support of Sri Kanshi Ram, who claimed to champion the cause of poor and Dalit. The Chief Minister announced the withdrawal of all cases instituted in U.P. and she has now been set free.

There is yet another case of Ms. Kiranjit Ahluwalia,[2] an Indian, married to one Dipak at Canada where they fell in love. The couple later shifted to Sussex (Great Britain). Kiranjit was being brutally tortured by her husband. Probably due to fear psychosis, one night while her husband was asleep, she sprinkled petrol on the legs of her husband and burned him. In consequence, he died after a few days of treatment in the hospital. She was sent to jail and after about a period of three and a half years in jail, she was acquitted by a British Court who took a liberal view of the matter and deviated from the beaten path of rigid application of law to judge her criminality. This woman has now taken a pledge to help oppressed women.

Therefore, barring the women belonging to some of the tribal community and nomads, as a general rule, female criminality is a function of poverty, maltreatment, involvement of male members of the family in criminal activities where the woman is required to play supportive role and sexual-exploitation. However, the involvement of females in criminal activities is very low. The following figures of Delhi Police, furnished in mid-1991 is quoted by way of example.[3]

This works out to 95% males against 5 per cent females as proclaimed offenders.

Other forms of crimes are abortion (particularly when the pregnancy is in consequence of pre-marital sex, or to a widow or on account to rape), murder through poisoning, killing of children (due to quarrel in the family and abject poverty). In such cases, the woman is found to attempt to commit suicide or commits suicide. In one case, the woman castrated her brother-in-law who had an evil eye on her and was attempting to have sexual intercourse. Killing or injuring a rapist by a woman has the protection of Section 100 of I.P.C. In stray cases, women having no child of her own, attempt to steal newly born babies from hospital.

Nature of Crime	Number of Proclaimed Offences		Total
	Male	Female	
Dacoity	72	—	72
Custodial Escape	4	—	4
Gambling	43	—	43
Burglary	292	3	295
Hurt	122	2	124
Immoral Traffic	18	29	47
Extortion	7	6	7
Kidnapping	161	8	169
Murder	145	1	146
Attemt to commit murder	58	—	58
NDPS Act	202	5	207
Robbery	130	3	133
Rape	27	1	28
Suicide	6	—	6
Theft	1102	37	1139
Others	2107	180	2287
Total	4993	269	5262

12.02 Police and Women

Police is empowered under the provisions of the Code of Criminal Procedure to investigate cognizable offences but the provisions in relation to women are that no woman shall be summoned to the police station, search of a woman suspect shall be conducted by a woman and medical examination shall be conducted with the consent of the woman. But inspite of it, abject disrespect has been found to have been shown to women suspects. According to a recent report, the story of three women, Surjit Kaur, Parmeshwari and Mohinder Kaur of Channa village (Patiala district) who were suspects as pick-pockets has gained importance from the act of the police in beating these helpless women in the police station and forcibly putting tattoo marks on their forehead as 'Jeb katri', allegedly in presence of the Superintendent of Police.[4] This has been flashed in the news papers of the country. The police are reported to have been claiming that these marks existed from before which the victims are challenging as false.

Now the situation is that these hapless women are living in self-imposed seclusion for they are ashamed of showing their faces to the people. The court has ordered for the removal of the tattoo mark at the cost of the state. However, unless the policemen who have resorted to the type of nefarious activities are punished, such atrocities are not going to be prevented for future victims. Inspite of the fact that laws are there, the implementation of those laws in a faithful manner is a must and there is a strong need for policing the police.

In the preceding pages, in other chapters, numerous instances of police brutalities have been cited.

12.03 Judiciary and Women

When we look back, it appears that the judiciary in a number of cases has applied the principle of benefit of doubt in favour of criminals which in some cases have evoked widespread resentment. Recent examples are the two decided cases of Mathura and Suman Rani who were sexually assaulted by policemen in the police station. In the former case, the accused were let off applying the principle of consent and the latter case, application of proviso to the Section 376 I.P.C. resulted in reducing the punishment to nearly the sentence already undergone. But in the present context, the situation seems to change altogether. To quote for instance, in a case, where the husband claimed for blood test in determination of paternity of the child the Supreme Court in an elaborate judgement has enunciated the following principles against such a proposition:[5]

(1) the courts in India cannot order blood test as a matter of course;
(2) where applications are made for such prayers in order to have roving enquiry, the prayer for blood-test cannot be entertained;
(3) there must be a strong prima-facie case in that the husband must establish non-access in order to dispel the presumption arising under Section 112 of the Evidence Act;
(4) the court must carefully examine as to what would be the consequence of ordering the blood test, whether it will have the effect of branding the child as a bastard and the mother as an unchaste woman; and
(5) no one can be compelled to give sample of blood for analysis.

12.04 Voluntary Organisations and Women

The various women organisations and voluntary organisations have started functioning effectively but they are not adequate. A few such organisations required to cater to the needs of 50 per cent of the total population of the country which is only a tip in the iceberg. What is required is the establishment of a large number of such organisations manned by dedicated workers from both the sexes with adequate means and resources at their command to implement such schemes like prevention of atrocities, dowry demands and dowry victimisation, education, health, family planning, employment, etc. It will not be out of place to mention that intake of liquor by the male members in a family leads to untold disasters and in some cases women have taken upon themselves to prevent the sale of liquors but such efforts by a very few are insufficient to cure the malady. Such schemes should be given a support and encouragement by the state. The states, if cannot totally ban the sale and intake of liquor, can restrict its use. It is reported that in Punjab with the return of peace, consumption of liquor, which had been controlled by the Militants, has recorded a phenomenal increase and against 30 odd liquor shops in the rural parts of the district in 1991, there are more than 500 shops operating in 1993 and illicit distillation is allowed unauthorisedly on payment of Rs. 2 to 3 thousands to the beat constable. According to an official report 56 deaths were reported in 80 villages in Majitha region.[6]

It is heartening to note that an organisation 'Yuvati Niwas Centre' run by a group of sisters belonging to the Religious to Mary Immaculate, the Bombay based body which works for the upliftment of women, has been providing vocational training to Adivasi girls. Alongwith the training, the girls work mostly as housemaids, to earn their livelihood. The girls have also participated in Delhi School Literacy project. Till the close of 1991 about 500 Adivasi girls have participated in the literacy programme and vocational training.[7]

The All India Women's Conference with its headquarters at Sarojini House, 6 Bhagwan Das Road, New Delhi-1, founded in 1926 by Margaret Cousins, an Irish Lady, who made India her home is rendering yeomen service with the objectives to:[8]

(1) work for a society based on the principle of social justice, integrity, equal rights and opportunities for all;
(2) secure recognition for the inherent rights of every human being; to work and achieve the essentials of life, such as food, clothing, housing, education, social amenities and security;
(3) support the claim of every citizen to the right of enjoying basic civil rights and liberties;
(4) create awareness among women so that they utilise to the fullest the Fundamental Rights conferred on them by the Constitution of the country;
(5) co-operate with peoples and organisations of the world for the implementation of these principles and
(6) strive to achieve these objectives as a charitable society.

It has 500 branches all over the country and a membership of more than 1,00,000. These are managing a number of projects on women and children, in rural and urban areas through its branches. Some of its activities are listed below:

(1) Short stay homes for women in distress,
(2) Old age homes,
(3) Family counselling centres,
(4) Working women's hostels,
(5) Adult literacy classes,
(6) Schools for tribal children,
(7) Centres for women artisans,
(8) Blind girls's training project,
(9) Nodal agency for propagation of smokeless chulha programme, bio-gas and solar cooker,
(10) Socio-economic projects such as printing press, textile printing press, candles making by leprosy affected people,
(11) Day care centres for children,
(12) Nutritious crops raising by and for lepers in collaboration with FAO,
(13) Margaret Housing Memorial Library—Documentation Centre,
(14) Environmental awareness, camps, clubs, etc.,
(15) Family welfare programmes, health programmes,
(16) Urban slum clearance projects,
(17) Legal awareness camps,
(18) Rural sanitation.

At Wardha, rural women are being trained in simple scientific technology aimed at reducing the drudgery of a village woman's daily chores. The training programme is organised in six different month-long training courses held in an atmosphere of caring, nurturance and freedom at the Centre of Science for villages (CVS) and the same is backed by the Department of Science and Technology (DST), New Delhi.

The training programme includes yoga classes, lectures on nutrition, health and sanitation, sessions on the status of women, equality of the sexes and importance of education besides visits to nature cure clinics, Gandhi's Sevashram and Vinoba Bhave's Paunar Ashram. A unique feature was the sympathetic hearing of the life-story of each woman, which enabled the trainers, all of whom are dedicated social scientists, to help and understand better.[9]

12.05 Women in the Modern Age

The idea of equality is a modern concept. Women all over the world do appear to have secured formal legal equality and political emancipation the moment they were entitled to the right to vote and active participation in politics and nation building exercises. The democratisation process began in the middle of the 18th Century in England through the revolutionary ideas in France in the light of the Lockean Theory of natural rights and liberties for women. Many countries in the world granted the right to vote to their women by the first quarter of the 20th Century which many progressive women group interpret the development as a beginning of a process which is bound to gain momentum in due course and much may be required to be done before full equality can be achieved.

The industrial revolution leading to the development of commercial economy provided a number of job opportunities to the people. The women commenced taking up jobs which were regarded as male bastion. This country had seen a very strong woman Prime Minister, several Ministers in the Centre as well as in States, female Judges and Chief Justices in various High Courts of the country including one in the Supreme Court. In the field of classical music there were a large number of women vocalists but no instrumentalists or player of percussion instruments. In the forties and fifties, there was one sitar player (Kalyani Roy), a violin player (Sishir Kanadhar Dey), two sarod players (Saran Rani and Annapoorna Shanker) but now there are a large number of instrumentalist playing not only sitar, violin or sarod but such instruments like sehnai, flute, nad-swaram, pakhawaj, tabla and sarangi. However, the women have not achieved a situation of substantive equality with men in the areas of economic independence, occupational status and administrative and political power.

The achievement of substantive equality with men are largely dependent upon the sociological definition of the role of women within the household wherein some jobs are considered purely meant for women only.

The functional relationship between man and woman is largely responsible for the subordinate role of the women. In social setting, the task of running a home and rearing children is generally considered a woman's field of work and finds no economic recognition. The usual division of work between man and woman is confined to external and internal spheres respectively. Some women take up jobs outside their homes but often there is discrimination between the wages in many countries. However, the job outside the home is paid for, the jobs performed inside the home are unpaid and is not recognised as labour or contribution by way of earning. The socicty regards women as predominantly nurturing expressive functions and intellectually aggressive women are classed as deviants.

Some feminists view abolition of the household and child-rearing tasks as crucial to achieving true equality for women. This seems drastic and unnatural. But home and family should be regarded as the responsibilities of both and both should be trained to share the responsibilities. The idea of patriarchal family where the man is supposed to dominate and the woman is supposed to be dominated and render services at the command and whims of the husband should be discarded. The idea that motherhood and rearing of child are the only or the most important roles of women should be discarded and the girls should also be provided the same opportunity for pursuing a career depending upon the capabilities and talents and this is the most reasonable aspect of the matter.[10] There are reports that there should be 30 percent reservation for women but one pertinent question is why it should be so? Those who want to achieve anything by reservation or through any concession are devoid of self confidence or are having less developed personalities. Women do not have less developed capabilities that they will fail to compete with men in academic field or for a job. Rather they have better concentration on their jobs. We will strongly plead against the reservation of jobs but will always like the idea of giving equal opportunity to women in education, training and exposure to the situations requiring their performance. The author informally knows a case, where a woman was selected by the UPSC for a Class I post under the Government of India and the Head of the Institution approached the authority for not issuing the appointment letter and to withhold the appointment and make fresh selection as the selected candidate, being a woman, would not be able to discharge the functions of the office effectively. However, the Issuing Authority of the appointment letter disagreed and directed the head of the institution not to raise this question and provide all the necessary facilities to the selected candidate after she joins to enable her to discharge her duties in an effective manner. Incidentally, the selected candidate joined the post and is discharging her duties in the most efficient manner.

The technological advancements in the present century has given greater freedom to the society and women, too have been benefited from it. The domestic chores have become easy with the fuel gas, washing machine, carpet cleaner and other electric gadgets. The family can now afford to plan the size of the family. The developments in fields of bio-technology and medical science can assist to get rid of the unwanted child or a child having defect at the early embryonic stage.

The society, by and large, should pay necessary attention to implement the following schemes in the larger interest of nation:

(1) adequate training to both men and women for managing homes and this aspect should be viewed with necessary seriousness;
(2) there should be good, reliable and proper and inexpensive child care system so that the working men and women can pay adequate attention to their jobs;

(3) there should be family care units and/or institutions and provisions for payment of maintenance in the event of unemployment, destitution and death of the breadwinner of the family;

(4) equal rights to the property and inheritance and an access to their earning and savings.

The crux of the matter is that a complete transformation is needed in women so that they must cease to see themselves in the role of mother and wife only. It is only with the functionalist view of the woman that women can achieve the status of equality in all spheres viz; political, social and economical.

REFERENCES

1. S. Malhotra, "Metamorphism of Phoolan Devi", *Hindustan Times* (Delhi) dated June 3, 1989.
2. Harjit Kaur, "Pati Ki Hatyari, Phir Bhi Nirdosh", *Grih Shobha* (Hindi) Jan, 1993 pp. 94–98.
3. Girija Shanker Kaura, "Crime, No more a Man's world", *Hindustan Times* (Delhi), dated July 10, 1993.
4. Harpreet Singh, "Shame drives women to seclusion", *The Hindustan Times* (New Delhi), dated Jan. 29, 1994.
5. *Goutam Kandu* Vs. *The State of W.B. and Another*, AIR 1993 SC 2295.
6. Ajay Bhardwaj, "Hooch flows as peace returns to Punjab" *The Times of India News Service*, Times of *India* (Delhi Ed.), dated 27.1.1994.
7. Arati Bhargava, "Earning to live a life of dignity" *Hindustan Times* (Delhi ed.), dated December 1, 1991
8. Source, A.I.W.C, Sarojini House, 6 Bhagwan Das Road, New Delhi-1
9. Gargi Parsai (in Wardha), "Science for village woman, *Hindustan Times* (Delhi Ed.), dated 15.3.1987.
10. Dr. Sushmita Ramaswamy, "Managing Office and Health" *Hindustan Times*, (Delhi Ed.), dated Dec. 18, 1993.